78   1   0

20260.

REMAINS

𝕳istorical and 𝕷iterary

CONNECTED WITH
THE PALATINE COUNTIES OF

𝕷ancaster and 𝕮hester

VOLUME XXXVI – THIRD SERIES

MANCHESTER

𝕻rinted for the 𝕮hetham 𝕾ociety

in association with the Lancashire and Cheshire Antiquarian Society

1992

W. H. CHALONER, 1986

PALATINATE STUDIES

CHAPTERS IN THE SOCIAL AND INDUSTRIAL HISTORY
OF LANCASHIRE AND CHESHIRE

W. H. CHALONER

Selected and edited by
W. R. WARD

MANCHESTER

𝔓𝔯𝔦𝔫𝔱𝔢𝔡 𝔣𝔬𝔯 𝔱𝔥𝔢 ℭ𝔥𝔢𝔱𝔥𝔞𝔪 𝔖𝔬𝔠𝔦𝔢𝔱𝔶

in association with the Lancashire and Cheshire Antiquarian Society

1992

The Chetham Society

The Chetham Society was founded in 1843 to publish 'Remains Historical and Literary connected with the Palatine Counties of Lancaster and Chester'. In practice its publishing has been largely historical and for over a century in addition to a wide variety of historical documents, letters and journals it has included numerous monographs based on original research. Membership of the society is open to individuals and institutions upon the payment of an annual subscription. Current members are entitled to a copy of each new volume upon its publication. Details of membership are available from the Honorary Treasurer, The Chetham Society, c/o Chetham's Library, Long Millgate, Manchester M3 1SB.

Palatinate Studies
Chapters in the Social and Industrial History of Lancashire and Cheshire

by W. H. Chaloner

Copyright © The Chetham Society, 1992
Text copyright © W. H. Chaloner, 1992

Published for the Chetham Society by Carnegie Publishing Ltd., 18 Maynard St., Preston
Designed and typeset by Carnegie Publishing Limited, 18 Maynard Street, Preston
Printed in the UK by T. Snape & Co. Ltd., Preston
ISBN 0-948789-85-9

British Library Cataloguing-in-Publication Data
A CIP catalogue record for this book is available from the British Library

CONTENTS

LIST OF ILLUSTRATIONS

PROFESSOR WILLIAM HENRY CHALONER
1914–87

Memorial publications which have already appeared have done much to
show why Bill Chaloner evoked a deep if light-hearted affection among his
friends and professional colleagues. The volume of his papers edited by Dr
D. A. Farnie and Dr W. O. Henderson shows to a demonstration the range of
the scholarly expertise which he acquired.[1] The tribute to him published by
the Lancashire and Cheshire Antiquarian Society generously acknowledges
his services as editor over a whole working lifetime, attempts the bold feat
of collecting his scattered and multifarious writings into a single list, and
features many delightful recollections of a man who was a 'character' by
nature as well as by aspiration.[2] The Council of the Chetham Society has
also felt it right to acknowledge its indebtedness to Professor Chaloner for
long and valuable services as a member of its Council from 1953 and of its
Publications Committee from 1970. Many young scholars as well as members of the Society and the general public have reason to be grateful for the
sharp eye he kept on work in progress which ought ultimately to take its
place in the Society's series. The present selection of his contributions to the
history of Lancashire and Cheshire illustrates the fact that he was as generous with his aid to friends and neighbours as he was to young scholars, and
that when there was an occasion for a local celebration he would support it
by a workmanlike and scholarly essay. Of course the man whose most
substantial work concerned *The social and economic development of Crewe,
1780–1923*[3] became the leading modern historian of that region of his
generation, and much of his success in tracing new sources derived from an
astonishing range of local acquaintances; this in turn grew from a generous

---

1 *Industry and Innovation,* Frank Cass, London, 1990.
2 *Transactions of the Lancashire and Cheshire Antiquarian Society* 85 (1988), pp. 1–105.
3 Manchester University Press, 1950; 2nd ed. 1973.

and genial willingness to serve. Not all the essays here reprinted are readily available elsewhere, but, brought together, they will continue to support the historiography of the author's native region, and refresh recollections of the author himself.

W. R. WARD

ACKNOWLEDGEMENTS AND SOURCES

The Chetham Society gratefully acknowledges the permissions received for the reproduction of the articles here reprinted, and expresses its particular thanks to Mrs Joan Chaloner. Thanks are given also to the librarians and private individuals who have traced and supplied new photographs for this volume, and to Mr E. A. Rose for compiling the index. Every effort has been made to trace parties with an interest in the copyright of the articles and the Society apologises if any infringement has inadvertently occurred.

The chapters which follow were originally published in the following: Chapter I, Crewe Congregational Church Centenary Celebrations Committee, 1947; Chapter II, the Mayor of Crewe's Charity Committee, 1948; Chapters III, IV and V, the Lancashire and Cheshire Antiquarian Society, see *Transactions,* vols. lxi (1951), pp. 121–36; lxii (1952), pp. 133–56 and lxiii (1953), pp. 52–109; and lxxi (1963), pp. 58–74; Chapter VI, the Historic Society of Lancashire and Cheshire, see *Transactions,* vol. cxii (1961), pp. 110–45; Chapter VII, Manchester University Press, 1973; Chapter VIII, Frank Cass & Co. Ltd., as the introduction to *The Autobiography of Samuel Bamford* (two vols., 1976). See vol. 1, pp. 9–45.

The illustrations have been reproduced by courtesy of the following: frontispiece, Mrs Joan Chaloner, photograph by Mr Gordon Chaloner; plates 1–4, Macclesfield Museum Trust; plates 5–7, The Salt Museum, Northwich; plates 8 and 9, the University of Manchester; plate 10, Mr W. J. Smith.

EDITORIAL NOTE

The texts have been reprinted with the minimum of alteration, but typographical errors have been corrected and occasional minor changes have been made to suit the new context. The articles were written over a twenty-year period during which Professor Chaloner used different methods of presenting references. The variations are not confusing and have been preferred to an imposed uniformity. Insertions in square brackets are by Professor Chaloner; those in angled brackets are editorial.

John H. G. Archer,
Joint General Editor, Chetham Society

CHAPTER I

THE HISTORY OF THE CREWE CONGREGATIONAL CHURCH, 1841–1947

Each Congregational Church is a self-contained, democratically-governed union of believers in God revealed as the Father, Son and the Holy Spirit in the Scriptures; in the words of the *Declaration of Faith and Church Order* adopted by the brethren assembled at the general meeting of the Congregational Union in London, on May 10th, 1833, these believers, men and women, hold:

> that the New Testament authorises every Christian Church to elect its own officers, to manage all its own affairs,

and:

> that the only officers placed by the apostles over individual churches, are the ... pastors, and the deacons ... and that to these, as the officers of the Church, is committed respectively the administration of its spiritual and temporal concerns.

In the nineteenth century the various Nonconformist types of church government, of which the oldest was Congregationalism, played an important part in training ordinary men and women in citizenship, in the ways and means of managing their own affairs peacefully and with general consent. The devoted pioneers who built the Nonconformist chapels had as their counterparts in the economic world the small groups of earnest men who founded the local friendly societies, trade unions and co-operative stores. The membership of chapel and trade often overlapped, and the business experience gained in solving the financial problems of a church sometimes proved useful in more worldly spheres.

In the minutes of church meetings, which in the case of Crewe Congregational Church, exist from 1855 onwards, we can see this religious self-government at work. It became more democratic as the nineteenth century advanced. For example, although the Crewe Congregational Church meeting elected the deacons from the beginning, these officers held their posts until they died, or resigned, e.g., on August 31st, 1861 deacon James Swan resigned and was replaced by John Eaton. The church meeting was also the body which issued unanimous invitations to prospective ministers to assume the pastorate of Crewe, and accepted new members from the Sunday School, the outside world, and other churches. On December 2nd, 1869, the Crewe church meeting decided to increase the number of deacons to five.[1] In addition, the method of election was henceforward to be 'by voting papers containing the names of all the accredited male members of the church, one paper to be sent to every member who has been in communion during the past six months.' James Robertson, John Eaton, Mark Sudworth, W. Smith and John Heath were the first deacons elected under the new system on December 30th, 1869. Three years later (January 2nd, 1873), the church meeting decided to hold the election of deacons in this manner every three years. As an instance of the extremely democratic character of the Congregational form of church government, the following resolution, dated June 30th, 1875, should be noted:

> That young persons received into Church fellowship do not possess the power of voting at meetings until they reach the age of 17 years.

Crewe Congregational Church is a product of what is called the 'New Dissent' of the early nineteenth century. During the mid-eighteenth century 'Old Dissent,' or the 'Older Nonconformity' in Cheshire, represented by Independency or Congregationalism, Presbyterianism and Unitarianism, was at a low ebb. Between 1717 and 1772 only one new Nonconformist chapel had been built in the county. This was at Hale, and replaced the one at Ringway which had been seized by the Episcopalians. On the other hand, the three chapels at Middlewich, Bromborough and Upton had ceased to count as effective religious forces between the same years. On July 24th 1773, the Rev. John Chidlaw wrote of Cheshire:

> The Dissenting interest in this county in general is in a very declining languishing state, and some of the congregations are likely to drop very soon.

---

1 The exact number of deacons in the early days is not known. The deacons were increased from eight to twelve in 1905.

This state of affairs changed for the better in the course of the early nineteenth century. Stimulated to some extent by the example of the Methodists and the Evangelical movement in the Church of England, the Congregational ministers and laymen of Cheshire established in 1806 the Cheshire County Union of Congregational Churches, which had as its object the 'diffusion of Christianity, in connection with Congregational principles, in the County of Chester.'[2]

One of the earliest and most vigorous workers for the Cheshire Union was that famous evangelist, the Rev. William Silvester of Sandbach, 'a man, not of polish and erudition, but of heart and soul, upright and earnest and ready to make any sacrifice in the cause of his divine Lord.' He began his mission in Haslington in 1807, and soon gathered together a large and attentive congregation. By 1810 the congregation was financially strong enough to build a chapel and Haslington, once noted for profaneness, dissipation, drunkenness, cock-fighting and riot, a 'spot devoid of the common civilities of life,' had undergone a spiritual transformation. In the circumstances, it was natural that the Rev. William Silvester should, in 1841, turn his attention to the religious needs of the newly-founded industrial colony and railway junction of Crewe,[3] where hundreds of labourers and builders, drawn from the length and breadth of the country, were erecting workshops and houses to accommodate the Grand Junction Railway Company's mechanics and woodworkers from Edgehill. In 1841, the members of the Congregational Church at Middlewich repaid a debt of £200 to the Cheshire Union, and:

> ... it was deemed advisable to apportion a small part of this sum for the immediate purchase of a piece of land, which had been offered on most advantageous terms, at Crewe. The rapidly increasing character, and central position of that village, seemed to call for this measure, and the value of this plot of ground for many purposes, in furtherance of the objects of the Union, render this opportunity a subject for congratulation.[4]

2 The purpose of the Union is more adequately described by the name which it adopted at a meeting in the Independent Chapel at Crewe on Thursday, April 27th, 1848 – 'The Cheshire Congregational Home Missionary Society.' The old title came back in the course of the 1850s.

3 He had preached occasionally at Coppenhall from 1807 onwards.

4 *Report of the Cheshire Union of Congregational Churches* (1842), p. 4. This piece of land, south of Chester Bridge, and on the West side of Exchange Street (then called Oak Street) is said to have been secured through the instrumentality of Thomas Bostock of Haslington,

Pending the erection of a chapel, the Congregational services of the Rev. William Silvester and his fellow-missionaries at Crewe took place in the open air, sometimes on the vacant piece of land destined for the chapel, or in a room in a local hotel, in fact, in any room that could be secured for the purpose. In September 1846, the Rev. W. Silvester died, but the project that he and his Haslington supporters had begun came to fruition in the course of the following year. In the mid-1840s, a number of families holding Congregational views on matters of faith and church government had settled in Crewe, and with the help of the Cheshire Union, the worshippers at Crewe were able to build their first Independent chapel in Oak (Exchange) Street. This 'neat brick building' was opened for worship in June, 1847, by the Rev. Thomas Raffles, D.D., of Liverpool, who preached the opening sermon. The congregation for this ceremony was so large that the chapel would not accommodate the whole of it, and those present were compelled to adjourn to the bowling green at the nearby Oak Farm Inn, 'where the venerable minister delivered one of his eloquent discourses.' In a speech which he made at a public meeting held in the Town Hall the same evening, he declared, with the humour that was characteristic of him, that he had discovered a new thing under the sun that day, inasmuch as he had opened a new chapel and had not been within its walls! The chapel contained accommodation for 150 worshippers and in the *Cheshire Union Report* for 1852, the following information is given:

> The friends of Crewe have still remaining on their chapel a debt of £220, but they are earnest in desire and sanguine in hope, that by the generous aid of their friends in the county that debt will, at no distant day, be numbered among the things that were. (p. 3)

The mere provision of a permanent place of worship did not, however, solve all the troubles of the infant congregation, which was still without a permanent minister. Between September, 1846 and the end of 1849, students of the Lancashire Independent College at Manchester took the services, but this arrangement proved far from satisfactory. The one bright spot was the successful foundation of the Sunday School by a few devoted teachers early in 1848, and it is interesting to note that the proceeds of the first three recorded collections in the chapel (1849–51) went to sustain it. The Report of the Cheshire Union for the year ending September 30th, 1848, gives an

whose son, B. S. Bostock, also of Haslington, was an active Congregational worker and local preacher.

interesting survey of Congregationalism in Crewe at that time. Writing in October, 1848, the District Secretary said:

> ... the cause, being in its infancy, is yet weak; the average of hearers is 50, and of scholars in the Sabbath School 46; the appointment of a settled ministry is regarded, under God, as the great essential to the prosperity of the place.[5]

The compiler of the Report commented:

> We are concerned to add, that things there have not much improved since; but the reverse, and that so much so, that the hearers, at present, hardly number more than some 18 or 20. No church has been as yet formed at Crewe, and the friends there deem that, *viz.*, the formation of a church, which may act as a nucleus to gather to it those comers to the place who are already members of other churches, and a settled ministry ... essential to the very existence of the cause there.

In accordance with the desire expressed in the above document, Crewe Congregational Church was formed on May 13th, 1849, when an introductory address on the nature of a Christian Church was delivered by the Rev. John Robinson of Middlewich. The members then united in fellowship and the ordinance of the Lord's Supper was administered by the Rev. S. Bowen of Macclesfield, assisted by the Rev. John Simpson of Nantwich. When the first pastor, the Rev. Charles Bingley, of Middlesbrough-on-Tees, accepted the call on December 19th, 1849, the Crewe and Haslington congregations were united for ministerial purposes, services being held in the Crewe chapel in the morning and evening, and in the Haslington chapel in the afternoon.

It is recorded that the Rev. C. Bingley, who arrived in January, 1850, 'laboured with some success for the short time he remained,' but as he gave up the task in June, 1851, 'the various means' he adopted 'in the hope of securing a larger attendance from the inhabitants' met with a 'very limited success.' The congregation at Crewe in 1850 averaged from forty to fifty, while the church members at Crewe and Haslington together numbered only

---

5   p. 6. By 1849 it could be said: 'The Sabbath School continues to do well; scholars in attendance about 50, with 8 teachers.' It was held in the chapel until in September, 1861, a small schoolroom was opened at the rear of the main building. The first superintendent was James Swan and the first recorded list of teachers included Miss M. Bailey, Miss E. Bailey, Miss E. Eaton, Thomas Lindop, C. Turner, J. Robertson and F. Gavin. James Robertson (1815–1905) later became famous locally as the first working-man J.P., and served as treasurer of the Church from 1862 to 1904. He was succeeded as Treasurer by F. F. Ramage (1904–9) and Mr. T. Challinor (1909 to the present).

thirty. During this period (1848–51) Crewe remained in the depths of an economic depression due to the collapse of the railway boom and several of the most active and useful church members left the town. It is customary to think of the nineteenth century as a period when true religious feeling was more wide-spread and easier to awaken than it is in the twentieth century, but the Rev. C. Bingley noted in 1851:

> Amongst the mass of the population (of Crewe) there is an awful indifference to all matters of religion.[6]

Bingley was succeeded by a pastor of a very different stamp, the Rev. James Comper Gray, a true evangelist and the author of *The Class and Desk*, *The Biblical Museum*, and other publications dealing with Sunday School work, popular and useful in their time, however antiquated they may seem now. He received a unanimous invitation on July 7th, 1851, and aided by the growth and increased activity of the railway workshops, the Crewe Congregational Church flourished under his pastorate, as the *Cheshire Union Report* for 1852 reveals:

> Both the church and the congregation at Crewe are gradually increasing, as does also the Sunday School, which is under a very efficient management, connected with which are established a juvenile missionary society, a teachers' improvement class, and a meeting for the improvement of psalmody. A tract distribution society has been formed, and two weekly cottage lectures are being conducted regularly by the minister, and have a good average attendance.

Unfortunately for the cause in Crewe, the Rev. J. C. Gray received an invitation in 1854 to be assistant pastor to the Rev. Brewin Grant, of Highbury Chapel, Birmingham, and removed thither in May of that year.[7] Many of the troubles of the period from 1854 to 1868 can be traced to the departure of this energetic pastor after only three years' work in the town. For long it seemed as though the Church's roots could not spread in the soil in which it was planted. The succeeding pastor was the Rev. Frederick Hemming, from the U.S.A., who took charge towards the end of 1854. He laboured in true transatlantic style with 'much energy and vigour,' and some

---

6   This was by no means a purely transient phase. A writer in the *Cheshire Observer* of August 1st, 1863, remarked on 'the great number of intelligent mechanics in Crewe who stood outside all Church connections – either in indifference or hostility to Christianity.' See Appendix, p. 19.

7   Later he ministered to churches in Halifax and Bristol.

success, until August, 1857, when he returned to America. The Churches at Crewe and Haslington then remained without a pastor for more than three years, and passed through many vicissitudes. The Report of the Cheshire Union for 1858–9 contains the following amusing passage on the situation:

> . . . whether they (the churches at Crewe and Haslington) have been so long destitute because of seeking for some impossible combination of excellencies in the man, or for some unlikely unanimity amongst themselves, might be worth an inquiry on the part of the sub-committee.

By 1858–9 the average congregation had sunk to twenty-eight in the morning and thirty-eight in the evening, but the number of church members at Crewe alone had now reached thirty.[8] In 1859–60 another blow was struck at the prosperity of the town, and the Congregational cause in Crewe, in the shape of 'one of those fluxes by which it has been more than once depressed':

> The London and North-Western Railway has changed the place for its Coach-works (from Crewe to Wolverton), and six families connected with the Chapel have been taken away.[9]

At length the members met with a minister who was unanimously approved by the church, the Rev. Thomas Davison, of Stockton-on-Tees. He accepted the call and entered upon his work on December 2, 1860. His ministry proved longer and, therefore, more successful than that of any previous pastor. Many converts were added to the church, 'the majority of them young people.' In addition, prayer meetings for young people, a mothers' meeting (1861–2) and a class for young men conducted by one of the deacons all flourished during this period. It was in June, 1861 that the Sunday School room and vestry were opened behind the main chapel, largely because insufficient accommodation hampered the growth of the school. By 1863 the remaining debt on this new building and the redecoration of the chapel amounted to only £60, and the 'young disciples and others connected with the church and congregation' resolved to make an effort to pay it off.'[10]

---

8 In 1865 the membership at Crewe numbered forty-five.

9 *Cheshire Union Report*, 1859–60, p. 6. The Report for 1861–2 contains the following passage: 'As to things moral and spiritual, the brethren in Crewe have to lament a source of discouragement, well-nigh inseparable from the nature of the population – the removal of some of the most useful and promising young people (from the town) . . .' (pp. 4–5).

10 *Cheshire Union Report*, 1862–3, pp. 3–4

The Rev. T. Davison closed his pastorate at Crewe on October 30th, 1864, in order to accept a call from the church assembling at 'The Quinta,' in Denbighshire. Throughout 1865, the church remained leaderless, and the Cheshire Union, on which body the Crewe congregation still depended for an annual grant of £50, debated in that year:

the suggestion as to the severance of Haslington from Crewe, and its union to Wheelock, under the care of an evangelist.[11]

This severance of Haslington from Crewe was accordingly effected, and since 1865, therefore, Crewe has been completely independent of its 'Mother Church'.

Complete independence did not begin auspiciously. At a church meeting held on March 13th, 1866, it was found necessary to resolve 'that there be a Congregational Tea Party held on Good Friday for the purpose of trying to cultivate a more social feeling among the members of the congregation'! In addition, Crewe lost a promising and energetic new pastor. Early in 1866, the young Rev. Joseph John Thornton, of the Lancashire Independent College, had accepted the unanimous call of the Crewe members to become their pastor, and commenced his labours on the second Sunday in February. Unfortunately, he was stricken in the following July with such a severe and painful illness that on November 9th, 1866, he found himself unable to write his letter of resignation, and was obliged to dictate it to his father.[12]

The Rev. J. J. Thornton had only accepted the invitation to Crewe on four conditions, the first of which read:

That the Church and congregation unite with him in endeavouring to secure as soon as possible a new ecclesiastical building for their use in the worship of God.[13]

11 *Cheshire Union Report*, 1864–5, pp. 4–5.

12 The Rev. J. J. Thornton, who later accepted a call to Whitchurch, recovered, and revisited Crewe as late as 1917, i.e., over fifty years after his pastorate.

13 The remaining three conditions were as follows: '2. That each will do what lies in his power to promote the efficient working of the weekly offering. 3. That he only be required to undertake two services on the Sabbath. 4. That he have five Sabbaths for rest and relaxation in the year when the Church find supplies for the pulpit.' On May 1st, 1862, the pastor's salary had been raised to £95 per annum, in 1865 to £100, in 1873 to £150 (with six free Sundays), and in 1880 to £180, from which peak figure it was reduced to £150 in 1882, in view of financial difficulties 'and the meagre prospect of increasing . . . current income immediately.'

The task of presiding over the erection of the new church and of steering the young congregation out of the troubled waters of the 1860s fell to Thornton's successor, the Rev. William A. Blake, of Over, who was unanimously invited to become pastor at Crewe on July 21st, 1867. He entered upon his labours at Crewe on the second Sunday in September, and was ordained on February 11th, 1868. A considerable addition to the congregation followed, and it became even more urgent than it had been in 1866 to provide a new meeting-place. On February 20th, 1868, a special meeting of the Church and congregation resolved to remove the services to the Town Hall in Prince Albert Street in March.[14] The meeting also considered 'the project of a new Chapel,' and John Eaton, F. Dingley, John Pullan, John Heptinstall and W. Latham were appointed a committee to solicit subscriptions towards the new chapel fund in Crewe and the surrounding towns. The old chapel in Oak (Exchange) Street was sold to Frederick Cooke, a rising young solicitor from Winsford, for £500; in addition, he gave £25 as a donation to the new chapel (December, 1868).[15]

Vigorous efforts were now made to raise the necessary funds for the new building on Hightown, for which the architect's plans were approved, with alterations, on April 1st 1869. Later in the month the pastor and the deacons were appointed to 'procure names of respectable builders to tender for the erection of (the) new chapel,' of which the foundation stone was laid by Sir James Watts, of Manchester, on August 9th, 1869. The entire cost of the building, including land, architect's charges and fittings, amounted to £2,758 18s. 7½d., towards which the Lancashire and Cheshire Chapel Building Society gave a grant of £750.[16] The new chapel 'at the top of Victoria Street' was opened for service on February 9th, 1870, when sermons were preached by the Rev. R. W. Dale, M.A., of Carrs Lane Chapel, Birmingham, and chairman of the Congregational Union for that year, and the Rev. J. A. Macfadyen, M.A., of Manchester. Special services were held

---

14 On Saturday, February 9th, 1869, a disastrous fire occurred in the Town Hall, and the Congregationalists would have been temporarily homeless had it not been for the voluntary kindness of the Rev. Joseph Nadin, the Anglican vicar of Christ Church, in placing one of the Christ Church schoolrooms at their disposal. The congregation worshipped here for several Sundays; subsequently, the Corn Exchange and the Baptist Chapel in Oak Street were used, pending the opening of the new chapel in February, 1870.

15 The old chapel, rechristened 'Temple Chambers,' was used by Cooke as his legal offices, and for a time the Monks Coppenhall (Crewe) Local Board, the local governing authority of the period, and later the Borough Council, used to meet there. Cooke was Clerk to the Local Board and became first Town Clerk of Crewe in 1877. The building is now used as a place of worship by the Christadelphians.

16 W. F. Poulton, of Reading, was the architect, and A. P. Cotterill, of Crewe, the builder.

on the following two Sundays, and after the collections made on these three occasions there remained a debt of £100 only on the total cost. In the following year a successful special effort was made to free the building from this last encumbrance. The Rev. William A. Blake continued his work in Crewe for three years after the church was erected, and under his ministry the number of members continued to increase, and the religious organisations connected with the Church became well consolidated. He removed to 'a larger sphere of labour' in Stockport in March, 1873. Before bidding a final farewell to 'the Congregational Church assembling at Oak Street, Crewe,' it is interesting to dwell on certain aspects of religious worship during a period when church membership tended to occupy a more important place in the mind, and to exert a greater influence on the conduct, of the individual than it does now.

Let us begin, for example, with matters of church discipline. The minutes of the Church meetings, which have survived from 1855 onwards, reveal that non-attendance by members at Holy Communion might easily lead to expulsion from the Church, e.g., on February 27th, 1862:

> The pastor mentioned the names of some of the members of the Church who had absented themselves for some months from the Lord's Supper. James Swan has been waited upon by the pastor (and) requested the pastor to intimate to the church his wish to have his name withdrawn from the church book which was accordingly done. William Latham had been waited upon, but would give no satisfactory reason for his absence from the Lord's Supper. His case to stand over. A deputation was appointed by the Church (Mr. Eaton and Mr. Ridgway) to wait upon Mrs. Clucas and Mary Clucas respecting their absence from the Lord's table.

The result of these visitations was seen on the following May 8th and 29th, when:

> James Robertson presented a report of his interview with Mrs. Clucas and Mary Clucas which, proving perfectly satisfactory, it was unanimously resolved that Mrs. Clucas and her daughter be received into full communion.

> After a satisfactory statement made by James Robertson respecting an interview he had had with William Latham in reference to his absence from the Lord's Supper in which William Latham expressed his regret

and his earnest wish to return Brother Latham was unanimously received back into the fellowship of the Church.[17]

The change in the mid-nineteenth century Nonconformist attitude towards music in the chapel is particularly interesting. Until 1868 Crewe Congregational services were enlivened merely by hymn-singing and psalmody. It is true that at a church meeting held on February 26th, 1863, some daring but anonymous reformers proposed the introduction of 'instrumental music . . . into the service of the sanctuary,' but after some conversation on the subject on which the minister and the deacons expressed their wish 'that we should keep to our present congregational singing, it was resolved that the consideration of the subject should be laid aside for the present.'

Five years later, however, on July 30th, 1868, the church meeting asked W. Latham to form a choir, and information was sought as to the terms for the use of the organ in the Town Hall, where the church services were at that time held. On October 1st, 'Mr. Latham reported that his singing class was prepared to undertake the psalmody if the organ could be obtained.' On December 31st, 1868, it was moved by Mr. Yearsley and seconded by Mr. Dingley 'That the singing of the congregation be led by a choir,' of which W. Latham was appointed leader 'with the understanding that he is now responsible to the church for the conducting of the psalmody.' At the same time, the best thanks of the church were tendered to James Robertson 'for the able manner in which he has conducted the psalmody of the church for many years.' Chanting was introduced into the church services in 1877, when the church adopted *The Congregational Chant Book*. Even after the successful establishment of the choir the church had still to be provided with an organ, and James Robertson proposed, on June 3rd 1873, that 'the time has arrived when it is expedient to introduce a musical instrument into the church.' A resolution was carried on June 17th 'that we take steps to procure an organ for the church.' To raise funds for the proposed organ and to pay off the debt on the heating apparatus in the new chapel on Hightown, the members organised a bazaar. A harmonium was purchased 'on the three years' system'

17 On one occasion the Church took active cognizance of a matter of morals, e.g., at a church meeting held on September 1st, 1864, 'the pastor presented a report of his interview with . . . respecting the premature birth of his child. The pastor stated that . . . had expressed his deep penitence and that of his wife on account of their sin. It was resolved by the Church that while deeply sympathising with their erring brother and sister, and trusting that their penitence is sincere, still, to maintain the purity of the Church in the eyes of the world, it is desirable they should be suspended from Church fellowship for three months.

in 1875, but not until June 28th, 1876, was 'the scheme to obtain an organ' adopted; after this events moved quickly, for on February 28th, 1877, the church meeting resolved 'that there be an Organ recital on the opening of the organ,' and F. James was appointed the first organist (and also choirmaster) at a salary of £10 per annum.

In the early days of the congregation, general collections were only taken occasionally for special purposes, e.g., between September 16th, 1849, and December, 1851, only four general collections were taken, three of which were for the Sunday School, and one to reduce the chapel debt. From October, 1857, however, members of the Church and congregation were placed under an obligation to make a weekly offering towards the expenses of the church. 1881–2 saw a financial crisis in the affairs of the church, and it was decided to charge a minimum sum of one penny per Sunday, or one shilling per quarter for each regularly-occupied seat in the Church. At the same time, the pastor's salary was reduced to £150, and the number of general collections limited to four per year, for the Sunday School, the London Missionary Society, the Church Aid Home Missionary Society, and the Hospitals.

After six successful years, the Rev. W. A. Blake resigned his pastorate in March, 1873, to become leader of a church in Stockport, to the 'great regret' of the Crewe congregation. The following May, a student from Spring Hill College, Mr. A. W. Potts, accepted the unanimous invitation of the congregation to become its next pastor, and was ordained on October 13th, 1873. In the same year the Crewe church decided to enter the main current of the national movement by joining the Congregational Union of England and Wales. An earlier adherence in 1867 had lapsed.

The Rev. A. W. Potts' ministry proved to be the longest the Church has ever seen; it closed only with his death and was marked, after a bad start, by vigorous development and violent controversies.[18] At a time when most of the members of his congregation were either Liberal in politics, or thought that politics should not intrude upon religious worship, Mr. Potts, who was a man of strong opinions, made no secret of the fact that he opposed Home

18 On November 29th, 1877, a church meeting earnestly requested the pastor, who was disappointed at 'the non-progress in the Church' to reconsider his intended resignation, expressed its esteem and respect for him, together with a 'belief that under the influence of an extended mutual sympathy, affability and Christian earnestness, the future success of his ministry' might be secured. In 1888–9 a fierce quarrel broke out between the Rev. A. W. Potts and Jonathan Holliday, the superintendent of the Sunday School, during which the latter accused the pastor of telling 'a pack of lies.' The deacons supported Mr. Potts, and eventually effected both a reconciliation and a full apology from Mr. Holliday.

Rule for Ireland, and became an ardent Liberal Unionist.[19]

During the Rev. A. W. Potts' ministry several attempts were made to start a Congregational Mission in Crewe.[20] These efforts, if they had been successful, would have meant the eventual foundation of a second church. A preaching room in Frances Street had been taken and furnished towards the end of 1875, thanks to the financial aid of Thomas Hilditch. A committee of management from the parent church was nominated in the following March, and in May and June, 1876, the Cheshire County Union offered to send an evangelist to Crewe, and to pay his salary on appointment. The Frances Street Mission seems later to have been transferred to Nantwich Road, where it was definitely discontinued on June 27th, 1877. On December 11th, 1876, William Bacchus, a member and deacon of the Crewe Church, and a convert from the Wesleyan body, was declared 'a fit and proper person' to be recommended as the missionary of a second mission established in West Street. This West Street Mission flourished considerably and, in 1877, the Cheshire Union granted £50 towards the upkeep of the 'commodious and central building,' which had been fitted up there as a school and preaching room. A Mr. D'Ewart, Scripture reader from Denton, was appointed to take charge of it and, in 1878, the Union felt justified in raising the grant to £100. Unfortunately, D'Ewart 'turned out a disappointment,' whereupon a Mr. Moon of the Manchester Mission, took his place but in a much better room (July, 1878). He removed to Nantwich at the beginning of 1880, when the Mission was again placed under the management of a committee appointed by the Crewe Congregational Church. The Cheshire Union grant was reduced to £30 for supply preachers.[21] This amount was granted again in 1881, but the grant of £25 in 1882 proved to be the last.

There seems to have been a certain amount of friction on the subject of the Mission between the Executive Committee of the Cheshire Union and the Crewe Church. The financial situation of the Crewe Church was weak at

19 On March 2nd, 1904, the Church meeting unanimously adopted a resolution protesting against the Conservative Government's sanction to the ordinance authorising the introduction of Chinese labour into the Transvaal. See MS. Minutes of Church Meetings (1855–1919).

20 There had been attempts at evangelical work in 1864, when brothers Eaton, Cliffe, Griffiths, Parr and Dingley were appointed 'to visit the loiterers in the streets and invite them to attend the means of grace,' while brothers Mould and Roper were to 'look after the strangers who attend the chapel.' In 1870 'Cottage Meetings' had been held in various parts of the town.

21 Joseph Sibley took charge of the Mission in 1880–1, and W. Bacchus from 1881 until its discontinuance when he resigned from the diaconate and membership of the church, to be readmitted in 1892.

the time, and the missionary work tended to drain away enthusiastic members and badly-needed resources from the parent body, so that in spite of an offer of £50 from R. S. Hudson, of Bache Hall, Chester, it was decided in January, 1883, to discontinue the West Street Mission, on recommendation from a deputation of the Executive of the Cheshire Union. The Crewe congregation accepted an offer from the more active Wesleyans for the room and furniture. Whether this dissolution was a wise step or not must remain a matter of dispute, for the Mission members were on the point (September, 1882) of inviting a student from the Congregational Institute at Nottingham to become their evangelist, and had unanimously resolved to ask the officers and members of the parent chapel 'to permit us . . . to form ourselves into an Independent Church.'

The 1880s were marked by the foundation of two institutions which are inseparably connected with the Crewe Congregational Church. In 1886 the American Christian Endeavour movement was brought to the notice of the Rev. A. W. Potts by George Austin Charnock, a Crewe artisan who had emigrated to the U.S.A. some years previously, and later became a pastor of the Congregational Church, Bethany, California. The Rev. A. W. Potts organised No.1 branch (British section) of the movement in the course of 1887, and its early years are noteworthy for the work of Miss Annie Sudworth and Miss Emily Moore.[22] The 1880s also saw the foundation of the Juvenile Benefit Society in connection with the Church. This was a combined small fortnightly savings movement and insurance scheme to cover the cost of child burial, and averted many a humiliating application to the Poor Law or the pawnbroker, for funeral expenses often proved a crippling item in working-class budgets in those days of high birth-rates and a high level of infantile mortality. Based on the principle of the annual share-out, the 'J.B.S.' soon proved one of the most popular institutions in the town, being open both to members of the congregation and to the general public. Between 1894 and 1900 its membership increased from 1,896 to 3,689, and it still flourishes <1947>. The exact date of its foundation remains obscure, but it had evidently been in existence some time when first mentioned in the Church meeting minutes (January 22nd, 1890).

On Friday, May 27th, 1892, the church lost 'a most talented preacher and a man of strict integrity and uprightness' by the death of the Rev. A. W. Potts, at an age which gave promise of many more years of useful service. The

22 *Christian Endeavour Times*, December 31st, 1903, January 28th, 1904. Constant emigration meant that the Crewe Church had many links with Australia and the U.S.A.

respect and esteem in which the pastor was held may be judged from the number of messages of sympathy received from the other religious bodies in the town and county.

The succeeding pastorate was that of the Rev. A. E. Hawes of Wellingborough, who came to Crewe in May, 1893, when his salary was fixed at £150 with four free Sundays. He built on the solid foundation laid by the long ministry of the Rev. A. W. Potts, and during his tenure of office a new organ was installed at a cost of £500 to celebrate the jubilee year of the Congregational Chapel in Oak Street (1897). In 1900, F. James resigned his position as the church organist. He was succeeded in office by Mr. J. T. Peake, who carried on the tradition of long service until the 1940s. The organ has been blown by an electric motor since 1902. The earliest copy of the *Year Book of the Hightown Congregational Church, Crewe*, which has survived, dated January, 1894, reveals that the church possessed a flourishing Cricket Club, with a ground off Wistaston Road, founded in 1886, a Football Club founded in 1893, and a Young Men's Mutual Improvement Association formed the previous October.

Towards the close of the nineteenth century the tendency towards united action by all Nonconformist denominations became more evident. It was exemplified in the case of Crewe, both by a general house-to-house visitation scheme decided on by a combined meeting of the Nonconformist churches of the town in 1895, and by the foundation in 1897 of the Crewe and District Free Church Council, of which the Congregationalists in the area have been active members. In 1899 the Rev. A. E. Hawes succeeded in establishing a local edition of the *Congregational Magazine* (a previous attempt in 1870 to localise the *Christian Penny Magazine* had not been a success). The Rev. A. W. Potts for some years edited *Sun and Shield* in the interest of Congregationalism in West Cheshire.

The Rev. A. E. Hawes resigned in 1901, to accept a call to the Cheadle Hulme Congregational Church. He was succeeded by Mr. Herbert Cooper, a student from the Lancashire Independent College, Manchester, and a worker at the College Settlement in Hulme, who was ordained on October 8th, 1902. The Rev. Herbert Cooper's ministry was marked by increased efforts to evangelise the Crewe district. On September 20th, 1905, the pastor directed attention to the spiritual condition of the Church with which he considered the members should be profoundly dissatisfied. In the winter of 1905–6 he held week-night mission lectures with a view to deepening the spiritual life of the Church, and in 1906, the church meeting decided to advertise the services week by week for three months in one of the local newspapers, to ask the Sunday School teachers to consider the best means of inducing the scholars to attend the morning service, and to arrange for a free distribution of tracts by house-to-house visitation. At the same time, the Church supported the scheme of open-air services organised by the Crewe and District Free Church Council.

More lasting results were obtained from vigorous development of Sunday School work in 1904–8, by the vigorous partnership of Mr. and Mrs. T. E. Sackfield. Mrs. Sackfield (Miss Annie Sudworth) had joined the Church from the Sunday School at the age of sixteen in 1873. Her husband, T. E. Sackfield, joined the Church in 1882, was elected deacon in January, 1891, and Secretary of the Church in the following December, a post which he held for many years. After the opening of the new chapel in 1870, Sunday School services had been held in the large room underneath the church. Although a lecture room and a new class room were built on to the original structure in 1888 at a cost of over £500, raised by a 'grand Egyptian bazaar,' the school did not flourish as much as it might have done. Even the formation of a Boys' Brigade in 1893, and a Junior Endeavour Society in 1895, did little to increase enthusiasm and membership. Nevertheless, a very high proportion of Sunday School scholars became members of the Church at the age of seventeen and ensured a constant stream of new workers throughout the last quarter of the nineteenth century and early 1900s, thus replacing the constant wastage caused by migration, emigration, lapse and death.

A writer in one of the Crewe newspapers of 1908 wrote:

> ... of late it has been the wail of Churchmen of almost every sect and creed that the success of their Sunday Schools has tended rather to decrease than to increase. The cause of this anomaly has been the continual tolerance of old-fashioned methods, which instead of being attractive to the children, were of a dull and dreary character.

In the year 1872 there were 229 children and eighteen teachers on the books, but by 1904 this number of scholars had fallen to 212, of whom only thirty-six were infants. At this point Mr. and Mrs. Sackfield, aided by a devoted band of teachers, introduced the new methods on the model of those being introduced at the time into the secular day schools. The Sunday School was divided into three departments – the primary, the intermediate and the senior. In the primary or infant department 'it was felt that more illustrative teaching should be given in order to seize upon the imagination of the infants and to secure their interest in the Divine Truth.' Mrs. Sackfield took charge of the Primary Department, and by 1908 had fourteen assistants, who 'were to carry out Frederick Froebel's kindergarten principles, one of which was that a little child must be surrounded by an atmosphere of love, and another that they must treat the little child as a little child.' By the end of 1907 the effect of this new organisation showed itself, for the total number of Sunday scholars reached 311, of whom 109 were infants. By the autumn of 1908 the Sunday School included 169 infants. An entirely new kindergarten Sunday School on the northern side of the Church was, therefore, built at a cost of £472, and was opened on September 12th, 1908, by Francis Milne of Bowdon, chairman of the Cheshire Congregational Union.[23]

After six years of signal service the Rev. Herbert Cooper accepted a call to the Northgate Congregational Church at Chester in 1908. After his departure the pastorate remained vacant for twelve months until it was filled in November, 1909, by a young able and enthusiastic minister 'of progressive views and decided social sympathies' from Hanover Congregational Church, Stockport, the Rev. C. J. Barry. From the beginning of his short ministry of twenty months, the Rev. C. J. Barry, who was 'an optimist and a firm believer in Christian democracy,' made successful attempts to win the attention of non-churchgoers. On February 5th, 1911, with the financial backing of Mr. Frank A. Haworth, of Holmes Chapel, he inaugurated at his church the Crewe Men's Own Brotherhood. This was an undenominational religious organisation governed by a joint council of representatives of the Church and the Brotherhood. It was addressed on Sunday afternoons by speakers of local and national celebrity on the social and economic questions of the day, the subjects being treated from a broad religious angle. At various times between its foundation and the outbreak of the first World War packed meetings of the Brotherhood listened to lectures by the Marquis of Crewe, the Labour politician, J. A. Seddon, W. S. B. MacLaren, Liberal M.P. for the Crewe Division, 1910–12, and his Conservative successor, Ernest Craig (1912–18). The Brotherhood may be considered as one expression of the movement towards the 'Pleasant Sunday Afternoon' which marked the early twentieth century, and had been foreshadowed by an adult Sunday afternoon class formed by the Rev. A. W. Potts in 1889. At the end of February, 1922, the Brotherhood had about 1,000 members. By the end of the year it counted 1,400 adherents, and had taken over the Beech Street Institute as headquarters. For purposes of comparison, the resident membership of the Crewe Congregational Church in 1912 was 208. A Crewe Sisterhood was formed on the model of the Brotherhood in the course of 1918–20.

---

23 See *Crewe Guardian*, September 16, 1908, and *Crewe Chronicle*, September 19, 1908.

Much to the regret of the deacons and congregation, the Rev. C. J. Barry resigned the Crewe pastorate in September 1911, to become Superintendent of the Salford Central Mission at the invitation of the Manchester Congregational Board. He was succeeded in November 1911, by Mr. Joseph Pickthall, M.A., student of the Yorkshire United College, Bradford, who commenced his duties as pastor in the latter part of 1912 on the completion of his college course. The Rev. Joseph Pickthall, also inherited Barry's presidency of the Brotherhood (February 1912) and the beginning of his active pastorate coincided with the formation in September, 1912, of the Crewe and District Federation of Congregational Churches (Crewe, Nantwich, Haslington, Sandbach and Wheelock), which was in essence a scheme whereby three ministers sufficed to serve these five places of worship.

The financial problem still remained acute. In 1900, the Church deficit had to be met by appropriating the Ladies' Sewing Meeting Fund and throughout the first decade of the twentieth century frequent sales of work and bazaars were necessary to pay for the maintenance and extension of the fabric of the Church, and the provision of Divine Service.[24] This increased dependence on the money-raising efforts of women members of the church may be one of the reasons for the increasing part they played in church affairs. It was natural for the church to appoint a woman as its delegate to the Crewe Sick Nursing Association in 1898, or for ladies to serve on the first Sick and Absentee Visiting Committee to be elected in May, 1890, but in July, 1901, Congregational women members were appointed to the Crewe and District Free Church Council for the first time, while the minute books reveal increased activity on the part of lady representatives of the deacons during the same period.

The Rev. J. Pickthall's pastorate covered the major portion of the First World War, and for twelve months in 1915–16, he was absent as chaplain to H.M. Forces. On March 31st, 1918, he relinquished the charge at Crewe and accepted a call to the Hope Street Congregational Church, Wigan. After a vacancy of more than a year, the Rev. S. R. Laundy, of Stockport, accepted the pastorate in October, 1919, and laboured with much patience during the difficult post-war years, resigning in September, 1929. He was succeeded by the Rev. W. W. Evans (July 1930 to March 1939) and the Rev. F. W. Robinson (July 1940 to August 1944). After a vacancy of more than two years the Church was fortunate enough to secure the services of a young and

---

24 On October 1st, 1913, a scheme of self-assessment under the envelope system was adopted for raising the money required for the maintenance of divine worship.

enthusiastic RAF padre, the Rev. G. A. Thomas, in whose pastorate these centenary celebrations of the opening of the Oak Street Chapel in 1847 are being held. He has a unique opportunity in these difficult post-war years for carrying on and strengthening a Christian fellowship which has weathered the strains and storms of a century.

A NOTE ON THE CHURCH AND THE TOWN

Three members of the Church have served in the office of Mayor of Crewe for the following years:

Richard Whittle, 1879–80, 1884–5.

James H. Moore, 1899–1900, 1902–3.

Harry Hoptroff, 1906–8.

It is an interesting commentary on the nineteenth-century connection between Nonconformity and politics that these three citizens were prominent Liberals.

APPENDIX

When pessimists deplore the present-day apathy of the public towards matters of religion it is instructive to remember that even in April, 1914, a former Crewe Congregational minister could say:

> . . . it was perfectly true that for the past hundred years we had been living in times of religious disintegration. The increase of scientific investigation into religion was gradually bringing about an atmosphere and attitude which made people imagine that everything concerning it was open to question.[25]

G. Faulkner Armitage, in his inaugural address as chairman of the Cheshire Congregational Union, on April 8th, 1914, went into greater detail, and foreshadowed more recent denunciations of modern distractions a follows:

> He dwelt on the power of the Press, and referred to the harm done by a certain type of Sunday newspaper. Many other things competing with the churches for the people did not hide themselves in back streets or country lanes. Nor were the managers content just to open their doors for the public to come in as they chose They proclaimed with no uncertain sound the merits of their establishments. Those

25 Rev. Herbert Cooper, of Chester, quoted in the *Crewe Guardian*, April 14th, 1914.

places fed the public with high-spiced stuff and spoiled their taste for the simple services of the churches. He also criticised theatre and music hall performances. Football drew crowds in uncounted numbers. Had not the churches something to offer better worth having that? Merely to open their places of worship at certain hours that they, who had become fixed in their religious habits, were accustomed to, was quite futile, and to blame the people for not coming in was worse. The motor with its allurements, was monopolising too much of the spare time and money of one class to be good for it. They were shocked to observe the shameless manner men and women flaunted their reckless Sabbath-breaking customs in the eyes of the public. A great section of the community was doing its part in destroying the Sabbath peace on any road and in every village within a radius of fifty miles of a town or wealthy suburb. They could only hope as time went on those who enjoyed the motor would grow weary of rushing about, and would settle down to a rational use, and a more considerate feeling for the remainder of the world.[26]

BIBLIOGRAPHY

MS. Minutes of Church Meetings (1855–1919), 6 vols.

MS. Minutes of Deacons' Meetings (1889–1917), 5 vols.

Church Membership Roll (1849–1893).

Crewe Congregational Year Books, 1894, 1896–1900.

Annual Reports of the Cheshire Union of Congregational Churches, 1816–1865 (various dates).

Crewe Guardian newspaper, March 30th, 1878 (article by John Eaton, on Crewe Congregational Church).

F. J. Powicke: *A History of the Cheshire County Union of Congregational Churches* (1907).

W. Urwick: *Historical Sketches of Nonconformity in the County Palatine of Chester* (1864).

26 *Cheshire Observer*, April 11th, 1914.

CHAPTER II

BRIDGET BOSTOCK,
THE 'WHITE WITCH' OF COPPENHALL
NEAR NANTWICH IN CHESHIRE, 1748–9

Two kinds of witch are usually distinguished – the 'black witch', the doer of evil, and the 'white witch', the doer of good. Bridget Bostock, if indeed she can be called a witch at all, belonged to the second category, and the strange story of this faith-healer of South Cheshire is fairly well known to students of such matters. Her activities acquired a nation-wide fame in 1748, when, in Thomas Pennant's words, 'multitudes resorted to her from all parts, and kept her salival glands in full employ'. Miss Christina Hole has indicated the significance of her career admirably in the following passage:

> The distinction between the true white witch and the religious faith-healer was often very fine. Many cures were effected, or at least attempted, by a combination of prayer and magic. In the eighteenth century Bridget Bostock, of Church Coppenhall, Cheshire, cured diseases and cast out devils by prayer and the use of her own spittle. The latter was, of course, purely magical, the belief in the power of spittle being very ancient and still dimly remembered in the schoolboy's habit of spitting on his hands before a fight. To spit three times at a malicious witch was a form of protection, and to spit on the first money received during the day not only sealed the bargain but also destroyed any possible evil attaching to the coins. Bridget Bostock . . . was usually described as a white witch but it seems clear that she was a religious woman, and though she employed magic, she undoubtedly saw nothing diabolical or wicked in her own activities.[1]

---

1 *Witchcraft in England* (1945), pp. 106–7; see also Christina Hole: *Traditions and customs of Cheshire* (1937), p. 175. The licking or smearing of warts with spittle before breakfasting or cleaning one's teeth is still recommended as a folk-cure in parts of the country.

Up to the present, however, no handy account of 'the Cheshire Python-ess', embodying the most relevant portions of the evidence, has been compiled. The present record therefore consists chiefly of extracts from the *Gentleman's Magazine* for 1748 and 1749. Parts of the Rev. George Reade's letter to the editor of the *Gentleman's Magazine* and portions of the comment in *Old England*, indicated either by stops or asterisks, have been omitted as of little interest. The letter by 'J. T.' has been condensed for the same reason.

A search of the parish registers of Barthomley, Church Minshull, Coppenhall, Nantwich, Warmingham, Wistaston and Wybunbury failed to reveal the entries for Miss Bridget's christening and burial, although the names 'Bridget and 'Bostock' are of frequent occurrence from the seventeenth to the early nineteenth century in the district round Coppenhall.[2] The position is further complicated by the possibility that 'Bridget' may not have been the Christian name given to her on baptism. Cases have occurred in modern Coppenhall of persons who were popularly known by Christian names which did not appear on their birth and baptismal certificates. All we can say at the moment is that she was born about 1685 and died at some date between 1749 and the 1780s. The land-tax return for Church Coppenhall township dated 1787, and preserved at the County Record Office in Chester Castle, describes a house and land owned by James Bostock and occupied by Acton Bostock, jun., as 'Late Bridget Bostock's, Doctres[s]'. The holding paid 18s. 8d. to a land tax of 4s. in the £, and may have been the 'great hall house' to which she had removed in 1749. As far as can be ascertained, she left no will, although the wills of James Bostock (1786) and Acton Bostock (1799), both described as of 'Church Coppenhall, Yeoman', are preserved in the Court of Probate at Chester.[3]

RISE TO FAME

Gentleman's Magazine, September 1748, page 413.

London, Aug. 30, The following Paragraph appear'd in the Newspapers. 'Middlewych in Cheshire, Aug. 28.

2 E.g., Abigail, daughter of Ottiwell and Jane Bostock, baptised on March 23rd, 1683/4; Elizabeth, daughter of John and Elizabeth Bostock, jun., baptised on January 7th, 1697/8 (Warmingham Parish Registers).

3 *Lancashire and Cheshire Record Society*, Vol. 44, p. 14, Vol. 45, p. 19. This farmer, James Bostock, who was buried in Coppenhall churchyard on October 28th, 1787, may have been her nephew.

There is risen up in this country a great doctress, an old woman, who is resorted to by people of all ranks and degrees, to be cur'd of ALL diseases; she lives four miles from hence, and has been in this great fame about 2 months; she has several hundreds of patients in a day out of all the country round for 30 miles: I went to see her yesterday out of curiosity, and believe near 600 people were with her. I believe all the country are gone stark mad. The chief thing she cures with is fasting spittle and "God bless you with faith".'

September 1748, pages 413–14.

Extract of a letter from 'Namptwich' in Cheshire, dated August 24, 1748.

'Old Bridget Bostock fills the country with as much talk as the rebels did.[4] She hath, all her life-time, made it her business to cure her neighbours of sore legs, and other disorders; but her reputation seems now so wonderfully to increase, that people come to her from far and near. A year ago she had, as I remember, about 40 under her care, which I found afterwards increased to 100 a week, and then to 160. Sunday se'ennight, after dinner, my wife and I went to this doctress's house and were told my Mr. S——, and Tom M——, who kept the door, and let people in by fives and sixes, that they had, that day, told[5] 600 she had administer'd to, besides her making a cheese. She, at length, grew so very faint (for she never breaks her fast 'till she has done) that, at six o'clock, she was obliged to give over, tho' there were then more than 60 persons whom she had not meddled with. Monday last she had 700, and every day now pretty near that number. She cures the blind, the deaf, the lame of all sorts, the rheumatic, king's evil,[6] hysteric fits, falling fits, shortness of breath, dropsy, palsy, leprosy, cancers, and, in short, almost every thing, except the French disease,[7] which she will not meddle with; and all the means she uses for cure are, only stroking with her fasting spittle, and praying for them. It is hardly credible to think what cures she daily performs: some people grow well whilst

4 A reference to the Jacobite Rebellion of 1745–6
5 'Told' = counted.
6 'King's evil' = scrofula, which was, until 1714, believed to be healed by the touch of the reigning monarch of England. Dr. Samuel Johnson was touched for this disease by Queen Anne, without result. (D. Guthrie: *A history of medicine* (1945), pp. 210–11).
7 'French disease' = syphilis.

in the house, others on the road home; and, it is said, none miss: people come 60 miles round. In our lane, where there have not been two coaches seen before these twelve years, now three or four pass in a day; and the poor come by cart-loads. She is about 70 years of age, and keeps old Bostock's house, who allow'd her 35s. a year wages: and, tho' money is offered her, yet she takes none for her cures. Her dress is very plain; she wears a flannel waistcoat, a green linsey apron, a pair of clogs, and a plain cap, tied with a half-penny lace. So many people of fashion come now to her, that several of the poor country people make a comfortable subsistence by holding their horses. In short, the poor, the rich, the lame, the blind and the deaf, all pray for her, and bless her; but the doctors curse her.'[8]

September 1748, page 414.

We have received a Confirmation of these Accounts, as follows:
'Sɪʀ   Sandbach, Chesh. Sept. 16.

The old doctress, Bridget Bostock, lives at Coppenhall, between this place and Namptwich, being three miles from each. She is a very plain woman, about 64, and hath followed doctoring for some years to some few people in the neighbourhood. About a quarter of a year ago she came into great fame, for curing of most diseases, by rubbing the place with the fasting spittle of her mouth, and praying for them; she hath had 6 or 700 of a day, and it hath been so throng'd, that a great many people have come, that have stay'd a day or two before they could get to her. She now speaks to none but those that have been with her afore-time, and we hear she will not (till next April) excepting such, and those for deafness. The Rev. Mr Wm. Harding, minister of Coppenhall, gives her a very great character, and saith, that she is one that is a constant frequenter of his church.[9] A son of his was cured of his lameness by her immediately after he had been with her, when all other doctors could do him no service; Mrs. Gradwell, of Liverpool,

8   See also the version in *The Whitehall Evening Post, or London Intelligencer* newspaper, No. 401, Sept. 3rd to 6th, 1748, a copy of which may be inspected at the Nantwich Public Library.

9   William Harding was curate of Coppenhall from October, 1729, until his death on July 9th, 1775; the rectors at this time were absentees. His remuneration is said to have been about £50 per annum, with the use of the Rectory and grounds, on which he brought up a large family (six sons, one daughter). He was 'remembered with much pleasure and respect' (Coppenhall Parish Registers; *Crewe Guardian* newspaper, Aug. 31st, 1878).

hath wonderfully recover'd her sight, by the assistance of the said doctress. She helps and heals, in a wonderful manner, all persons that come to her, and doth more service to the world than all other doctors besides. Some of this neighbourhood have received great benefit; but others have been with her but little.'

THE SCEPTICAL PARSON

Gentleman's Magazine, October 1748, pages 448–51.

MR. URBAN,[10]
'In your Magazine for October, you are desired to insert the following, by Your constant Reader,

G. R.[11]   Over Peover, Sept. 26

It has been made a question by some, whether the extraordinary cures, ascribed to the famous Bridget Bostock, of Coppenhall, be natural or supernatural effects. I propose here to inquire, and hope to give such a resolution of the matter, as may satisfy reasonable and considering people.

The means she ordinarily makes use of, are to rub the parts affected with her fasting spittle, and to bless or pray for every one that attends her.

Now, whatever natural efficiency or sanative virtue any person may suppose to be in her hand, or her spittle, yet, that these are not the means by which any cure is effected, nor even necessary to be applied, I think it is undeniably evident from this plain matter of fact. Before she practised this way, she used only to take the names of her patients, and to make a short prayer for every one in particular; and I have been assured by a near neighbour, and one who has constantly attended her, that she cured with as much certainty and success then, without even so much as seeing the person, as she has done since. He likewise told me, that of late, when she has been attended by such crouds of people,

---

10 'Sylvanus Urban' – the Editor's 'nom-de-plume'.

11 'G. R.', who begins and ends his letter, here abbreviated, with Latin quotations, uses the word 'papist', and shows a turn for theological controversy, can be identified as the Rev. George Reade, M.A. (1715–1796), vicar of Over Peover from about 1739 to 1790, and rector of Baddiley 1759–96. Both these Cheshire livings were in the gift of the great Mainwaring family (Ormerod: *Hist. Ches.*, Vol III., ed. 1882, p. 458; list of incumbents at Over Peover).

that she could not possibly administer to all, some were sent away with her blessing only, it being all she was able to give them; and he believed it intirely sufficient. Nay, in several cases, such as convulsions, hystericks, and falling fits, she never requires more than the patient's name, and her prayer does the business. The only reason given for altering her first method is, because her patients presently became so numerous, that she could not, in her own phrase, think of them all. From hence it appears, that the application of her hand, and her fasting spittle, is a mere ineffectual ceremony, and that all the supposed efficacy lies in her blessing and her prayer, or words, whatever the form may be, which she makes use of. There is then no natural power in the means she uses to produce the effects pretended: . . .

Her cures then, if any be performed, must be supernatural or miraculous effects . . . (*Then G. R. argues that her cures cannot be miracles*) . . . A miracle is a conspicuous, instantaneous, a compleat and perfect work. It is conspicuous, and obvious to the senses of every spectator; her pretended cures are not so: . . . most of her pretended cures advance by time and slow degrees: . . . [and] . . . are so different [from miracles], that, to my certain knowledge, several persons have relapsed; and this is so incontestable, that for these ten days past she has admitted but few, except her old patients.

Besides, there is no instance upon record, and it is indeed absurd to suppose, that any person should be favoured with a power of working miracles, and not know that he is possessed of such a power, nor from whence it is derived, nor for what end it was given: But this however is the case of our Copnall doctress. Her wonder-working power she ascribes to the stars, and thinks she can effect any cure, only because she fancies herself born under a lucky planet. So gross is her ignorance.

* * * * *

But after all, why may we not suppose her endowed with this gift of healing, upon account of preserving her virginity to an advanced age? There are some persons weak enough to think so. . . . And yet I can hardly think that virginity has any such virtue annex'd to it: for if that were so, what a rare number of doctresses, both old and young, should we have in every town!

It is now, I hope, sufficiently proved, that the cures, said to be wrought by this old woman, are neither natural nor supernatural effects. The consequence, I am afraid, will be, that then they are none at all. And I cannot help it: for I never heard of a third sort, really distinct from those mentioned. That this, in short, is the truth of the case, I am fully convinced upon good grounds, and a careful enquiry; insomuch that I dare challenge her warmest advocates, to produce a single instance of a cure, that can be fairly proved to be wrought by her means.

But yet I will not deny, that several persons may have received a good deal of benefit, by going to her and attending her. A gentle walk, or an easy ride, at a fine season of the year, might greatly relieve some, who perhaps, for a long time before, had used no such exercise. She requires a very great degree of Faith in her patients; . . . Now, in many cases, where the imagination has any power to assist, this faith, one may conceive, together with that air of confidence and assurance, which she and the people about her put on, will strangely heighten and invigorate it, and very much promote the cure, if not entirely effect it. . . . In other cases, nothing could happen to any of her patients, but what would as certainly have happen'd, if they had staid at home.

* * * * *

But here, I fancy, some body may be ready to say, Why is this scribbler so warm and zealous in the cause? If he does not like to be spit upon by the old woman, why should he thus spit at her? I warrant you he is some doctor.

My answer is, whatever the writer be, he can see no reason for the doctors being so much against her, . . . for 'tis likely, if she proceeds in the same way she has lately done, that she will create them more business, than twenty quacks, attended by all their train of tumblers, rope-dancers, and merry-andrews, could do.'

ANOTHER SCEPTIC, AND A PERSONAL INTERVIEW WITH BRIDGET BOSTOCK

October, 1748, same pages as above:

From the *General Evening Post*, Oct. 18.

'SIR,   Bewdley, Oct. 14.

Notwithstanding what is asserted in letters from Cheshire . . . of the famous Bridget Bostock, who, they say, cures all diseases, I can assure you 'tis an imposition, and downright falsehood; and tho' most in the neighbourhood may be willing to abet the cheat, for the sake of the advantage they may receive from such numbers continually flocking thither, yet many of them are so honest as to confess the truth, and own they believe her to have no just claim to any extraordinary healing power.

About a week since, I had the curiosity to go with a friend, about a mile out of our way, to see this miraculous woman. When we came to the house, we were informed by a young fellow who kept the door, that she would see no more that day; but being admitted after a little parley, we saw an old shrivelled creature seated in an elbow-chair, in a most dirty attire, and her petticoats not reaching above half-way down her legs. – At sight of us, she looked very much discomposed, and said she would meddle with no body more that day (imagining, I suppose, we wanted to have the blessing of her gums); we told her we had no complaint, but came purely to have the satisfaction of seeing and conversing with so extraordinary a woman. At first she was somewhat reserved, but, after a little time, she conversed with us pretty freely for above half an hour.

There were great numbers of scraps of paper stuck up on the walls, whereon the patients (or some body for them) had written their names, and the disorders they were afflicted with, which most people that come there take for so many cures performed by Dame Bridget; but she honestly told us they were only so many remembrancers for her to pray for them, and that she had nearly a bushel more above stairs. How ridiculous this is, and how it tends to deceive the vulgar, let any one judge. Indeed I scarce think the old woman can read writing, but if she can, I defy her to make out one in ten of those papers.

She says she does not pretend to cure all disorders, nor will promise wholly to cure any, but believes with her fasting spittle, and by praying for them (if they have faith) she may do them good; that she did not desire such numbers of people to come after her, but that somebody had put her in the *Gazette*, since which she could scarcely have any rest.

I told her, I heard she put off great numbers that came four-score or a hundred miles, with the frivolous excuse of not meddling with such disorders till after such a time; this I represented as a great unkindness to those poor creatures (some of whom I had seen on the roads, who indeed were miserable objects) if she had it in her power to relieve them; she reply'd, very sharply, "What do I care? I did not send for them; let them stay if they will."

An instance I was witness to myself, will enable us to judge of the virtue of her fasting spittle. There came in a woman of the neighbourhood, who had a little redness on her forehead, about as big as a crown-piece, but no swelling, which Bridget called St. Anthony's Fire; and having then some foul earthen dishes in her hand (out of which, I suppose, she had been eating) she immediately put them down: "Come", says she to the patient, "I'll rub it, however, with my spittle, tho' I have eat a bit of meat, it will do as well".

Upon the whole, she appears to me to be a very ignorant creature, tho' (by the bye) she seems to have been instructed by some more artful persons, being sometimes much on her guard.

The noise that this silly woman has made, even among the vulgar, is surprising; but, that any person who pretends to any degree of sense, should be so deluded as to go near an hundred miles after her, is still more surprising.'

November, 1748, page 513.

J.T. wrote a long letter in support of Bridget Bostock, and argued that, if as, G.R. alleged, she required 'a great degree of faith in her patients', so did Jesus Christ; then he entered into a long disquisition on healing and salvation by faith.

August 1749, page 343.

Extract from a letter from Oxfordshire, August 20.

'About a month since Mr. Christopher Lucas, a gardener in Thame, carried the following persons into Cheshire, to Mrs.[12] Bridget Bostock (who has now taken a great hall house) to have them cured, 1. his own wife, with an incurable palsie; 2. Mary Canon, the daughter of Thomas Canon, bell-man of the town, who hath been blind for 5 years; 3. the wife of Mr. Samuel Dudley, a grocer, with a pluresie in her side, turned out uncurable, from the hospitals in and about London. – The latter is come home cured but the other two remain as they were, and are likely to continue so.

Yours, D. H.'

---

12 Although she was sometimes described as 'Dame' or 'Mrs.', Bridget Bostock was a spinster.

THE CREDULOUS BARONET

Old England, a London newspaper edited by a journalist who hid his identity under the name and style of '*Argus Centoculi, Inspector-General of Great-Britain*,' contains a front-page article in its issue No. 259 of Saturday, April 15, 1749, which enables us to connect Bridget Bostock with a 'very credulous and eccentric, but otherwise a very worthy man', Sir John Pryce Bt., of Newtown Hall, Montgomeryshire.

Sir John, the fifth baronet, the son of Sir Vaughan Pryce, Bt., was born about 1698–99. He succeeded to the title and estates on his father's death, April 30, 1720. His first wife, Miss Elizabeth Powel, died on April 22, 1731, and in 1737 he took as his second wife Mary Morris, the daughter of John Morris, a farmer, of Wern Goch, Berriew. There is a tradition that he met his second wife while taking shelter under a tree during a storm, and taking a fancy to her, married her. She died on August 3, 1739, aged 24 years. Her epitaph refers to the 'Cloud of Infamy which had been cast upon her Character by Envious and Malicious persons' and states that her decease was 'most unfortunately occasioned by their unjust aspersions'. From this it has been surmised that, owing to her humble origin, Sir John, while she lived, kept his marriage with her a secret; and that it was generally supposed that she was only his concubine, not his wife, a fact which preyed upon her mind and caused her death of a broken heart, within two years of her marriage. It is said that he had his two first wives embalmed, and kept them in his room, one on each side of his bed.

On July 6, 1741, Sir John addressed a letter to the Rev. William Felton, curate of Newtown, who was then lying dangerously ill, and did indeed die the very next day, requesting that after his (Felton's) death and entry into Heaven

> . . . you will do me the favour to acquaint my two Dear Wives, both of which you will be sure to find within those happy Regions, and questionless within the same mansion too, that I retain the same tender Affections and the same Honour and Esteem for their Memories which I ever did for their persons, and to tell the latter that I earnestly desire, if she can obtain the Divine permission, that she will appear to me, to discover the persons who have wronged her and to put me into a proper method of vindicating those wrongs which robb'd her of her life and me of all my happiness in this world . . .

Before long, however, he was so far consoled as to become enamoured of

Eleanor, widow of Roger Jones of Buckland, Breconshire. This lady is said to have declined the honour of his hand until her defunct but embalmed rivals were committed to their proper resting-places. Be that as it may, Sir John married her on December 19, 1741, at the parish church of Llansantffraid, Breconshire. She brought him a marriage portion of £15,000, and after about 1743 he appears to have quitted Newtown, and taken up residence at Buckland, Breconshire. The third Lady Pryce died in 1748, and soon afterwards Sir John wrote a letter to the Cheshire doctress, then at the height of her fame. This letter was printed, but without the sender's name and address, by the editor of *Old England*, with the following preliminary comment:

Two happy Days in Marriage are allow'd
A Wife in Wedding Sheets and in a Shroud:
How then can Wedlock-State be thought accurst
When the last Day's as happy as the first?

The following Letter is put into my Hands by a Gentleman who vouches for it's Genuineness. It was wrote by a Person of Consideration and some Dignity in his Country, to a poor, indigent, old Woman, whose Spittle and Prayers the Roman Catholics, in the North-West parts of England, set up as Universal Medicines, to heal all Sorts of Distempers whatsoever, affecting human kind, and never known to have failed. The spreading Fame of this miraculous Doctress, and her cheap Medicine, reached the Ears of all Sorts of Condition of People, thro' the Nation, and even the Minds of so many, as to render the poor Creature very uneasy by their Followings, in order to be spit upon. This Occurrence often put me in Mind of the poor Woodman in the Farce of *'The Mock-Doctor'*, who was cudgelled into the Faculty and Knowledge of Medicine at once; and it seems this poor Woman was as unwilling as the Woodman to prescribe, till she was forced to adapt the Conceit of other People,and do as they entreated her. Thus many a good old Woman was formerly overpowered by the Opinion of others, to believe and confess herself a Witch. I should not have wondered if the Infatuation of Mrs. Bostock's Power of healing had run only among the credulous Vulgar, who love to deceive and be deceived; but to find People of Education and good Sense join in the public Cry, is somewhat astonishing, as there is no accounting for it in a rational Way, without recurring to the Operations of an Enthusiastic Brain. But I give the Letter in the Words I received it.

'To Mrs. [Bridget] Bostock, at Namptwich, Cheshire.
Madam,

   Being very well informed by various Accounts, both public and
private, that you have performed several wonderful Cures, even when
Physicians have failed; and that you do it by the Force and Efficacy of
your Prayers mostly, if not altogether, the outward Means you use
being generally supposed to be inadequate to the Effects produced; –
I cannot but look upon such Operations to be miraculous; and if so,
why may not an infinitely good and gracious God enable you to raise
the Dead, as well as heal the Sick, give Sight to the Blind, and Hearing
to the Deaf? For since he is pleased to hear your Prayers in some Cases
so beneficial to Mankind, there is the same Reason to expect it in
others, and consequently in that I have particularly mentioned, namely
raising the Dead. Now, as I have lately lost a Wife whom I most dearly
loved, my Children one of the best of Stepmothers, all her near
Relations a Friend whom they greatly esteemed, and the Poor a
charitable Benefactress; I entreat you, for God Almighty's Sake, that
you will be so good as to come here, if your actual Presence is
absolutely requisite; if not, that you will offer up your Prayers to the
Throne of Grace on my Behalf, that God would vouchsafe to raise my
poor departed Wife Dame E[leanor] P[ryce], from the Dead. This is
one of the greatest Acts of Charity you can possibly do, for my Heart
is ready to burst with Grief at the Consideration of so great a Loss.
This would be doing myself and all her Relations and Friends such an
extraordinary Kindness, as would necessarily engage our daily Prayer
for your Preservation, as the least Gratuity we could make you for so
great a Benefit; tho' were any other compatible with the Nature of the
Thing, and durst we offer or you accept, we should think nothing too
much to give, to the utmost of our Abilities; but I suppose this is not
lawful even to attempt, and I wish that the bare Mention of it is not
offensive both to God and you. If your immediate Presence is absolutely necessary, pray let me know it at the Return of the Post, that I
may send a Coach and Six and Servants to attend you here, with
Orders to defray your Expences in a Manner most suitable to your
own Desire; or if your Prayers will be as effectual at the Distance you
are from me, pray signify the same in a Letter directed by way of
London, to, good Madam,

   Your unfortunate and afflicted petitioner and humble Servant,
   [John Pryce]
   [Buckland,] Dec. 1, 1748.

P.S. [Pray direct your Letter to Sir John Pryce, Bar't., at Buckland in Brecknockshire, South Wales.] God Almighty prosper this your undertaking and all others intended for the Benefit of mankind and may He long continue such an useful person upon Earth and afterwards crown you with Eternal Glory in the Kingdom of Heaven, for Jesus Christ's sake. Amen.'[13]

The editor of *Old England* continued:

I make no doubt but a ludicrous Construction of this Letter will occur to the Wags of the Town, who will be more merry than wise upon the Subject. All the old Jokes upon Matrimony will be revived, and an Emulation for coining new ones will prevail among our Smatterers in Wit. We shall have them say, That a dead Wife is much better than a living one; and that many a good Man would be glad to make the Gentleman a Compliment of his Wife to repair his Loss, if Wives were transferable; or perhaps to exchange a living for his dead Wife. I know very well, that our Libertines will wonder at the Gentleman's Singularity, in being so very sollicitous to raise what most Men of Fashion would give half their Worth to lay; and that if Mrs. Bostock's Spittle could operate in this last Way, she would have much more Business upon her Hands, tho' she might endanger her Health by spitting herself into a Consumption in a little Time. But as I apprehend, that our old Batchelors will be the severest on this Occasion, I must tell them, with Shakespear in '*Macbeth*', *You have no Wife to lose*, and consequently are no competent Judges of the Loss of a good Wife. As a Parody on what Dryden says of the Pleasure in being mad, I say, *There is a Pleasure in being married which none but married Men know*. I must therefore warn our Batchelors to forbear their Invectives against a State they are wholly ignorant of, and measure only from outward Appearances, extravagantly enlarged and overstrained by a fertile Imagination . . .

But one can't resolve in what Light to consider this extraordinary Letter, as the Writer does in no wise appear to be an ignorant Person,

13 This letter is also printed, in an incomplete and garbled form, in Thomas Pennant: *Tours in Wales* (1778–81), Vol. III (Part III), pp. 189–191 (edition of 1810), and in a fuller and more correct version in *Archaeologia Cambrensis*, Vol. V (second series), 1854, pp. 108–9, from which the portions in square brackets have been added. There are other slight differences between the *Old England* version and the *Archaeologia Cambrensis* version, the most important being that in Bridget Bostock's address, which is given in the latter publication as 'near Whitchurch, Shropshire'.

but manifestly in the opposite Class; since a Strain of good Sense, as well as good Argument, run thro' the whole Letter, tho' conducted on wrong Principles. That nothing is impossible to God is a divine Maxim, and an Attempt to purchase the Spirit we find severely punished in the Case of Simon Magus in the Gospel. Upon these Topics the Gentleman seems to ground his Application and Hopes of Success. 'Tis no bad Reasoning to conclude, and consequently believe, that a Person favoured by Heaven one way, may be still further enabled to do Good among Mankind. Diseases may be healed by human Means so long as Breath remains in the Patient, but when that is gone nothing but supernatural Power can restore it. This, we read in the New Testament, hath been frequently done; – but this we are not to expect in these Days, for we are taught that Miracles have ceased. I will not enter into the Merits of the Dispute which is now on foot, in relation to Miracles, further than to say with Sir Roger de Coverley, that *much may be said on both Sides;* which I apprehend is all the Satisfaction we are to expect from the Debates of the learned Pens engaged in the Question.

If we should allow the Gentleman a Share of good Sense, we must at the same Time give up his Judgment, which seems to have been impaired from the melancholy Contemplation of his Loss working upon a disordered Imagination, and Misapplication of what he had read, into a State of Enthusiasm; for what is there that the jaundiced Eye of Enthusiasm will not see, it's fanciful Ear not hear, or it's fanatical Mind not conceive? . . .

It is asserted by two authorities that Bridget Bostock actually visited Sir John's house in Wales to 'bring back to life his dead lady, who was then coffined in a room therein . . . but upon this occasion, at all events, her art failed her, poor Lady Eleanor Pryce being quietly buried with other dead members of her family, to make room for a successor, who refused to wed Sir John, until the remains of his former lady had been removed to mother earth for safety.'[14]

In the absence of any contemporary evidence these statements must be accepted with reserve. At the time of his death, which took place on October 28, 1761, Sir John was apparently on the eve of being married to a fourth wife, Miss Martha Harries of Haverfordwest, to whom he left by his will dated June 20, 1760, nearly all the property he had power to devise. In the

14 *Bye Gones*, Vol. I, August 1878, p. 80.

will he referred to her as his 'most dear and most entirely beloved and intended wife', and it is significant that in a deed executed in 1765 he is described as 'late of Haverfordwest'.[15]

15 The material on Sir John Pryce is to be found in *Collections historical and archaeological relating to Montgomeryshire* (Powysland Club), Vol. XVI (1883), pp. 39–45, 283–92.

CHAPTER III

THE CHESHIRE ACTIVITIES OF MATTHEW BOULTON AND JAMES WATT OF SOHO, NEAR BIRMINGHAM, 1776–1817

In 1775 Matthew Boulton and James Watt, of Soho, near Birmingham, entered into partnership to carry on the business of supplying and erecting Watt's improved separate condenser steam engine, the patent for which, originally granted in 1769, had been extended by Act of Parliament in 1775 for twenty-five years.[1] Watt's steam engine was not the first to be put to commercial use. Pumping engines of the Newcomen, or atmospheric, type had been erected in considerable numbers in Great Britain since 1712, although, with the exception of one, replaced just before 1766, at Norbury colliery, south of Stockport,[2] it does not appear that any were set to work in Cheshire. Engines on the old, or Newcomen, construction continued to be erected, chiefly in colliery districts, long after 1775. Watt's engines, however, did the same amount of work as Newcomen engines of the same size with the consumption of only one-quarter to one-third of the fuel. This represented a great financial saving in districts where coal was scarce and dear. The early Watt engines were, like atmospheric engines, of the reciprocating type, working with an up-and-down motion, pumping water from one level to another. They could only be made to drive machinery indirectly, i.e., by replenishing mill dams which drove water-wheels, or by directly pumping the tail water back on to the wheel. Boulton and Watt erected only one engine of the reciprocating type in Cheshire. In 1781 Watt improved his

---

1 For Boulton and Watt and the steam engine, see E. Roll: *An early experiment in industrial organization* (1930); H. W. Dickinson and Rhys Jenkins: *James Watt and the steam engine* (1927); H. W. Dickinson: *James Watt* (1935); and H. W. Dickinson: *Matthew Boulton* (1936).

2 Anon.: *History of inland navigations*, 1st ed., 1766, part ii, p. 18; *Manchester Mercury*, 9 Oct., 1764, p. 4.

steam engine by making it rotative, so that it could be applied to driving machinery directly. Between 1785 and 1817 thirty Boulton and Watt rotary engines of the sun-and-planet, beam-crank and side-lever independent types were set to work in the county of Chester, with a total horse-power of somewhere between 523 and 529. Of these, seventeen were erected in or near Stockport.[3] The firm of Boulton and Watt therefore played an important part in stimulating the Industrial Revolution in Cheshire.

THE THURLWOOD (LAWTON) BEAM PUMPING ENGINE

In November 1776, soon after the new partnership had commenced operations, Watt received an enquiry from N. Henshall of Knypersley, Staffs., near Lawton in Cheshire,[4] about a steam engine to be erected for a friend of Henshall's.[5] This friend was apparently Edward Salmon of Hassall Hall, near Lawton, who was in partnership with a certain Dr. Penlington in the concern known as Lawton Salt Works at Thurlwood, 3½ miles S.E. of Sandbach, near the newly-opened Trent and Mersey, or Grand Trunk Canal.[6] In the course of 1777 Boulton and Watt agreed to erect a pumping engine of 4 h.p., with an 18" diam. cylinder, stroke 3' 2", which was cast and bored at John and William Wilkinson's foundry at Bersham near Wrexham. The whole engine cost £400, of which £300 was for the engine and materials and £100 for Boulton and Watt's licence to use the same for the duration of the patent. There was a good deal of delay in erecting the engine, but on January 31, 1778, James Watt wrote to Salmon:

> I intend to be at Lawton on Tuesday evening or Wednesday morning. One of our workmen, James Law, sets out on Sunday afternoon and will be at Lawton on Monday. I feel very much for your disappointment and had the causes of my delay in coming to you threatened

3 For fuller details see Appendix 1, pp. 45–9.

4 Lawton is five miles S.E. of Sandbach.

5 Watt to Henshall, Nov. 12, 1776; see also Watt to Henshall, April 27, 1777.
    The references to letters in this and succeeding footnotes are from the Boulton and Watt letter books and in-letters in the Birmingham Public Library (hereafter referred to as B. and W. Coll.)

6 The Red Bull inn at Lawton was once a stage on the packhorse route between the Potteries and the ports on the River Mersey, and after the cutting of the canal remained a transport centre of some importance. For example, the Macclesfield Copper Company held from John Lawton the twenty-one-year lease, from February 2, 1789, of a warehouse with a crane and other conveniences 'situate on the Staffordshire Canal, near to the Red Bull, in Lawton.' (Bill of Sale, 1801.)

anything less than the ruin of our affairs, I should have merited a reproach on that account.

In April 1778 we learn that Watt had been 'so busy' in Cheshire that certain engineering drawings had been delayed,[7] but the engine was apparently set to work early in that month and gave complete satisfaction. Boulton and Watt were well aware of the value of publicity, provided it was combined with a certain degree of secrecy, for when Salmon wished to put something in the newspapers about the machine, Watt replied (April 9, 1778):

If you insert anything about us in the advertisement I would not have more than the following: We hear from Lawton Salt-works that Mr. S. has now completed his new works on the banks of the Staffordshire canal, which are esteemed to be the most complete in their way of any in the county: the reservoir of brine is situated 100 yards above the brine in the pit and higher than the canal. It is filled with brine by a small fire engine constructed by Boulton and Watt of Birmingham which does its business with great ease and a very small consumption of fuel.[8]

The details which found their way into print were fortunately more ample than the above, for *The history of inland navigations, particularly that of the Duke of Bridgewater*[9] contains the following:

Extract of a letter from Manchester, June 25, 1779.
. . . nor can I pass silently over the capital and new-erected salt-works, built upon the banks of the navigable canal at Thurlwood in Cheshire, the property of Messrs. Salmon and Penlington. In an adjoining valley they have fixed a fire engine, constructed by Messrs. Boulton and Watt, which, in the waste of three hundredweight of coals, (value

7   Logan Henderson to Gilbert Meason, April 4, 1778; see also Watt to John Wilkinson, Feb. 24, 1777; Boulton to Salmon, Feb. 16. 1777; Watt to Salmon, March 28, Oct. 27, 1777.

8   See also Boulton to Edward Salmon, April 16, 1778; Watt to Salmon, Aug. 13, 1779, Sept. 11, 1780, Jan. 7, July 18, Dec. 23, 1783; receipt for £400 and licence dated Birmingham, Aug. 25, 1779; Watt to Weston, Aug. 21, 1779. It is interesting to know that Salmon sent a present of Cheshire cheese, for Watt wrote on August 13, 1779: 'My cheese proved very good; one is still untouched.'

9   Anon.: 3rd edition (1779), p. 102. The first (1766) and third editions of this anonymous work are ascribed by the *British Museum Catalogue of Printed Books* to James Brindley (1716–1772), the Duke of Bridgewater's famous canal engineer, but this is open to doubt. There was a second edition in 1769.

nine-pence) does in twelve hours throw up to the height of a hundred yards, not less than twenty-four thousand gallons of brine; which is received in a very large reservoir and from thence conveyed to the salt-pans, where the salt is extracted and loaded into barges, in which it is carried into Staffordshire, Derbyshire, and the neighbouring counties.

By 1800 the Lawton saltworks and the steam engine attached to them had become the property of the Rev. Sir Thomas Broughton, Bt., of Doddington Hall, N. Staffs. (d.1813), head of the Delves-Broughton family, for in that year he asked Boulton and Watt to despatch an engineer to inspect it.[10]

The performance of Salmon's engine soon brought enquiries from another industrialist in the area. On May 3, 1779, James Paddey of Street, who operated a water-driven hammer, wrote to Boulton and Watt:

> I have a forge situated within about a mile of Lawton salt-works where you erected an engine for Mr. Salmon . . . though we do a great deal of business [we] are notwithstanding in the summer time much distressed for water. I have some thoughts of erecting a fire engine upon your construction to return at least a part of my water into the pool again.

Owing to pressure of other work Boulton and Watt had to decline the job of helping to refill Paddey's hammer-pond.[11]

This seasonal irregularity of water supply also lost another Cheshire forge the distinction of being the iron-works to supply the boiler-plates for the first Boulton and Watt engine to be erected abroad. On February 12, 1779, Watt ordered eighty-eight boiler-plates, which were to be used in conjunction with a pumping engine on a coal mine owned by Mons. Jary of Nantes in Brittany, from Nicholas Ryder, of Marston Forge, two miles N.E. of Northwich, 'to be delivered in Chester in 3 weeks at furthest.'[12] Ryder

---

10 Boulton and Watt to Broughton, Oct. 10, 1800. See also E. Hughes: *Studies in administration and finance, 1558–1825* (1934), pp. 361, 475. In 1782 Salmon wrote to Boulton requesting him to refuse to erect a steam engine for an unnamed rival. Watt replied (Jan. 7, 1783): '. . . we look upon ourselves, as so far servants of the public, in consequence of the exclusive privilege granted to us, as not to dare avowedly to refuse to serve any person who offers an adequate compensation for our trouble.' But on December 23, 1783, Watt wrote to Salmon as follows: 'No application has ever been made to us from the quarter you mention, and if any comes, we shall decline it if possible, or at least make them pay properly for it, but we will not do it at all if we can avoid it by any fair means.'

11 See their reply to Paddey, Letter Book (Office), 1778–80, p. 177.

12 See also Watt to Ryder, Jan. 27, 1779, Ryder to Watt, Feb. 2, 1779. Twenty more plates were ordered on April 19, 1779 (Watt to Ryder).

was engaged, presumably, in manufacturing and repairing the large iron salt pans used by the Cheshire salt-boilers. On March 30, 1779, however, Ryder wrote to Watt:

> I have been very short of water through this exceeding dry weather . . .
> I shall take it as a favour if you can give me two months to finish the complement of plates.

By the end of May we find more excuses. Ryder became 'exceedingly uneasy' at the contents of a letter he received from Watt:

> I had begun making your plates and had got pretty forward . . . when I was called upon by a particular customer and one, too, who had some connections with me, for some boiler plates, much like those prepared for you, and lying under some necessary obligations, [I] was obliged to let my friend have them. This is therefore to request that if possible you would indulge me with a little longer time, being at present rather short of water and very full of orders.[13]

It is somewhat surprising that Watt did not finally lose patience with Ryder until September 1779, when he transferred the order to Job Parsons,[14] of Burton-on-Trent, and wrote to John Wilkinson:

> I . . . will . . . set Mr. Ryder down in the black book for non-efficiency.[15]

THE ROTATIVE ENGINES, 1785–1817

No further Boulton and Watt engines were erected in Cheshire until 1785, when Samuel Walker, George Walker, and Hugh Ley, corn and flour merchants of Chester, entered into an agreement dated June 1, whereby for a payment of £50 per annum they received Boulton and Watt's licence to use a 14 h.p. rotative engine 'able to grind 14 Winchester bushels of wheat into flour in one hour.'[16] Either the firm or the engine was not particularly successful, for George Walker was trying to dispose of the latter some years later.

On January 1, 1789, John Gilbert of Worsley in Lancashire, agent to the Duke of Bridgewater, agreed on behalf of himself and partners to pay

---

13 Ryder to Watt, May 29, 1779; see also Watt to Ryder, March 7 – Sept. 16, 1779, *passim.*
14 Parsons became Boulton and Watt's standby in boilermaking (see Dickinson and Jenkins: *op. cit.*, p. 237).
15 Watt to Wilkinson, Sept. 20, 1779.
16 See agreement in B. and W. Coll.

Boulton and Watt £50 per annum for licence to use a 10 h.p. engine for the purpose of drawing or winding rock salt and pumping brine and water out of 'a certain salt mine called Marston Rockpits situated near Northwich on the Trent and Mersey canal.'[17]

Then from the beginning of 1791, with the adaptation of steam power to various processes of the rapidly expanding cotton industry, there was a run of orders for engines for Cheshire which lasted until the financial crisis of 1792–3. The well-known Samuel Oldknow of Stockport and Mellor was the first in the field, with an 8 h.p. engine for his mill in the Higher Hillgate, Stockport (February 1791), where it was apparently used for winding hanks of cotton and driving carding engines.[18] In December 1798, Oldknow was obviously in great financial difficulties, as he had fallen two years in arrears with the yearly rent of £40 on the engine and he did not pay up until September 1799.[19] By 1798 both mill and engine had been leased to the firm of Parker, Sykes and Co., from whom they passed into the possession, firstly of the famous William Radcliffe of Mellor and his partner Thomas Ross of Montrose, and secondly, after Radcliffe's bankruptcy in 1807, to J. B. Spencer and Co.

No orders for engines for Cheshire were received between April 1792 and May 1795. In the latter month Michael Bott of Burton-on-Trent, Moses Birch of Barton-under-Needwood, Staffs., and Edward Bower and Joseph Randell of Birmingham ordered what eventually became a 26 h.p. engine for £1,060 to convert their cotton-spinning mill established at Nantwich about 1788 from water- to steam-power.[20] There was some opposition to the introduction of the steam engine into Nantwich, for Bott, Birch and Co.

---

17 See agreement in B. and W. Coll. There is a short description of either this mine or Thomas Marshall's mine (see Appendix) in John Mawe's *Mineralogy of Derbyshire* (1802), pp. 162–3.

18 G. Unwin and others: *Samuel Oldknow and the Arkwrights*, pp. 128–9, 130–2, 147, 199–200, 148–50.

19 Gregory Watt to Oldknow, Dec. 7, 1798, Sept. 20, 1799. The mill and its engine were advertised for sale in 1798.

20 Bott was probably related to the Charles and John Bott who were partners in a cotton-spinning mill at Tutbury in Staffs. (A. Redford: *Labour Migration in England*, p. 26; J. Hall: *History of the town and parish of Nantwich*, 1883, pp. 241–2; Sir Oswald Mosley: *History of the castle, priory and town of Tutbury* (1832), pp. 310–11). The Nantwich area was a point where Lancashire and Midlands investors met, both during the early cotton boom and the early railway age (1825–50). Ralph Fogg, cotton merchant of 5, Bank Street, and Crow Alley, Manchester, had also started a cotton mill in Nantwich about 1785. It was, however, destroyed by fire in 1792 and never rebuilt (W. H. Chaloner: *History of the cotton manufacture in Nantwich, 1785–1874* (1938), published in *Johnson's Almanack and Directory*, 1938, pp. 135–48.).

addressed the following query to Boulton and Watt on June 17, 1795:

> Whether they have known an instance of the inhabitants of any place preventing a steam engine being erected or recovered damages by actions at law for injury done by the erection of any engine for the reasons of the smoke being injurious to vegetation, to fruits, or impregnating the air with noxious vapours, and if they think the joint efforts of the inhabitants of this town can prevent our intentions.

Boulton and Watt's reply, though not preserved, was evidently reassuring, because the engine was set to work in the course of 1796, when the mill contained 1,600 spindles. It was enlarged in 1797 and 1799, and a second engine of 36 h.p. installed in 1816–17. This cotton mill ceased operation only 1874.

It is sometimes very difficult to discover what operations the engines supplied to textile mills actually performed. Let us take the case of Abraham Illingworth of Stockport. He ordered two steam engines for his cotton mills, presumably for carding and spinning, from Boulton and Watt in quick succession (10 h.p. August 1791; 21 h.p. April 1792), and went bankrupt in 1793. His assignees leased the mill containing the first of these engines to John Dumbell, of Mersey Mills, Warrington. On March 3, 1796, James Lawson, one of Boulton and Watt's engine erectors reported to James Watt, jun.:

> . . . according to the account of Mr. Robinson, the manager and, I believe, partner with Mr. Dumbell . . . they are doing very well, and have the mill almost full. The power is let out to different people at so much a carding engine according to its size.[21]

The second mill and its engine (which had only been set to work on July 8, 1794) were also paying well in 1796 – 'the power is all let out,' reported Lawson. Illingworth had by then bought back the premises and was trying to get full possession of them.[22]

---

21 This Mr. Robinson, whom Lawson described to James Watt, jun. (March 28, 1796) as a man who 'knows nothing of business (he is one of the Stockport Bank Company),' was probably either John Robinson (d. 1823), or Thomas Robinson (d. 1837), grocer and cotton spinner, Mayor of Stockport in 1820, who built Spring Bank Mill and was an original director of the Stockport Gas Company.

22 Lawson to James Watt, jun., March 3, 16, 28, 1796. In 1801 one of Illingworth's engines was advertised for sale as capable of developing 'a power sufficient to turn at a proper speed, one hundred carding machines of the sort now used' (*Manchester Mercury*, Aug. 25, 1801, p. 1, col. 4). Some details concerning the first four Stockport engines are given in J.

Thomas Hope, hat manufacturer of Stockport, who ordered two engines (12 h.p. October 1797; 24 h.p. November 1798) for cotton spinning, also proceeded to lease out the power he had purchased, for in February 1799 one of his factories was in the occupation of Joseph Sykes who moved to the second when the new and more powerful Boulton and Watt engine was bought, and we find Abraham Binns in occupation of Hope's first factory in 1804.

Another Stockport capitalist who stands out as eager to take advantage of the new form of power was Jeremiah Bury, cotton check manufacturer, who later became a master cotton spinner on a considerable scale.[23] He ordered his first engine in September 1791 (8 h.p.), a 30 h.p. engine in July 1801, and one of 20 h.p. in 1804. He ordered a fourth of 14 h.p. in June 1809.

Lastly we come to the amusing story of the 'pirate' engine at Poynton. In the course of 1795 Boulton and Watt discovered that several engineering concerns, including those of Joseph Thackeray of Garratt, Chorlton-on-Medlock, Messrs. Bateman and Sherratt of Salford, and John Wilkinson of Bersham, near Wrexham, had been infringing Watt's patent for separate condenser steam engines, thus causing a serious loss both of revenue and reputation to the Midlands firm, for the unlicensed engines were for the most part neither constructed nor serviced as efficiently as the products of Soho. In order to be in a position to prosecute if necessary, Boulton and Watt had to collect evidence and therefore sent agents into the localities where these 'pirate' engines were known to be, or suspected of being, in operation. Their representative for Lancashire, Cheshire and part of Yorkshire was James Lawson, who was something of a character, and his letters to his masters are full of amusing sketches of the Lancashire mill owners and engineers whom he was interviewing. Dressed like a jockey, he carried with him a liberal supply of half-crowns for corruptible engine-minders. On March 24, 1796 he wrote to James Watt, jun.:

> I intend riding tomorrow to see Sir G. Warren's[24] engine [at Bullock's Smithy[25]], the last I know of.

Aikin: *A description of the country . . . round Manchester* (1795), p. 446; J. Butterworth: *History and description of . . . Stockport*, (1827), pp. 281–2; and H. Heginbotham: *Stockport, ancient and modern*, vol. ii, p. 323.

23 See Unwin and others: *op. cit.*, p. 39. According to Butterworth, Bury also manufactured muslins and ginghams (*op. cit.*, p. 281).

24 Sir George Warren, M.P., of Poynton, Cheshire (1735–1801), lord of the manors of Stockport and Poynton and the owner of flourishing coal mines in the area.

25 Now, regrettably, known by the more genteel name of Hazel Grove.

Next day he wrote again to young Watt, this time from Stockport (March 25):

I have now nearly finished my *espionage*, having just seen the engine on [a] coal mine near Bullock's Smithy, which has an air pump and condenser exactly similar to Boulton and Watt's, only, like all the rest, well concealed.

In going to see it I observed very near it a small winding engine with conductors in the pit,[26] same as you saw at Kippax. This engine I said I came to see.

I found at the place the landlord of a neighbouring ale house half drunk (being Good Friday and consequently a holiday), who sent for the engine man (and also for some ale) to set the winding engine to work. In the meantime I examined the pumping one – it is [a] 40 inch cylinder, 6 foot stroke and has been at work just thirty weeks this day, the landlord remembering well the day it was set to work. It was working well, about 12 strokes per minute.

It is satisfying to know that Lawson's activities bore fruit in this case. Thomas Jones, Boulton and Watt's attorney in Manchester, took up the matter with the lessee of the mine, Nathaniel Wright,[27] who

said he could not afford to pay your annual premium for the use of your principles and gave me notice he would give them up and I was afterwards informed by Sherratt that the engine was altered to the old [i.e. atmospheric] principles. From your letter I find that you have not received for the time he infringed on you and therefore I write by this post to him desiring payment.[28]

26 An early instance of pitshaft guide rails. These had been patented by John Curr of Sheffield Park Colliery in 1788 (T. S. Ashton and J. Sykes: *The coal industry of the eighteenth century* (1929), p. 65).

27 Nathaniel Wright, gentleman, of Brabyns Hall, Low Marple, died on July 16, 1818 (J. P. Earwaker: *East Cheshire*, vol. II, p. 56). Wright was the lessee of collieries in Norbury, Middlewood and Poynton belonging to T. P. Leigh, as well as lessee of other collieries in Poynton and Worth belonging to Sir George Warren and, after Warren's death, to Viscount and Viscountess Warren-Bulkeley (see Burton MSS., vol. V, p. 491 – lease of mines from T. P. Leigh, June 1, 1795 for twenty-eight years; vol. V, p. 501 – two underlookers at Wright's Norbury engine-pit killed, Mar. 4, 1797 (Manchester Public Library); lease of mines from the Warren-Bulkeleys, 1810, for twenty-one years – Vernon Park Museum, Stockport). I am indebted for the above references to Miss P. Giles.

28 Thomas Jones, Manchester, to Boulton and Watt, Oct. 18, 1796.

APPENDIX NO. 1

CHRONOLOGICAL LIST OF BOULTON AND WATT ENGINES ERECTED IN CHESHIRE, 1778–1817

Compiled from the Boulton and Watt Letter Books and the Steam Engine Book in Birmingham Public Library.

Person or partnership for whom originally built.	Nominal horse-power and type.	Location.	Purpose.	Approximate date of order for erection.	Other remarks.
1. Edward Salmon and Dr. Pennington.	4, reciprocating beam.	Thurlwood, near Lawton.	Pumping brine.	1777.	Set to work in 1778.
2. Samuel and George Walker and Hugh Ley, corn and flour merchants	14, rotative, sun and planet.	Chester.	Grinding corn.	Feb. 1785.	Agreement dated June 1, 1785.
3. John Gilbert of Worsley, Lancs., and partners.	10, rotative, sun and planet.	Marston Rockpits, near Northwich.	Winding rock salt and pumping brine and water out of salt mine; able to raise 9 cwts. of salt (1 cwt. = 130 lbs.) 120 yards.	1788 (?)	Agreement dated Jan. 1, 1789.
4. Samuel Oldknow.	8, rotative, sun and planet.	Higher Hillgate, Stockport.	'Carding, roving, and spinning of cotton.'	Feb. 1791.	Agreement dated March 1, 1791.
5. Abraham Illingworth (No. 1).	10, rotative, sun and planet.	Stockport ('Dumbell's engine' at Top-o'-th'-Hill).	Cotton mill.	Aug. 1791.	Agreement dated Nov. 1, 1791.

Person or partnership for whom originally built.	Nominal horse-power and type.	Location.	Purpose.	Approximate date of order for erection.	Other remarks.
6. Jeremiah Bury and Co. (No. 1).	8, rotative, sun and planet.	Stockport (Hope Hill Mill, Heaton Norris).	To be 'employed in the preparation and spinning of cotton, wool, silk, or flax.'	Sept. 1791.	Agreement dated March 1, 1792.
7. Alexander Hunt.	10, rotative, sun and planet.	Stockport.	Cotton mill.	Dec. 1791.	Agreement dated March 1, 1792.
8. Abraham Illingworth (No. 2).	21, rotative, sun and planet.	Stockport ('Park Engline').	Cotton mill.	April 1792.	Agreement dated Sept. 1, 1792.
9. Messrs. Bott, Birch, Bower, and Randell (No. 1).	24 (later 26), rotative, sun and planet.	Nantwich.	Cotton Spinning.	May (?) 1795.	Agreement dated May 1, 1795.
10. Thomas Marshall.	8, rotative, (beam crank).	Northwich.	Salt mine winding (required 'to draw 1200 lb. 115 yards deep at the utmost.')	July 1796.	Agreement dated Aug. 1, 1796.
11. Thomas Horrocks.	16, rotative, sun and planet.	Stockport (Park).	Cotton mill.	Oct. 1796.	Agreement dated Nov. 1, 1796.
12. Thomas Hope, hat manufacturer (No. 1).	12, rotative, sun and planet.	Stockport (Carr Mills).	Cotton spinning.	Aug. 1, 1797.	Agreement dated Aug. 1, 1797.
13. Thomas Hope, hat manufacturer (No. 2).	24, rotative, sun and planet.	Stockport (Carr Mills).	Cotton mill.	Nov. 1798.	Agreement dated Jan. 1, 1799; engine erected by end of 1799.

Person or partnership for whom originally built.	Nominal horse-power and type.	Location.	Purpose.	Approximate date of order for erection.	Other remarks.
14. Charles Lees and Co.	16 or 20, rotative, (beam crank).	Stockport.	Cotton mill.	April 1799.	Engine erected in 1800.
15. Thomas Walker, — Ward and Co.	16, rotative, sun and planet.	Chester.	Lead manufactory.	April 1799.	In 1811 the materials of this engine were sold to Mr. Lucock of 'Kidcrow' (i.e. Kidsgrove) colliery, N. Staffs.
16. Thomas Slate.	6, rotative, (beam crank).	Congleton.	Silk mill.	July 1800.	Engine set to work in 1801.
17. Daintry, Ryle and Co. (No. 1).	32, rotative, sun and planet.	Macclesfield.	Cotton mill.	March 1801.	
18. Jeremiah Bury and Co. (No. 2).	30, rotative, sun and planet.	Stockport (Hope Hill Mill, Heaton Norris).	Cotton mill.	July 1801.	
19. Daintry, Ryle and Co. (No. 2).	40, rotative, (beam crank).	Macclesfield.	Cotton mill.	July 1802.	
20. Samuel Cheetham (No. 1).	10, rotative, (beam crank).	Stockport (Park Mills).	Cotton mill.	Early in 1802.	Erection of engine completed by Dec. 1802.
21. Joseph and Samuel Ashton.	6, rotative, side-lever independent.	Portwood, Stockport.	Cotton mill.	1802.	Engine at work by April, 1803.
22. J. and G. Pearson.	20, rotative, (beam crank).	Macclesfield.	Silk mill.	Oct. 1804.	

Person or partnership for whom originally built.	Nominal horse-power and type.	Location.	Purpose.	Approximate date of order for erection.	Other remarks.
23. William Crowther.	10, rotative, (beam crank).	Heaton Norris, near Stockport.	Silk mill.	Oct. 1804.	
24. Daintry, Wood and Daintry (No. 3).	20, rotative, (beam crank).	Macclesfield.	Cotton mill.	Feb. 1805.	
25. Jeremiah Bury and Co. (No. 3).	20, rotative, side-lever independent.	Stockport (Hope Hill Mill, Heaton Norris).	Cotton mill.	1803.	Not set to work until 1805; originally ordered as a 6 h.p. but by 1805 raised to 20 h.p.
26. Samuel Cheetham (No. 2).	20, rotative, (beam crank).	Stockport (Park Mills).	Cotton mill.	July 1806.	Engine at work by mid-1807.
27. William Howard.	36, rotative, (beam crank).	Stockport.	Cotton mill.	Aug. 1807.	
28. Thomas Walker and Co. (No. 2).	20, uncertain, probably rotative, (beam crank).	Chester.	Lead manufactory.	1808.	
29. Jesse Drakeford.	6, rotative, side-lever independent.	Congleton.	Silk mill.	(Sept. 1802) see next column.	This engine was originally ordered by and erected for Marriott and Robinson at Manchester but was sold to Drakeford at some date before Feb. 1809.

Person or partnership for whom originally built.	Nominal horse-power and type.	Location.	Purpose.	Approximate date of order for erection.	Other remarks.
30. Jeremiah Bury and Co. (No. 4).	14, rotative, (beam crank).	Stockport (Hope Hill Mill, Heaton Norris).	Cotton mill.	June 1809.	
31. Bott, Birch and Co. (No. 2).	36, rotative, (beam crank).	Nantwich.	Cotton spinning.	April 1815.	Engine not erected until 1816–17.

APPENDIX NO. 2

BOULTON AND WATT'S LICENCE FOR THEIR FIRST CHESHIRE ENGINE

(From the Boulton and Watt Letter Book (1778–80) in the Birmingham Public Library.)

Birmingham, August 25, 1779.

Rec. from Messrs. Salmon and Penlington at sundry times four hundred pounds fifteen shillings and three pence being in full for the materials and workmanship furnished by us for a steam engine and erected by them at Lawton saltworks and for our licence to use the same

	[£	s.	d.]	
Engine and Materials	300.	15.	3.	Boulton and Watt
Licence to use the same	100.	0.	0.	
	400.	15.	3.	

We Matthew Boulton and James Watt engineers of Soho in the county of Stafford do hereby grant to Edward Salmon Esq. and to all the other proprietors of Thirlewood, alias Lawton Saltworks in the county of Chester and their administrators executors and assigns, our licence and authority to use work and exercise at the said saltworks in such a manner as may seem good to them for and during the remainder now to come and unexpired of the term of twenty-five years, for which an exclusive privilege for the use of certain new invented steam engines was vested in the said James Watt by Act of Parliament, a steam engine of the said James Watt's invention as described in the said Act of Parliament having a cylinder 18 inches diameter and four feet long erected by us for the use of the said Edward Salmon and his said partners at the said saltworks at Thirlewood aforesaid and we hereby also acknowledge the receipt of £100 being the stipulated price of this licence. In witness whereof we have subscribed this licence on the twenty-fifth day of August one thousand seven hundred and seventy nine years.

James Watt.

CHAPTER IV

CHARLES ROE OF MACCLESFIELD (1715–81): AN EIGHTEENTH-CENTURY INDUSTRIALIST

PART I: 1715–66

CHARLES ROE AND THE SILK MANUFACTURE

In writing economic history there has been a tendency to concentrate on the study of the foremost figures in eighteenth-century British industry – Arkwright, Boulton, Watt, Wedgwood, Wilkinson and the rest. These great men had, however, many contemporaries who seemed vastly more important at the time in which they lived than they do to us, and have in fact simply fallen into undeserved oblivion. Charles Roe of Macclesfield is one of these men – a large-scale industrialist who founded a firm which by 1787 had interests in England, Wales, Scotland and Ireland.

Charles Roe was born at Castleton in Derbyshire on 7 May 1715 and baptized in the parish church there on 2 June 1715 as the son of the Rev. Thomas Roe, M.A., vicar of Castleton, and Mary his wife.[1] He was the

---

1   J. P. Earwaker (*East Cheshire*, Vol. II, p. 509) gives the date of Charles Roe's baptism (wrongly) as 5 January 1715. The Rev. Thomas Roe, born in 1670, was the son of Robert Roe, of Aston, co. Salop, and lord of the manor of Hadley in the same county. He matriculated at All Souls, Oxford, on 11 November 1685, and was vicar of Castleton from 1698 until his death. He married Mary, daughter of the Rev. Kittlesby Turner of Knutsford on 6 October 1698 (*Cheshire Sheaf*, 1935, pp. 72–3, 74–5). We may draw some conclusions about the Rev. Thomas Roe's character from the following entry he made in Castleton Parish Register: 'Edale Chappel was built in the year 1633 and consecrated on Trinity Sunday 1634. Memorandum that on the 1st day of December 1718 John Mellor of Edale showed me his father-in-law's will, whose name was Thomas Creswill, wherein instead of Edale Chappel it is called Edale Church, which will he told me was drawn up by Edward Ashton of Lady Booth. What the designe was in writing it Edale Church, I know not, but am of opinion 'twas no good one to Castleton, the Mother Church, of which I am the unworthy Vicar. (signed) Tho: Roe.'

CHARLES ROE (1715–81)
From the oil-painting by Joseph Wright of Derby in Christ Church, Macclesfield.

youngest child of his parents. Apart from Frances (1701–19), Robert (1705–18), and John Roe (1707), whose baptisms and early deaths are recorded in the Castleton registers, he had three brothers and a sister, Mary, born in 1712.[2] Of his eldest brother, Thomas, nothing is known beyond the fact of

2   For Mary Roe, see footnote 29.

his baptism on 7 March 1700. William Roe, the second son, who was born on 10 August 1703, graduated B.A. at Oxford in 1724, took holy orders and was curate at Macclesfield from 1724 until his death in 1730. James Roe, born on 18 June 1711, took the degree of B.A. at Cambridge in 1732 (M.A. 1736) and on 31 July 1733 was presented to the living of Disley, which he retained until his death in 1765. He was also appointed minster and prime curate of Macclesfield in 1756.[3]

The Rev. Thomas Roe died on 23 May 1723, aged 52, when Charles was only eight years old. His widow followed him to the grave in 1724.[4] Nothing is known about Charles Roe's life from the date of his baptism until 8 October 1742, when he was admitted a freeman of Macclesfield and described as 'gent'. From later sources it appears that he was a manufacturer of silk twist and of mohair – and silk-covered buttons. As he was also described in 1744 as a 'button merchant,' it seems likely that he was a middleman engaged in organising and financing the production and sale of buttons under the domestic or putting-out system of industry. From being a button merchant, Roe began to manufacture the valuable raw material with which the best buttons were covered.

John Corry, in his *History of Macclesfield* (1817),[5] said of Charles Roe, in a sentence which has been uncritically repeated by almost every subsequent writer on the subject, that 'in the year 1756 he commenced the business of silk throwster in a building at the northern end of Park Green. This was the first silk mill erected in Macclesfield and from that circumstance the extensive street which now reaches from Park Green to the Market-place was called Mill-street.'[6]

It is now possible to prove that Roe erected a mill for the throwing of raw silk by water-power in 1743–4, twelve years earlier than the date given by Corry. The throwing of raw silk, i.e., the manufacture of organzine or silk thread on machines turned by water-power, had been introduced into this country from Italy in 1717 through the efforts of John (d.1722) and Sir Thomas Lombe (1685–1739). Sir Thomas Lombe's patent for the machine

3   *Cheshire Sheaf*, 1935, pp. 74–5; Earwaker, op. cit., Vol. II, p. 506.

4   *Cheshire Sheaf*, 1935, pp. 74–5; Foden MSS. The Rev. Thomas Roe was buried at Castleton on 25 May 1723 (Castleton Par. Reg.).

5   Earwaker, op. cit., Vol. II, p. 509; Royal Depot Mills MSS. (lease of 1744); John Corry, *The History of Macclesfield* (1817), p. 64.

6   Op. cit., pp. 64–5. There had been silk throwsters by hand in Macclesfield before 1743–4, and Samuel Smiles mentions 'a small silk-mill at Macclesfield, the property of Mr. Michael Daintry' as being in existence in the autumn of 1735 (*Lives of the Engineers*, Vol. 1 (1904 edn.), p. 162), but gives no details as the whether it was on Lombe's principles.

expired in 1732, and by that time his factory and the machines they contained, situated on an island in the River Derwent at Derby, had become famous throughout England.[7]

Corry stated that 'having obtained a perfect model of the machinery employed in the silk mill at Derby, he (Roe) engaged a skilful mechanic, who erected a complete machine.'[8] Unfortunately this is the sole evidence upon which we have to rely. It has been suggested that Roe's mill was erected by James Brindley (1716–72), the famous canal engineer; Brindley was apprenticed to Abraham Bennett, wheelwright, of Sutton near Macclesfield, between 1733 and 1740, and then served him as a journeyman until 1742. In 1742, however, he set up on his own at Leek, and although Smiles mentions the bare fact that after 1742 Brindley was 'employed in repairing and fitting up silk-throwing mills at Macclesfield, all of which were then driven by water,' no further details are at present available.[9] The discovery of the present whereabouts of Brindley's pocket memoranda books, which were in the possession of Joseph P. Mayer of Liverpool when Smiles wrote, might throw more light on the subject.[10]

Fortunately the original lease to Charles Roe of the site of what are now known as the Royal Depot Mills has survived, and from this document and subsequent deeds it is possible to extract trustworthy details of this pioneer enterprise. From the lease it appears that at some date between 13 July 1743 and 15 February 1744 Roe had (with the consent of the then lessee, John Pickering, twister of Macclesfield, and the owner of the land, Joseph Pickford, of Althill, Lancs.) 'taken down all the buildings;[11] on a piece of land in Macclesfield 'near to Pickford Bridge 26 yards long and 11 yards in breadth.[12] On this cleared space he had 'at a very great expense erected a large pile of buildings intended for a silk mill for throwing of raw silk by means of a wheel to be turned by water.' Roe also secured water rights in 'the brook, stream or water-course running by the side of the said building' together with certain rights over a 'sough or tunnel' (essential to the working

7 P. Mantoux, *The Industrial Revolution in the Eighteenth Century,* (1928), pp. 197–201. For the general background see G. B. Hertz, 'The English Silk Industry in the Eighteenth Century', in *English Historical Review,* Vol. XXIV, 1909, pp. 710–27.

8 Op. cit., p. 64.

9 Smiles, op. cit., p. 170.

10 Smiles, op. cit., p. 169.

11 These buildings consisted of a former dye-house, which had been converted into 'a shade or twisting house.' The person from whom Roe took over the premises was John Pickering, twister, of Macclesfield, to whom Pickford had granted a lease as from 4 September 1732.

12 By 1764 the area of the mill premises had expanded to 1,422 square yards.

of the water mill) which ran through property occupied by other tenants of Pickford.[13] To the lease is attached a note 'For Mr. Roe' dated December 14, 1744, from John Ward (1670–1748), of Capesthorne Hall, near Macclesfield, and the Inner Temple, 'the great conveyancer,' which ends: 'I wish you success in your mills.'[14]

From the documents examined there is no hint that Roe had a partner or partners in this enterprise at its commencement, but he had certainly entered into partnership with Samuel Lankford, silk merchant, by 1750. As from 25 March 1750, Roe and Lankford leased for 21 years at a rent of two guineas, Thomas, Earl Ffauconberg's corn mills at Sutton, in the parish of Prestbury, together with full power to divert and convey 'waste and useless water' from the Sutton mills for the use of their silk mills in Macclesfield.[15] This, and other evidence, suggests that the mills were in process of being enlarged in the early 1750s.[16] At some time between 1750 and 1762 Samuel Lankford died and was succeeded in the partnership by his son Harry Lankford of Mottram St. Andrew and later of 'The Fence within Hurdsfield.' During the same period Roe acquired two new partners, John Robinson, and William Stafford, both described as 'of Macclesfield, gent.', in 'the art and mystery of manufacturing raw silk and the trade of importing, buying and selling of raw and thrown silk.' Stafford, however, had no share in the capital stock of the enterprise before 1 January 1762, and may have been purely a manager until that date.

It seems evident that by the early 1760s Roe had decided, in view of the heavy capital investment demanded from 1758 onwards by his new venture

13 The transfer of the lease was made in return for a guinea consideration money paid to Pickford plus a yearly rent of £1 18s. 6d. and was to run for three lives, those of Charles Roe, Elizabeth his wife, and Joseph Pickford, Roe having the right to insert a new life within twelve months of the death of either of the other two persons. It was to run from 25 March 1744 (Royal Depot Mills MSS. Macclesfield).

14 For Ward, see *Trans. Historic Soc. of Lancs. and Ches.*, Vol. 100 (1948), pp. 63, 68–9, 71.

15 Royal Depot Mills MSS. This lease was renewed in 1762 to Charles Roe, Harry Lankford, John Robinson, Samuel Glover, William Greaves, and Samuel Huxley, and was to run for nineteen years from 5 April 1762, at £85 per annum.

16 Indenture dated 23 December 1753, containing a reference to an enlargement of the sough (Royal Depot Mills MSS). In addition, on 5 April 1754 Joseph Pickford had leased to Roe 'all those two closes . . . situate . . . in Macclesfield Park . . . , called The Highmost Brooke Meadow and the Little High Field . . . and also all those two other closes or parcels of land . . . in Macclesfield . . . called the Lower Dams and all that barn or parcel of building called Pickford Barn . . . near to a place called Pickford Bridge' for twenty-one years at a rent of £16 10s. per annum. On these premises soon afterwards Roe constructed 'a reservoir, dam or head of water . . . for the better supplying [of] the silk mills.' Part of Pickford Barn was also converted into a 'winding-room' for the partnership (Royal Depot Mills MSS.).

into the copper trade, to withdraw all his resources from the silk trade. Accordingly, on 1 January 1762, Roe, Lankford, and Robinson decided to surrender temporarily all their property in the silk mills into the hands of William Harper, a Macclesfield mercer, so that the value of respective shares in the enterprise could be assessed. At this date Roe held a two-fifths share, Lankford two-fifths and John Robinson one-fifth. After the deduction of bad and other debts £6,113 17s. 10d. was due to Roe, £7,848 17s. 2d. to Lankford and £2,649 3s. 2d. to Robinson, making a total of £16,611 18s. 2d.[17] Out of this total the silk mills, buildings, premises, machinery and utensils alone were valued at £2,800. As from 1 January 1762, William Stafford was admitted to a share in the partnership by his purchase of half Roe's share, or one-fifth. Harper's re-valuation was completed by 1764, for on 26 November of that year a new agreement was signed in which it was stated that the assets of the silk mill had been valued at £19,023 12s. 11½d.[18] On 24 July 1764 Roe had agreed to sell the other three partners his one-fifth share, valued at £3,435 9s. 2½d., for £3,808 15s. 3d., subject to deductions for what he had drawn out since the beginning of 1764. Lankford now owned a half share in the mill and the two other partners quarter shares. Roe liquidated his interest in the mill none too soon. A return dated 5 February 1765, published in the *Journals of the House of Commons* during a period of 'losing trade' in the British silk industry, gives the following details of the employment afforded by the firm and the machinery it had in operation:

A state of the silk mills belonging to Lankford, Robinson and Stafford, of Macclesfield, for four years past, on Sir Thomas Loom's [sic] construction[19]

Year		Dutch Mills	People Employed
1761	6 mills	2 Pair	350
1762	6 mills	2 Pair	350
1763	5 mills	1 Pair	280
1764	3 mills	1 Pair	[180]

17 Royal Depot Mills MSS. 'A General Account or Rest in writing hath been taken of the whole capital stock of the said . . . (partnership) . . . now remaining in the said joint trade, the particulars whereof are set forth and contained in three several books, commonly called Rest Books, subscribed by the said Charles Roe, Harry Lankford and John Robinson' (ibid.).

18 The later figure included a consideration for all profits due to Roe since 1 January 1764.

19 *J.H.C.*, Vol. XXX (1765–6), pp. 217, 219.

To judge by the number of persons employed the firm of Roe, Lankford, Robinson and Stafford was the fourth largest silk-throwing establishment in Macclesfield in 1761–2 and had moved up to the third largest in 1763–4, owing to the fact that another firm had suffered more severely from the depression which followed the end of the Seven Years' War.[20] On 16 July 1773 Messrs. Lankford, Robinson and Stafford, all 'late of Macclesfield,' were declared bankrupts. They were stated to make their living by buying raw and unmanufactured silk and throwing and twisting it and also by dealing in silks.[21]

During the period 1747–66 Charles Roe played an active part in the municipal life of Macclesfield. He was mayor of the town for the year 1747–48.[22] From that year until 10 September 1751, he was a fairly frequent attender at the public assemblies of the mayor, aldermen and burgesses. After the latter date he did not, apparently, attend again until 15 August 1755. On 3 October 1755 he was elected alderman for the municipal year 1755–56, an honour which was conferred on him for the years 1758–59, 1765–66 and 1774–5, although his attendances at corporation meetings after 1765 were infrequent. The shaky hand in which he signed his name as being present on 9 October 1772 suggests incomplete recovery from a recent illness. There is no record of his attendance after 22 September 1775.[23]

Although it is not possible to identify Charles Roe's residence in Macclesfield with complete certainty, it appears very likely that he lived in what is now No. 67, Roe Street. In 1810 this house was in the possession of his eldest son, William Roe of Liverpool, but was tenanted by Samuel Stone, gent.[24]

---

20 *J.H.C.*, Vol. XXX (1765), pp. 215–19.

21 Royal Depot Mills MSS. The deterioration in the firm's position since 1764 may be judged by the fact that its assignees in bankruptcy (Samuel Glover, merchant of Macclesfield, Samuel Wright, gentleman of Nether Knutsford, John Daintry, merchant of Leek, and William Greaves, a London merchant) sold half the concern for only £1,640 to Thomas Hicklin, merchant, of London, and William Ayton, jun., merchant, of Coleman Street, London, on 31 March 1775.

22 His signature appears for the first time in the Corporation Minute Book on 23 April 1748. His mayoral accounts were only handed in for audit on 4 October 1751 (Macclesfield Corporation Minute Book, Vol. I, 1734–68).

23 Macclesfield Corporation Minute Books, Vols, I and II (1743–68, 1769–1824).

24 Title deeds of nos. 63, 65, 67, Roe Street, Macclesfield (lease for 999 years by W. Roe of site of nos. 63 and 65 Roe Street to Nathaniel Pearson, 19 February 1810; abstract of title to no. 67, Roe Street, C. H. Henderson Roe, 1893). The writer was enabled to examine these through the courtesy of the owner, W. T. Boothby, Esq. and Messrs. May and Wain, solicitors, Macclesfield.

ESTABLISHMENT AND EARLY HISTORY OF THE
MACCLESFIELD COPPER COMPANY, 1758–66

The reasons which induced Roe and his partners to establish a copper-smelting works in Macclesfield are somewhat obscure. It is known that by the mid-1760s a crisis in Macclesfield's coal supply was reflected in rising prices for that commodity,[25] although by the 1790s the difficulty had been resolved, for it was then stated that the copper works consumed a large quantity of coal from the four separate seams which had been found 'upon a flat' at the bottom of the hills to the east of the town.[26]

The Macclesfield Copper Company at first depended for its competitive advantages upon the prospect of plentiful supplies of local ore from the copper mines of Alderley Edge. Of the Company's operations Henry Holland, in his *General View of the Agriculture of Cheshire*, wrote:

> Mr. Rowe . . . was at one time very sanguine in his expectations of success, and kept not less than forty or fifty men constantly employed; but upon the discovery of the great body of copper at the Parys mine . . . he suddenly gave up his concern at Alderley Edge, and took all his miners with him into Wales.[27]

The Company also secured ore from much further afield. The copper mine at Coniston in the Lake District was leased from Sir Michael le Fleming of Rydal Hall in 1758, and during eight of the years between that date and 1767 a total of 904 tons of ore was raised, on which Sir Michael received a royalty of one twelfth, amounting to £376. The ore was boated down the lake,

---

25 See pp. 151, 153 *infra*. For the general background, see H. Hamilton, *The English Brass and Copper Industries to 1800* (1926).

26 P. Barfoot and John Wilkes, *Universal British Directory*, 1790–98, Vol. III, p. 895.

27 P. 17 (edn. of 1813); Earwaker, op. cit., Vol. II, p. 611. This would date Roe's workings from about 1758 to 1768. There are some indications that the Macclesfield Copper Company also worked the copper mines at Kirkleyditch in the nearby township of Mottram St. Andrew (Earwaker, op. cit., Vol II, p. 357). For the general subject of the Mottram St. Andrew and Alderley Edge mines see H. Dewey and T. Eastwood, *Copper Ores of the Midlands, Wales, the Lake District and the Isle of Man* (Memoirs of the Geological Survey Special Reports on the mineral resources of Great Britain), Vol. XXX, 1925, pp. 5 and 6–16. Some evidence has been discovered to suggest that Roe had at one time bought copper ore from the Duke of Devonshire's great mine at Ecton Hill in Staffordshire, east of Leek (Mona Mine MSS., 3534, p. 40 – Roe to J. Cartwright, 9 July 1768). Roe had an interest in a group of Derbyshire lead mines (*Manchester Mercury*, 16 November 1773, p. 3, col. 1). See also C. Roeder, 'Prehistoric and subsequent mining at Alderley Edge . . .' (*Trans. L. & C. Ant. Soc.*, XIX, 107–11).

carried to Greenodd or Ulverston, and from thence shipped to the Mersey estuary. In a letter to John Moore, le Fleming's agent, dated 10 October 1761, Charles Roe stated that the Company had laid out a very large sum in making a sough or level, and were contemplating the construction of another 'without which the mine never can answer, under the best management upon earth.' Little mining appears to have taken place between 1770 and about 1792, when the Macclesfield Company, which still held the lease, showed a renewed interest in the mine. On 1 February 1792 over 283 tons of ore were on bank, but three years later Abraham Mills, the head of the Company, wrote to the agent offering to surrender the lease to the baronet because 'the Coniston Mine has for some time past been so unproductive that it has been determined to discontinue the working' (27 July 1795).[28]

Operations in Macclesfield itself began in 1758. At a public assembly of the mayor, aldermen and burgesses of the borough of Macclesfield held in the Guildhall on 19 August of that year it was agreed:

That Mr. Charles Roe and Mr. Rowland Atkinson[29] two of the burgesses of this Burrough (as far as in the said Mayor, aldermen and burgesses lies or they have the power to grant) may have liberty to inclose forty yards square out of the waste lands in Macclesfield . . . at or near a place on the Common there called Highledge and may erect thereon a smelting mill, paying to the Overseers of the Poor of Macclesfield . . . the sum of five shillings yearly for the use of the poor of Macclesfield . . . from the time the said building shall be inclosed and so long as the same shall remain standing and continue to be used as a smelting mill, or for any other purpose by them, the said Charles Roe and Rowland Atkinson or any other person or persons claiming under them or either of them.[30]

Very soon Roe and his partners began to extend the range of their activities. A 99-year lease of site in the township of Eaton, in Astbury parish, adjoining

28 W. G. Collingwood, 'The Keswick and Coniston Mines in 1600 and later,' in *Trans. Cumberland and Westmorland Antiq. and Arch. Soc.*, Vol. XXVIII, New Series, 1928, pp. 4–6, 31–2. The resumption of operations about 1792 is interesting in view of the Company's loss of Parys Mine in 1785 (See Part II in subsequent volume).

29 Rowland Atkinson, B.A. (Oxon), headmaster of Macclesfield Grammar School from 1749 until his death in 1773, was Charles Roe's brother-in-law, having married his sister Mary Roe, (born 23 December 1712) in 1748 (*Cheshire Sheaf*, 1935, p. 75; Earwaker, op. cit., Vol. II, p. 522 and footnote).

30 Macclesfield Corporation Minutes, Vol. I (1734–1768).

the Macclesfield–Congleton turnpike, was acquired in 1763 from Richard Ayton Lee at the moderate annual rent of £30 10s. To commemorate the siege of Havanah, the capital of Cuba, and its capture from the Spaniards by the British in 1762, the site was christened 'The Havannah.' Here, less than two miles from Congleton and over five miles from Macclesfield, a small industrial village was built, consisting of seven cottages with gardens, and both the manufacture of brass wire and the rolling of copper and brass sheets and bolts, with water power supplied by the 'whole River Dane,' were undertaken.[31]

Brass in the eighteenth century was an alloy of copper and zinc. The production of zinc demanded supplies of calamine (zinc carbonate), the ore from which it was smelted at the time. The River Weaver navigation toll books reveal shipments of calamine going up river to Northwich in 1757, but there were none between 3 Dec. 1757 and 17 October 1759, with the exception of a solitary consignment which paid toll at Northwich on 16 January 1759. From 17 October 1759, however, there are numerous ship-ments. Unfortunately the names of the owners of up-cargoes are not given until 1769, and some of the calamine may have been destined for Cheadle in Staffordshire.[32] There can be little doubt, however, that most of it was on its way to Macclesfield, for when the names of the owners of up-cargoes appear, as they do from 1769, all shipments of calamine are made on behalf of Charles Roe and Company.[33] They varied from only a few to over forty tons.

It is known that the Macclesfield Copper Company derived part at least of its calamine from 'Pennygarrick Gwin' mine near Mold in Flintshire,[34] and also from deposits at Moelydd and Llanymynech in Shropshire, S.W. of Oswestry, whence, it was stated in 1808, 'ores of lead and zink have been conveyed by the Stourport Canal to Birmingham, Macclesfield, and other

---

31 See also Daniel and Samuel Lysons: *Magna Britannia*, Vol. II, pt. 2 (1810), p. 427, from which it would appear that the Havannah was still in production at the time they wrote.

32 Weaver Shipments: Navigation Day Book, Vol. 6, 1757–61 (County Record Office, Chester).

33 See Northwich Tonnage of Up-Goods, Vol. 30, 1769–71 passim.

34 See letter dated 26 November 1777 from Charles Roe, Macclesfield, to Adam Woodward, agent at this mine. Sales of ore for six months of 1777 were about 40 tons. (The writer is indebted to Professor T. S. Ashton of the London School of Economics for a copy of this letter). It has proved impossible to locate this mine with certainty.

places'.[35] In 1800 the Macclesfield Company also owned a 'Calamine House' at Bonsall in Derbyshire.[36]

A second satellite establishment was founded in 1766, when a large tract of land and water-rights at Bosley, six miles due south of Macclesfield, were leased from the Earl of Harrington for 99 years at an annual rent of £25. Here the Company erected a mill for rolling and hammering copper, a rolling mill for dealing with brass and four brass battery mills. Abundant and constant water-power from two falls of 25ft. 3in. and 14ft. 9in. drove six water wheels, five of which were stated to be large ones, for the purpose of turning the machinery.[37] This industrial estate also included ten cottages for the workmen and what appears to have been the manager's house, to which was attached a small-holding of 16 acres.

CHARLES ROE AND THE MACCLESFIELD CANAL SCHEME, 1765–6

Charles Roe, copper merchant, was . . . examined as to the utility of the intended navigation, the quantity of copper ore . . . that may be carried upon it and the difference of expense in point of carriage to the owners (*Journals of the House of Lords*, Vol. 31, p. 350, 18 April 1766).

The establishment in Macclesfield of the copper-smelting industry, which involved hauling into the district large quantities of copper ore, calamine and coal, brought the question of a cheaper means of transport to the fore. In 1763 Macclesfield business men applied to the Duke of Bridgewater, requesting that he should cut a branch to Macclesfield from his proposed canal from Manchester to the Hempstones on the River Mersey, 'but as his navigation was not then carried into Cheshire, and as he had still very considerable difficulties to surmount . . . his Grace did not then think himself in a position to enter into farther engagements.'[38] It is not surprising,

---

35 G. Nicholson, *The Cambrian Traveller's Guide* (1st edn., 1808), col. 356. See also W. Davies, *General View of the Agriculture of North Wales* (1810), pp. 63–4. In 1792 calamine was 6 guineas per ton, in 1802 £10. The Rev. R. Warner, however, in *A Walk through Wales in August 1797* (1798), noted that no large-scale mining of any sort had been attempted at Llanymynech 'of late years' (p. 192).

36 Cheadle Brassware Co., Minute Book 1788–1831, 25 July 1800.

37 The Rev. W. Sutcliffe in his *Records of Bosley* (1865), p. 37, stated that James Brindley was partly responsible for the arrangements for harnessing 'the great water-power' of the original establishment, and this may well be correct, as Sutcliffe's account is otherwise well-informed.

38 *History of Inland Navigation*, 1st edn. (1766), part II, p. 11. According to a hostile

therefore, to find evidence that in 1765–6 Charles Roe was a vigorous supporter, and perhaps even the chief promoter, of an ambitious but unsuccessful scheme whereby Macclesfield was to be linked by canal not only with the River Weaver Navigation, but also with Stockport and Manchester.[39] The previous ten years had seen the successful completion of both the Sankey canal from St. Helens coalfield to the River Mersey (1755–7) and the Duke of Bridgewater's canal from Worsely to Manchester (1759–61). Since 1762 the Duke had been cutting his way from a point on his new canal at Longford Bridge in the township of Stretford, to the Hempstones in the township of Halton in Cheshire, on the south bank of the Mersey, thus opening canal communication between Manchester and the coast, with easier access to Liverpool in view. In 1765 this canal had not yet been completed, and the project for the Grand Trunk, or Staffordshire, Canal from Runcorn Gap on the Mersey to Wilden Ferry and Shardlow on the Trent, was still only a plan, although it had the powerful backing of the Duke, Earl Gower,[40] and Josiah Wedgwood, the great potter and head of the North Staffordshire merchants and industrialists who were supporting the scheme. The proposed Grand Trunk canal would complete the chain of waterways across England from the North Sea to the Irish Sea.[41]

interpretation of this action, '. . . his Grace . . . found himself interested, upon this occasion, to exclude the owners of other collieries from the benefits of water-carriage, and to prevent a communication with the Weaver, in order to secure to himself a more extensive and lucrative monopoly' (ibid., p. 15). The collieries in question were those of the Norbury area. Just before 1766 considerable capital expenditure had been incurred at Norbury colliery in the form of a newly-erected atmospheric steam pumping engine (ibid., p. 18).

39 The printed Bill for the scheme is entitled 'An Act for making a Navigable Cut, or Canal, from Witton-Bridge to the Towns of Nether Knutsford, Macclesfield and Stockport, in the County of Chester, and to Manchester in the County of Lancaster, 56pp.). This states that part of Witton Brook up to Witton Bridge had been rendered navigable under the River Weaver Navigation Act of 1721, and that the proposed canal was to go from Witton Bridge to Adam's Hill in Nether Knutsford, through the township of Mottram Andrew to Waters Green, on the left bank of the River Bollin in Macclesfield. From Mottram Andrew the other arm was to go via Petty Carr Green in Stockport to Newsham Barn in Manchester (pp. 1–3). The total length of the canal was to be 37 miles, and its width 5 yards at the top (Journals of the House of Commons, Vol. 30, p. 522).

40 Granville Leveson-Gower (1721–1803), second Earl Gower, created first Marquis of Stafford in 1786.

41 Josiah Wedgwood had been in touch with the River Weaver Trustees in the matter as early as 2 May 1765, and in July 1765 he had 'waited upon the Cheshire Gentn. at a meeting of the Commrs. for the Weaver Navigation at Northwich, who promised . . . to use their interest in favour of our design, provided we fall into their Navigation' (F. J. Wedgwood, The Personal Life of Josiah Wedgwood, ed. C. H. Herford, 1915, p. 78). Charles Roe wrote to Josiah Wedgwood on 4 December 1765, earnestly requesting his support for the Macclesfield scheme. Roe considered it 'morally impossible we should fail of success'. Since P.

In December 1765 an anonymous 'letter from Liverpool' to an unidentified newspaper alleged that in opposition to the Grand Trunk Canal: '. . . some Cheshire gentlemen, who are proprietors of the Northwich navigation (i.e., the River Weaver Trustees) . . . meditate a scheme for carrying that on from thence to Macclesfield, Stockport and Manchester, with a view to surround his Grace's navigation, and deprive the country of any possibility of ever having it extended either into Staffordshire or any other part'.[42] This scheme was energetically backed not only by Roe, but also by Sir George Warren, K.B. (1735–1801), lord of the manors of Stockport and Poynton, and the successful rival of the Duke of Bridgewater for the hand of the rich young heiress Miss Jane Revell, whom he had married in Edinburgh in 1758 after an elopement.

The writer of the 'letter from Liverpool' underwent correction by the pen of a later correspondent, who averred that the 'plain truth' was that 'some merchants and traders (not the set of gentlemen hinted at)' had indeed been the prime movers for a canal over the route described.[43] Their scheme had at first only been 'shewn to a few,' but they later inserted a notice in the *Manchester Mercury* of 12 November 1765 appointing the George Inn, Knutsford, and 12 noon on 3 December for a meeting at which the proposals would 'be produced in order to satisfy any gentleman who may be affected by the undertaking.'[44]

On 3 December 1765 more than forty 'gentlemen and traders' assembled as a result of this notice, and 'most of them . . . declared their approbation of it.' A second meeting 'of landowners and others, in the counties of Chester and Lancaster' at the George in Knutsford was called for 12 December 1765 and duly held. The draft Bill for the scheme was produced and 'plans of the proposed canal shewn.'[45] 'A great number of gentlemen, tradesmen and others' attended, and agreed unanimously that application should be made to Parliament for an Act empowering 'certain persons therein to be named' to construct the proposed canal. The estimated cost of £30,000 was to be raised by subscription, 'no person subscribing less than one hundred pounds; such

Mantoux used this letter (op. cit., p. 133 n.) it has been transferred to the John Rylands Library, Manchester (English MS. 1101). See also Wedgwood's letter of 12 December 1765 in the same collection and English MS. 1102, p. 160.

42 *History of Inland Navigations*, 1st edn. (1766), part I, p. 76.

43 *History of Inland Navigations*, 1st edn. (1766), part I, p. 80.

44 The advertisement was repeated on 19 and 26 November.

45 *Manchester Mercury*, December 10th, 1765, p. 4, col. 1; *History of Inland Navigations*, 1st edn. (1766), part I, pp. 80–1.

shares to be transferable, and the money to be advanced by calls as wanted.' A further meeting at the George was fixed for Boxing Day, in order to close the subscription list and to enable the subscribers to 'fix upon proper persons to be named undertakers, in trust for themselves and the rest of the subscribers.' It is significant that Charles Roe of Macclesfield was one of six persons appointed to receive subscriptions, the others being Jonathan Brayne, clerk to the River Weaver Navigation Trustees, Mr. Baxter of Knutsford, Mr. Robert Newton, solicitor of Stockport, and Messrs. Allen Vigor and Chippindall, solicitors of Manchester.[46]

For two reasons, however, what we may call the 'Roe-Warren scheme' automatically assumed the character of a rival to the canal projects of the Duke of Bridgewater.[47] In the first place, the Duke's agents were, in the early part of 1766, engaged in piloting through Parliament a bill empowering him to link Manchester and Stockport by constructing a branch canal from Sale Moor, in Cheshire, to Stockport.[48] In the second place, in the early part of 1766 the Duke abandoned his original plan of leading the Bridgewater Canal into the Mersey at the Hempstones. Instead, he undertook[49] to extend his canal to join the Grand Trunk canal at Preston Brook and to complete at his own cost the portion from Preston Brook, to the River Mersey at Runcorn Gap, thus obtaining a stranglehold over one end of this vital waterway. The bills for the Sale Moor to Stockport and the Grand Trunk canals were both passing through Parliament at the same time as the bill for the Roe-Warren scheme. Any canal which provided an alternative route linking Manchester, East Cheshire and North Staffordshire with the Mersey, was very likely to be hurtful to the Duke's interests, as it might decrease the volume of traffic on his proposed network.

But for the time being the outlook for the Roe–Warren scheme appeared good. The fusion of interest between those merchants and industrialists who supported the plan and the powerful landowners of Cheshire seemed

---

46 *Manchester Mercury*, 17 December 1765, p. 4, col. 1; repeated 24 December, p. 2, col. 1.

47 On 21st December, 1765, James Brindley wrote to John Gilbert, the Duke's agent: 'On Tusdey Sr. Georg [Warren] sent [Mr. Robert] Nuton in to Manchester to make what intrest he could for Sir Georg and to gather ye old [Mersey and Irwell] Navogtors togather to meet Sir Georg at Stoperd to make head a ganst His Grace' (S. Smiles, *Lives of the Engineers*, Vol. I, edn. 1904, p. 312).

48 This bill received the royal assent on 18 March 1766 (6 Geo. III, cap. 17), but the canal was never constructed. Brindley had made 'an ochilor survey' of its route as early as 8 January 1762 (Smiles, op. cit., Vol. I, edn. 1904, p. 232).

49 By clause 84 in the Grand Trunk Act (6 Geo. III, cap. 96, royal assent May 14, 1766) The Hempstones was 2,500 yards east of Runcorn Gap.

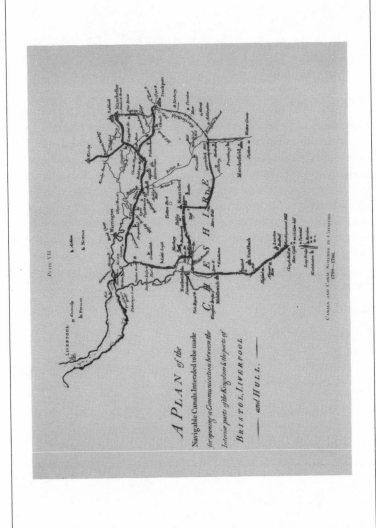

CANALS AND CANAL SCHEMES IN CHESHIRE, 1759-66.

complete, when, on 5 December 1765, a meeting of the River Weaver trustees at Northwich resolved to advertise publicly their unanimous resolution:

> . . . that the scheme for an intended canal navigation from Maccles-field to Mottram Andrew, from there to Stockport (and) to Manches-ter, and from the same point in Mottram Andrew by the nearest way (consistent with the levels) to join the Weaver Navigation at or near Northwich, will be beneficial to the public and the navigation of the River Weaver and they approve thereof and will concur in every proper measure to support that undertaking.[50]

It was hardly an exaggeration to state that the Macclesfield canal scheme had been taken up not only by 'a great body of traders and merchants,' but also by 'a considerable number of persons of the highest rank and property' in Cheshire and Lancashire.[51]

One of the supporters of the Macclesfield scheme, John Stafford, a Macclesfield solicitor, attended the famous meeting of 30 December 1765 at Wolseley Bridge which decided to promote the Grand Trunk Canal. In his report on the meeting to a fellow solicitor, S. Wright of Knutsford, he was not very optimistic:

> And as to the Macclesfield scheme, it was not even so much as once mentioned, so contemptible are we in the eyes of the great schemers of Staffordshire; for my own part I was not sorry for it; but my neighbour Roe wishes he had been there, and thinks he could have made it very evident, that our scheme will show the Burslamites etc. the way into the Weaver; as it will give them an opportunity at the crossing of the two canals[52] to go to Liverpool either by Northwich or the

---

50 Arley MSS. The Trustees ordered their clerk, Jonathan Brayne, to send copies of their resolution to Samuel Egerton of Tatton and Charles Cholmondeley, the county M.P.s. The resolution was published in the *Manchester Mercury*, 17 Dec. 1765, p. 4., col. 1. It is significant that Sir George Warren was present at this meeting of the Weaver trustees.

51 *History of Inland Navigations*, 1st edn. (1766), part II, p. 27. Cf. '. . . the promoters of this navigation . . . are owners of the greatest part of the lands through which it is to be made' (ibid., p. 17).

52 Clause 97 of the Grand Trunk Canal Act (6 Geo. III, cap. 96, 14 May 1766) laid it down that the Grand Trunk was to cross the proposed Witton Bridge–Macclesfield canal by an aqueduct with an arch of 15 feet span, in which the level of the water was not to be more than 9 feet above the normal level of the water in Wincham Brook, alongside which the Witton Bridge–Macclesfield canal was to run. The actual spot where the two canals were to cross was 'between . . . Wincham Bridge, situate on a brook called Wincham Brook or Peover Eye, and a certain mill called Cranage or Wincham Mill,' also on the same brook and

Hempstones as they please, and their own interest (the surest director) will certainly lead them to Northwich, as they may go by that course to Liverpool upon much easier terms than the other, the tonnage upon the [Grand Trunk] canal till it joins the Duke's being proposed to be 1s. 6d. for every ten miles, and when it comes into the Dukes 'tis 2s. 6d.; unless he thinks proper to lower it, which he may very well afford, if he can draw all the carriage from the Whielden (i.e. Grand Trunk) canal into his.[53]

The Duke's agents dangled the prospect of a branch twelve miles long from the proposed Sale Moor – Stockport canal to run from Cheadle to Macclesfield before the supporters of the Witton Bridge – Macclesfield scheme, who replied with catalogues of the work the Duke already had in hand but uncompleted ('which is to be finished, God knows when,' as one of them commented).[54]

A petition begging leave to introduce Roe's scheme as a bill was duly presented to Parliament on 15 January 1766 by 'several gentlemen, land-owners, merchants, manufacturers, traders and inhabitants' of Manchester, Stockport, Macclesfield, Knutsford and parts adjacent.[55] Stress was laid on the importance of extending direct communication by water from the port of Liverpool to these centres, with particular reference to the cheaper transport of cheese, salt, timber, coal, lime, flag, slate, and stone from the interior of Cheshire, Yorkshire, Derbyshire and Nottinghamshire. Great play was made by the promoters of the petition with the crisis in Macclesfield's coal supply:

> The town of Macclesfield, where some thousands of poor are em-
> ployed is in imminent danger of losing its manufactures for the want
> of that commodity; what coal mines they had near them, being some
> entirely, others nearly exhausted.

The new canal would enable fresh supplies from the collieries of Norbury, Poynton, and Worth to be tapped. The Norbury pits alone, it was estimated, could furnish at least 10,000 tons annually at only 4d. a cwt., instead of the 7d. actually being charged at Macclesfield and Knutsford.[56]

---

about a mile to the east of the Witton Bridge wharves. There was a similar clause in the Witton Bridge–Macclesfield Bill (p. 52).

53 Arley MSS.
54 *History of Inland Navigations*, 1st edn. (1766), part II, pp. 13–14, 15–16, 91.
55 *Journals of the House of Commons*, Vol. 30 (1765–6), p. 453.
56 *History of Inland Navigations* (1766) part II, p. 30. Owing to the approaching exhaustion of the Macclesfield coal pits it was alleged that 'the present price of coals there is one-third at least higher than it was ten years ago' (ibid., p. 8).

Although Charles Roe was not among the intended proprietors of the canal, at least four of his business associates were (Harry Lankford, Rowland Atkinson, John Robinson, and William Stafford).[57] Roe, however, was named as one of the numerous commissioners appointed to settle disputes which might arise out of the compulsory purchase of land under the measure, as were Harry Lankford and William Stafford, together with a number of the remaining shareholders.[58]

In the Commons the petition was referred to a Committee which included Samuel Egerton, Sir George Warren and Sir William Meredith. On 3 February the Commons received a petition supporting it from 'several gentlemen, merchants, traders and manufacturers of Liverpool.'[59]

The Commons' committee on the petition reported on 10 February that it had examined Hugh Oldham, who said that he had made a survey of the country through which the intended canal was to pass and considered that vessels of from 15 to 20 tons burden would be able to use it at all times.[60] John Golburn (or Golbourne) of Chester, engineer to the River Dee Navigation, estimated that the cost would be £44,000, at £1,200 per mile.[61]

From a letter written by John Stafford to Sir Peter Warburton of Arley Hall near Knutsford, it is possible to gain a more vivid picture than that given by the *Commons' Journals*. Evidently the projectors had not been too happy in their choice of surveyor, for Stafford wrote from London on 8 February:

Hond. Sir,

Yesterday our petition came before the Committee to whom it was referred. Lord Strange attended and seemed quite hearty with us. Our Surveyor [Hugh Oldham] who produced the plan, was a little confused in one point, tho' it was not a very material one, but Mr. Roe's testimony as to the utility of the scheme seemed to give great

---

57 The remaining prospective shareholders were Sir William Meredith, Sir Peter Leicester, Sir George Warren, John Arden, John Crewe, Richard Davenport, Samuel Egerton, Peter Legh of Booths, George Legh, Matthew Booth, John Brocklehurst, John Burscoe, Elizabeth Burgess, Philip Dean, William Hall, Robert Harrop, Ralph Nicholson, Daniel Nixon, Robert Nixon, William Norton, Edward Pitts, Thomas Royle, George Statham, John Thornicroft, John Twemlow, Thomas Weston and Frances Wright, widow (p. 2 of Bill).

58 Pp. 7–8 of Bill.

59 *J.H.C.*, Vol. 30, p. 510–11.

60 Water for the canal was to be taken from the River Bollin at Macclesfield, from Handford Brook and from other streams near it (Bill, p. 3).

61 *J.H.C.*, Vol. 30, pp. 522–3. The shareholders were to raise £50,000 in £100 shares, with power to borrow a further £10,000 (Bill, pp. 15–17).

satisfaction – and I think we gain ground upon the Noble Duke and shall be able to face him and his managers when we come next before the Committee . . . It was very fortunate that Mr. Golborn[62] and Mr. Pownal came up when they did for without their assistance we should have been very defective in evidence. And as we had a specimen yesterday of what we may expect a good deal of in the progress of this affair . . . we find it advisable to send down Mr. Golborn to go along with our Surveyor thro' the whole course of the canal that he may make his observations, and come perfectly prepared for the next Committee. He had only seen a part of the course before . . . [63]

In his evidence Charles Roe dealt with the case of '12 lime kilns at Buxton and four at the Forest near Chapel on the Frith,' which were producing 174,720 horse-loads of lime annually, 120,000 of which he estimated would be carried on the canal at a saving of 3d. per horse-load. On other merchandise two-thirds of the cost of carriage would be saved, and there would be 'double the quantity of goods . . . carried, to what is now by land carriage.' And he concluded '. . . there is a large silk and other manufactories in the town and neighbourhood of Macclesfield, and a very extensive one in the copper way, which employ 15,000 people, who by means of this canal, will be supplied with coals and other necessaries, at a cheaper rate.'[64]

As a result of this evidence, the Commons gave leave to bring in a Bill and, after the first reading, a committee was appointed which included a majority of M.P.s named either as shareholders or commissioners in the printed bill.[65] The bill was read a second time (3 March 1766),[66] but on 18 March 1766 several petitions were presented against it from interested parties in Manchester, Stockport, Congleton, and Middlewich, on the grounds that the Trent and Mersey and Sale Moor to Stockport canal

---

62 Golburn also gave evidence in support of the Bill before the House of Lords (*J.H.L.*, Vol 31, p. 350).

63 Arley MSS. During the Committee of 7 February the Duke's managers 'gave all the trouble they could.' It would seem that the Duke's agents had also been busy stirring up trouble among the landowners along the Manchester–Stockport section of Roe's scheme (see notices of meetings called for 23 and 30 Dec. 1765 and 6 Jan. 1766, in *Manchester Mercury*, 17, 24, and 31 Dec. 1765.

64 *J.H.C.*, Vol. 30, p. 523.

65 Ibid., pp. 523, 588.

66 Ibid., pp. 605, 618.

schemes then before Parliament were preferable as being a 'more safe, easy, expeditious and less expensive' method of achieving the same end.[67]

In spite of this opposition the Committee on the bill approved it, with amendments; it was read a third time on 27 March, and after being approved, was sent to the House of Lords for their concurrence.[68]

Here the real difficulties began. The Duke of Bridgewater was present at every meeting in the Lords at which the bill was discussed. Immediately after its first reading in the Lords on 14 April, his Grace's petition against it was considered, together with two from owners and occupiers of estates and mills in Lancashire and Cheshire, and from gentlemen, merchants manufacturers and tradesmen living in or near the 'great trading towns' of Manchester, Stockport, Congleton and Middlewich.[69] On 18 April Mr. Dunning, K.C., acting on behalf of the Duke, was allowed to call the Duke's surveyor, James Brindley, to give evidence against the bill. Brindley was examined as to 'the number of locks there must necessarily be made' upon the proposed canal,[70] as to 'the difference there will be in the price of carriage on the Duke of Bridgewater's navigation and the new one, the great injury the Duke's navigation is likely to receive by the taking of certain streams into the new canal which the Duke hath at a great expense and difficulty brought into his navigation, the impracticability of carrying on the new navigation without taking in those brooks; and as to the depriving of several mills for grinding corn of water, by the taking in of those streams, and the impossibility of his Grace's extending his navigation any farther, in case the said streams should be taken in.'[71]

From the subsequent cross-examination by counsel for the bill, Mr. Graham, it appears that, whereas the promoters of the Macclesfield scheme counted upon obtaining a substantial portion of their revenue from the traffic

---

67 Ibid., p. 668–9. See also p. 686, 24 March 1766 (petition of unnamed landowners against the bill).

68 Ibid., pp. 693–4, 701.

69 *Journals of the House of Lords*, Vol. 31, p. 338.

70 It is evident that a considerable number would have been required. See *J.H.L.*, Vol. 31, p. 350 (Golburn's evidence). Roe was examined before the House of Lords on 18 April 1766 'as to the time it will take on passing each lock' (ibid). Elsewhere it was stated '. . . from Macclesfield to Northwich, near 20 miles (in which part the greatest number of locks will be) a vessel may be navigated in about 12 hours' (*History of Inland Navigations*, 1st edn. (1766), part II, p. 29).

71 *J.H.L.*, Vol. 31, p. 350. Four hostile witnesses were called to give evidence concerning alleged damage to corn mills (John Simpson, James Wainwright, Thomas Cash, and Francis Mason).

in lime, this valuable source of agricultural improvement was carried toll-free on the Duke's navigations. After Graham had finished examining Hugh Oldham on technical problems concerning the proposed canal, Mr. Ruffhead asked Oldham insinuating questions 'as to his ever having made a navigable canal before' and 'as to the general character of Mr. Brindley as an engineer.' Charles Roe's evidence was much the same as that given before the Commons, but in addition he stressed the advantages which collieries near its banks would derive from the scheme.[72] Roe was also asked questions concerning the number of vessels which might be expected to pass along the canal every day.[73]

The hearing of counsel was then adjourned until 21 April 1766, when a Mr. Davenport gave evidence in support of the bill and was answered by the two opposing counsel. The bill was then shelved indefinitely by the resolution 'That the House be put into a committee upon the said bill on this day three months.'[74] Nothing further can be discovered concerning the scheme, and it can be said that the industrial development of Macclesfield was sacrificed to the Duke of Bridgewater's megalomaniac desire to be 'the largest dealer as a carrier in Europe.'[75] Nevertheless, the Macclesfield Copper Company made use of the Grand Trunk Canal, for in 1789 they secured a 21-year lease of 'all that warehouse, with the crane and other conveniences, situate on the Staffordshire canal, near to the Red Bull in Lawton,' from John Lawton, at a yearly rent of 2s. 6d., and renewable at the same rate.[76]

72 Cf. 'Henry Richards was . . . examined as to the want of coals at Macclesfield, and what quantity may be brought by the intended navigation' (ibid.).

73 Ibid.

74 Ibid., p. 353.

75 Letter quoted in T. S. Willan: *The Navigation of the River Weaver in the Eighteenth Century* (Chetham Society), 1951, pp. 93, 203. And see also *History of Inland Navigations* (1766), part II, p. 28: '. . . the true motives of this opposition will be found in the private interest of his Grace the Duke of Bridgewater . . . For if the communication of the proposed canal with the River Weaver be prevented, and the collieries in Norbury and other parts in that neighbourhood excluded from the benefit of water-carriage, and there is no other navigation for the conveyance of corn, meal and other provisions from Cheshire to Manchester market but by the Duke's canal, the design of his Grace's friends will be answered, and the monopoly they have in view secured.'

76 Bill of Sale of Macclesfield copper works. The lease, which was dated 2 February 1789, may have been a renewal of an earlier one.

PART II: 1767–1811

THE LATER HISTORY OF THE MACCLESFIELD COPPER COMPANY, 1767–1811

In 1767 the Macclesfield Company was among the eight brass and copper concerns which petitioned the King against the proposed grant of a royal charter of incorporation to the Warmley Copper Company of Gloucestershire.[77] This petition reveals that Charles Roe and Rowland Atkinson had been joined in the partnership by Robert Hodgson, Bryan Hodgson, John Walker, a Liverpool merchant, and certain other unnamed persons who stated:[78]

> . . . your petitioners have been preparing buildings, making wares,[79] mills and machinery to carry on the copper and brass manufactory betwixt nine and ten years and have already expended therein the sum of £15,500 and upwards, and have still a considerable sum to add before the works are compleated, when they hope and believe from what they have experienced to be able to make the several articles of this business in a very compleat manner.[80]

A description of the works on Macclesfield Common dating from the 1790s, gives some indication of their extent in their heyday:

> On the said common there is also a large building, with an open counter-yard in the middle of about thirty yards square, called the Smelting House, where they first melt down the copper ore, and make large quantities of shot or pellets; they also make large white bricks

---

77 A. B. Dubois: *The English business company after the Bubble Act, 1720–1800*, 1938, 30–1, 75.

78 R. Dalton and S. H. Hamer state (*The provincial token coinage of the 18th century*, I, 1910, 8) that the 'original partners' in the Macclesfield Copper Company were Charles Roe, Robert Hodgson, Bryan Hodgson, Rowland Atkinson, John Walker, Joseph Stockdale and Cookson Atkinson, but do not quote any authority. Stockdale may have been related to Charles Roe's second wife. On 1 May 1772, the Macclesfield Copper Company consisted of Charles Roe, William Roe, his eldest son, Bryan and Robert Hodgson, Rowland and Cookson Atkinson, Edward Pitts, Legh Dickinson, Thomas Weaver, and John Jeffreys (15 Geo. III, cap. 91, 1775).

79 I.e. weirs.

80 Public Record Office, State Papers Domestic, Entry Books (S.P. 44), vol. 266A, 31–33.

for the purpose of making their ovens, and deep large pots in the form of garden pots, but much larger, to melt their copper ore in. Between this and the brass houses stands a large windmill[81] for grinding the ore; next is the Balamy[82] Houses, a large range of buildings one story high where they wash and filter the ore several times over in running water. Next are the brass houses, being a number of lofty buildings, where they make the ore [sic] into copper sheets for ships, pan bottoms and brass wire, and they make large quantities of brass nails; before these houses are three large reservoirs of water for the supply of the works, and the range of dwelling houses for the workmen.[83]

In 1792 the traveller-diarist John Byng obtained a 'ticket' to view the Macclesfield copper works, 'where I took an accurate and gratifying survey, of their mixing, melting and flat'ning the copper; a most unwholesome employ, for which the workmen are meanly pay'd as the best earn but 14s. per week.'[84]

It seems fairly obvious that the local copper ores soon proved insufficient to supply all the needs of the company. In October 1763 Roe and Hodgson travelled to North Wales and inspected Parys Mountain in Anglesey, which was known to contain copper ore, although the owner, Sir Nicholas Bayly, Bt. (d.1782) of Plasnewydd, Anglesey, had lost money in prospecting for workable supplies of it. Bayly also owned a joint interest with the Earl of Powis in the lead mine at Penrhyn Du in the parish of Llanengan in Lleyn, Caernarvonshire, in which Roe and Hodgson were also interested. Bayly is said to have made it a condition of his consent to the Penryhn Du lease that the Cheshire adventurers should also take a lease of his Cerrig-y-bleiddiau Farm estate on the eastern portion of Parys Mountain. A clause in the lease of Cerrig-y-bleiddiau bound the lessees to make 'a spirited trial' there for ore. It is stated that the Macclesfield Company agreed to this condition only with reluctance, but the whole story must be regarded with suspicion.[85] The

---

81 Sails weighing 2 cwt. for this windmill came up the River Weaver from the Mersey estuary in 1776 on Charles Roe's account *per* the flat *Hopewell* (Weaver Shipments: Northwick Tonnage of Up-Goods, Vol. 34, 4 March 1776).

82 An obvious misprint for 'Calamy', i.e. calamine.

83 Barfoot and Wilkes, *Universal British Directory*, III, 895. This description of the works is identical with that found on pages 438–9 of Dr. J. Aikin's *Description of the country from thirty to forty miles round Manchester* (1795). The site of the windmill is perpetuated in the present Windmill Square, Macclesfield. Nearby are Windmill Street, Calamine Street and Place, Brass-house Street and Copper Street.

84 *The Torrington Diaries*, abridged edn., 1954, 438.

85 Mona Mine MSS 3534 – Cartwright's expense account for Oct. 1763; A. H. Dodd, *The*

actual lease of this portion of Parys Mountain to the Macclesfield Copper
Company has not been discovered, but it is known to have been for 21 years
from 10 October 1764, at a reserved rent of one-eighth of the produce. In
practice this meant that the Macclesfield Company paid a 'duty', i.e. royalty,
of one-eighth of the ore extracted to Sir Nicholas. Mining began there
towards the end of April 1765.[86]

In the case of Penrhyn Du a vigorous attempt was made to work the lead
ores from 1765 onwards with the help of skilled miners from Derbyshire.
The Company paid a 'duty' of one-tenth to the owners after deduction of
freight, and the ores were shipped directly from the workings on the southern shore of Lleyn. The Macclesfield men decided, however, to give up
mining at Penrhyn Du, which does not appear to have been very profitable,
as from Michaelmas 1767.[87]

The following advertisement from *Williamson's Liverpool Advertiser* of
21 June 1765 shows that the Company had succeeded in securing a foothold
in that important market:

John Walker, of Hanover Street, Liverpool, begs to inform the publick
that he has now got an assortment of rowl'd [sic] copper from Charles
Rowe, Esq. and Co.['s] Works near Congleton, and will always have a
regular and constant supply of all sorts; where braziers may depend
upon being served on the lowest terms and copper of the best quality;
plates for sheathing are roll'd to any thickness required . . .[88]

In 1767 Roe and his partners began to erect a copper smelting plant on
the bank of the Mersey estuary at Liverpool. The date is significant. It was

Industrial Revolution in North Wales, 1933, 154–5. The story concerning the conditional
lease appears for the first time in Thomas Pennant's *Tour in Wales*, II, 1st ed., 1781, 266, and
has been repeated by all subsequent writers, e.g. A. G. L. Lentin, *Briefe über die Insel
Anglesea*, 1800, 37–8, 42; W. Davies, *General View of the Agriculture of North Wales*, 1810,
46. See also Mona Mine Letters, II, i, 1267 (U.C.N.W., Bangor).

86 Mona Mine MSS 3544 – 'Observations &c respecting the Mines' (undated, but from
    internal evidence apparently written between 1782 and 1785); Mona Mine MSS 3534 –
    Cartwright's expense account for 1765; Mona Mine MSS 1267.

87 Mona Mine MSS 3534, 7–8, 41, 89. The actual lease was not surrendered until Dec. 1768 –
    ibid., 42, 96. It apparently ran from Michaelmas 1764.

88 Roe and Co. shipped 2 tons of copper in 8 casks down the River Weaver on 10 and 16 April
    1765, and from 27 September 1765 onwards there are frequent shipments of copper, brass,
    wire, copper bottoms, brass sheets and neptunes down the river on John Walker's account
    (Weaver Shipments: Navigation Day Book, vol. 8 (1765–1769) passim). In Gore's *Liver-
    pool Directory* of 1769, the smelting firm is described as 'Walker & Co., Copper Works,
    South Shore.'

one year after the defeat of the canal scheme; the new smelter would cut out the necessity of transporting all the ore up to Macclesfield. These smelting works at Liverpool are said to have been opened on 1 January 1768, and the copper produced there was shipped to Macclesfield for further treatment.[89]

Shortly after the Liverpool works began production it became known that the Macclesfield Company had had an amazing and unexpected 'strike'. According to the accepted version, on St. Chad's Day, 2 March 1768, a team of workmen superintended by the Company's mining agent, an experienced Derbyshire miner named Jonathan Roose, discovered an abundant vein of copper ore in Parys Mountain near the place later called 'The Golden Venture'.[90] Against the authenticity of this dramatic story must be set the undoubted fact that, on 15 February 1768, over a fortnight before the alleged date of the 'strike', John Cartwright, Sir Nicholas's agent, had been despatched by his master to Macclesfield 'to purchase share of Paris Mountain Mine'.[91] In addition, the erection of the Macclesfield Company's new smelter at Liverpool in 1767 suggests that the partners were well aware of Parys Mountain's buried riches long before 2 March 1768.[92] Cartwright set out for Macclesfield a second time a few days after the strike 'by Sir

---

89 The works stood 'upon the piece of land now (1792) used as a timber yard bounded on the north by the new street, which leads from the bottom of Sparling Street to the King's Dock, on the east by Wapping, on the south by other timber yards, on the west by the quay of the King's Dock' (Holt and Gregson Papers, xix, 75, no. 77, letter of John Johnson to John Holt, 20 September 1792 – Picton Library, Liverpool). Eye's *Plan of Liverpool* (1768) 'shows a copper works on the west side of the South Shore (the original name for Wapping), and between the bottom of the now-destroyed Crosbie Street and one of the small tidal basins that were there then but were swept away when the old King's Dock (the predecessor of the present Wapping and King's Docks) was made' (*Cheshire Sheaf*, 1922, 68).

90 A. H. Dodd, op. cit., 154–5. The memorial tablet to Roe in Christ Church, Macclesfield states: 'By an intuitive kind of knowledge he acquired an intimate acquaintance with the mineral strata of the earth; and was esteemed, by competent judges, greatly to excel in the art of mining. In that line his concerns were extensive; and the land owners, as well as proprietors, of the valuable mine in the Isle of Anglesea, are indebted to him for the discovery.' Whether this implies anything more than that he was the formal head of the Company it is impossible to say. W. Davies (op. cit., 46) alleges that Roose received 'positive orders' from the Macclesfield partners 'to desist and discharge the miners. Contrary to his masters' injunctions, as the farewell attempt, he collected his whole mining force to one favourite spot; there he sunk, and there within seven feet of the surface he discovered the body of ore'. There is a letter from Jonathan Roose to Cartwright dated March 16, 1768, i.e. written only a few days after the 'strike', in Mona Mine MSS 3534, 35–6.

91 Mona Mine MSS 3534.

92 This problem has been examined in detail by Dr. J. R. Harris in 'The Copper Industry in North Wales and Lancashire, 1760–1815' (Ph.D thesis, University of Manchester, 1952).

Nicholas Bayly's order to Mr. Roe with an unlimited power to purchase
shares of the copper mine at Parys Mountain'. According to Cartwright's
account, Roe promised to lay this request before the Company. In May John
Denman of Holywell, the Macclesfield Company's agent, Cartwright and
Roose viewed the mine and 'all joined in the opinion it would be for the best
to admit Sir Nicholas into a share of the mine'. Denman and Roose promised
to 'enterseed' with Roe and the rest of his Company for Bayly to have
one-eighth share. To this the Company agreed on condition that Bayly paid
one-eighth of the calls levied to meet the running costs of the mine. Roe
informed Cartwright of this decision in June 1768, but the mean and
irascible baronet overreached himself:

> ... About 2 or 3 days afterwards Mr. Roe and Mr. Denman came to
> Plasnewydd to speak to Sir Nicholas and Mr. Roe told him that the Co.
> had come to a resolution to let him have 1/8, upon which Sir Nicholas
> said he would have 1/4, upon which some dispute happened and I
> went with Mr. Roe to the stables to take horse and told him to make
> himself easy ... and furthermore told Mr. Roe and Mr. Denman that I
> would use all my interest with my master to have everything
> reconciled ...

The unfortunate Cartwright evidently overrated his influence over Bayly
and underrated the business acumen of Charles Roe, for on 9 July Roe wrote
to him[93] that the Company 'had come to a resolution to continue their shares
[as before], upon which my master ordered me to go over to Macclesfield
and settle with them for the 1/8 share'. Here Cartwright saw Roe, Atkinson
and Hodgson, and was told by the last-named that 'Sir Nicholas Bayly had
no right to 1/8 share of the mine, neither should he have any share'.[94] Bayly,
however, was still making attempts to retrieve his position as late as December 1768, as the following extract from a letter dated 7 January 1769 shows.
After informing Bayly that the Company had fixed its shares as before Roe
continued:

> ... Nor shall we ever alter them from any claim you can make.
> Neither shall we hold any more conference with Cartwright. But as
> you (we find) are desirous to buy 1/8 share at the prime cost – tho' we
> believe the same to be worth some thousand pounds, our inclination to

93 Mona Mine MSS 3534, 40, where a full copy of Roe's letter is given.
94 Mona Mine MSS 3534, 37–9. This last visit to Macclesfield apparently took place in August
    1768 (ibid., 42).

live in harmony and friendship (and no other, for we will defend our rights) leads us to make the proposals to you, Sir, which you'll find on the other side. We have made an effective workmanship since we began in your estate (and, more than any other Company would have done) we at last succeeded – I should think to the full of your expectations. What could we do (or you expect) more? Excuse my saying you'll have no more offers (these refused) from the Company,

    I am, for them and myself,

    Yours to command,

    Chas. Roe.[95]

The proposals referred to are set forth in the Mona Mine MSS[96], and included a condition that the lease of 1764 should be cancelled, to be replaced by a fresh one to run until 1790. As they were rejected by Bayly, it is not proposed to detail them here. Curiously enough, Bayly, who was joint owner of the rest of Parys Mountain, is later said to have 'made an offer to Roe and Co., of the moiety of Paris Mine on the same terms on which it is let to [John] Dawes,[97] and they rejected it'.[98] By 1782 the Macclesfield Company was dividing net profits to the amount of £15,000 a year and even the landlord's duty of one-eighth was producing £3,000 a year for Bayly's successor, the Earl of Uxbridge, which suggests that the annual expense of working the mine was about £6,000. Thomas Harrison, the compiler of 'Observations &c. regarding the Mine'[99] commented bitterly:

The lease [to Roe and Co.] seems to have been very incautiously and improperly drawn, for the lessees are under no covenants for working the mine so as to clear away the ore as they go on. It is therefore obvious that they may and no doubt they will, take that which is to be come at in the easiest way and at the least expense; and leave what is more difficult to be raised and more expensive behind; consequently on any future letting, a less duty must suffice; and they have a power of plundering with a vengeance and of which they will no doubt take the advantage.

95 Mona Mine MSS 3534. 103–4.
96 3534, 105–6. See also ibid. – letter of Roe and Co. to Sir Nicholas Bayly requiring a definite reply by 20 March.
97 Of Dawes, Devayne and Co., London bankers.
98 Mona Mine MSS 3544.
99 Mona Mine MSS. 3544. Harrison's authorship of this anonymous paper seems to be attested by his letter to the Earl of Uxbridge, 22 November 1787 (Bangor MSS, cat. iv, 3010, U.C.N.W.), the language of which is identical.

Between 9 December 1782 and 10 October 1785 the Macclesfield Company handed over to the Earl of Uxbridge 'duty' ores which sold for £15,261, or at the rate of £5,549 *per annum*. This portion of Parys Mountain seems never to have reached such a sustained height of productivity again.[100] Although it was comparatively easy to work, the Anglesey ore had a low copper content compared with say, Cornish ore, and at first Roe and Company calcined it on the top of Parys Mountain in a wasteful manner 'in open kilns; and the sulphureous fumes escaping, mixing with the atmosphere, and by condensation falling on the soil, spread universal sterility over several hundreds of acres of the lands adjoining'.[101] The calcined ore was then shipped to Liverpool for smelting.

Roe and Co. also obtained part of their ore supply from Cornwall. Yearly purchase varied greatly – from a minimum of 159 tons in 1767 to a maximum of 913 tons in 1773, the last yar for which figures are available.[102] The Company continued to purchase Cornish ore even when Parys Mountain's resources were being fully exploited, for on 4 October 1781 James Watt wrote from Cosgarne to John Turner, John Wilkinson's manager at Bersham Foundry in Denbighshire:

. . . there will be a vessel at Liverpool with ore from this county [Cornwall] for Messrs. Roe and Company.[103]

The Macclesfield Company was still one of the eleven smelting concerns bidding for Cornish copper ore in 1798–99.[104]

All did not go smoothly, however, at Liverpool. During the Lancaster Lent Assizes in 1770 the Corporation of Liverpool were plaintiffs and the Macclesfield Copper Company defendants as 'proprietors of the copper-works

---

100 Bangor MSS, cat. iv, 3028.

101 W. Davies, op. cit., 49. In 1774 Thomas Williams, later to become the 'copper king', invited Roe to bid for copper ore from the western portion of Parys Mountain (Williams to C. Roe, 27 July 1774 – Kinmel Papers, U.C.N.W., Bangor).

102 Figures for Roe and Co.'s purchases of Cornish ore between 1765 and 1773 have been calculated by R. O. Roberts (Statistics showing the amounts of copper ore sold publicly in Cornwall, to various firms, between 1729 and 1784 – MS), to whom the author is grateful for permission to use the figures.

103 Boulton and Watt Coll., Birmingham Public Library. The *Manchester Mercury* of 15 July 1794 records the arrival at Liverpool of a coasting vessel, *The Glory*, from Chester, with a cargo of 37 tons of calamine and 16 tons of lead on Roe and Co.'s account.

104 See *Report from the Committee appointed to enquire into the state of the copper mines and copper trade of this Kingdom (Great Britain)*, 1799 (Reports from Committees of the House of Commons, X, 1803), 684–701, passim.

contiguous to that town.'[105] Thirty-five witnesses for the plaintiffs were
examined, 'who proved beyond a doubt, that the noxious effluvia of the said
works, were pernicious to health, injurious to the herbage, and a nuisance to
the neighbourhood.' Roe and Co. agreed to discontinue 'the calcining part'
immediately and were 'allowed two years to remove the works to a more
remote situation.' Later in the year the works were advertised for sale.[106]

The verdict at Lancaster Assizes had evidently been to some extent a
foregone conclusion, for there is documentary evidence that Charles Roe
was already in negotiation with an agent of Viscount Molyneux[107] during
the latter part of 1769, concerning a lease of '500 yards of the shore under
Toxteth park, adjoining the Corporation liberties', i.e. on the banks of the
Mersey estuary south of Liverpool and about a mile from the former site.
Roe was fairly optimistic:

> . . . you apprehended we should build furnaces there, but in the first
> place I believe we shan't be obliged to remove our furnaces, but if we
> should be . . . we would not build on the said 500 yards and a clause
> may be inserted to forbid it. We should choose, in case removing
> them, Knott's Hole.[108]

Roe wanted the 500 yards' length of strand to extend 'as far into the sea or
river as we choose to take in – and 30 or 40 yards of land in the fields, above
high-water mark . . . necessary to complete . . . walls or yards'.[109]

After negotiations lasting some months, Lord Molyneux leased to Charles Roe and Company a strip consisting of portions of 'the Lower Croft, the
Roughs and the Great Sea Hey', 150 yards by 30 yards, all part of Toxteth
Park, together with the foreshore, part of which was intended to be used '. . .
for a reservoir for water to scour or cleanse such dock or docks[110] or other
sluices, as should or might be made within the said premises', for 80 years

---

105 *Annual Register*, XIII (1770), pt. 1, 96–7. Complaints had started in 1768 (*Liverpool Chronicle*, 8–15 Sept. 1768).

106 *Gore's Liverpool Advertiser*, 7 Sept. 1770.

107 Charles William, 8th Viscount Molyneux (1748–95). He became the first Earl of Sefton in 1771.

108 Charles Roe, Macclesfield, to James Chadwick, Mount Pleasant, Liverpool, 30 Dec. 1769 (D.D.M. 50/19, Molyneux Papers, Lancashire County Record Office, Preston). Roe was in competition for this piece of land with a syndicate of Liverpool merchants who wanted 'a spot of ground for a timber yard' (D.D.M. 50/17, 50/18, 10–14 Oct. 1769).

109 D.D.M. 50/20, Chas. Roe to Thos. Chadwick, Burgh, near Chorley, 6 Jan. 1770.

110 These docks and quays were unfinished in 1773 (D.D.M. 50/22). Two plans of the works and their surroundings are included in the Molyneux Papers.

certain, as from Michaelmas 1770, at £7 10s. per annum.[111] The Company
took possession of the land in 1770 and transferred the copper works from
the old site in 1771,[112] although the actual date of the indenture of lease was
as late as 1 May 1772, and the Earl of Sefton seems to have waived any
payment of rent until 1774.[113]

This lease was supplemented by a second and more extensive one,
granted by the Earl of Sefton to Charles Roe alone, as from 29 September,
1773. The land covered by this lease consisted of four lots (nos. 25 to 28
inclusive) in Toxteth Park, which was 'intended and agreed to be converted
into a town or village called Harrington'.[114] The lease was to run for 80
years certain at the annual rent of £65, with a fine payable every 20 years
and increasing in geometrical progression.[115] The total area of the four lots
was nearly 54 acres (704 yards long by 235 yards deep), and the copper
works stood on lot 27.[116] Roe and Company undertook to build substantial
'dwelling-houses, warehouses and other houses with conveniences and
appointments thereto' on the portion of the land fronting Sefton Street
during Roe's tenancy and upon the rest of the land 'such houses, docks,
wharfs, quays, timber yards or other yards, works, conveniences and
improvements as he or they shall think fit or proper'. In addition no person
except Charles Roe was to have any right 'to inclose below the aforesaid lots
towards the River Mersey'[117] and 'no merchandise, etc.' could 'be landed at
the slips, terminating the streets to the river, without paying . . . a

111 15 Geo. III, c.91 (1775) – *An act to confirm several building leases, already granted by the
Rt. Hon. the Earl of Sefton.* For confirmation see D.D.M. 50/20, 50/21, 50/23, 50/33.

112 Holt and Gregson Papers, loc. cit.

113 15 Geo. III c.91 (1775) – date of lease. Cf. C. Roe to W. Turner, Warrington, 31 Dec. 1773:
'Please to give my compliments to Mr. Chadwick and remind him that when I last saw him
at Liverpool that he reckoned upon more than two years of the three (that were to pass
without paying rent) to be elapsed since our bargain was agreed upon, and that his Lordship
said he would only give us one year from that time' (D.D.M. 50/22).

114 D.D.M. 50/30. Roe wrote on 31 Dec. 1773 to W. Turner of Warrington: '. . . my agreement
for the shore (in 1770) was the very cause of their thinking of building a town' (D.D.M.
50/22).

115 D.D.M. 50/23, 50/30. The fine payable on 29 Sept. 1793, was £130, that payable on 29 Sept.
1813, £260, on 29 Sept. 1833, £520, and so on.

116 Roe sold lot 28 for £600 and his son, William Roe, asked £8000 for the remaining term of
his lease of nos. 25–27 in 1789, when the Corporation of Liverpool commenced abortive
negotiations to purchase 'from Messrs. Roe and Co. the lease they hold under your Lordship
of the shore, which they enclosed near Harrington, with an intent to make a large dock and
bason thereon, and quays of great extent' (Thomas Smyth, Lord Mayor of Liverpool, to Earl
of Sefton, 22 Oct. 1789 (D.D.M. 50/26; see also D.D.M. 50/27).

117 D.D.M. 50/30.

compensation' to the Macclesfield Company.[118]

The Company smelted copper at the Harrington works until 1792–3. Robert Morris, who visited Roe and Co.'s works on 25 May 1774, left the following account of them:

> . . . The Works are single, and seem very cool and well contrived . . . Here they called the Regulus Metal, saying 'now this is not copper, but it will be copper next melting'. They roast or calcine all their ore. Most of the ore they have from Cornwall. A good deal from Anglesea, and from Flintshire. Most from these 2 places comes in a burnt state to them; and then it is of a red Color. I also saw some ore from Cornwall, which was red, that they said had not been burnt before it came. They have their Coal from the works up the river near Warrington. They said, they made more copper, than at Patten's Works. But they seemed not to know . . . they have but one foreman, who has 20 shillings, for the 7 days of the week. The men when they come here to work first have immediately 15 pence per day for the 12 hours for the first year; after which they have 16 pence a day, and can expect to rise no more. A Labourer in a stone quarry told me his wages were 18 pence a day. Close to the Copper-works, there is a neat row of small houses, to the number, as far as I can now guess, of about 12 or 14 for the workmen. There did not seem to be above 20 workmen employ'd at a time in the whole works. I forgot to reckon the number of Furnaces, but the works are not even so large as those at Middlebank at Swansea . . .[119]

The effect of the establishment of the Liverpool smelter in 1767–8 on the movement in copper ore up the River Weaver is particularly interesting. There were no shipments of copper ore up the Weaver throughout 1757 and 1758. From 4 October 1759 shipments of copper ore begin, and from March 1760 except during the winter there were few months which did not see the arrival of at least one cargo of ore at Northwich, in amounts normally ranging from about 20 to 40 tons at a time. From 29 August 1759 small consignments of copper in casks began to travel downstream on the second stage of the journey from Macclesfield. The first shipment of copper ore definitely stated to be for Roe and Company paid toll at Northwich on 27

118 William Roe, Fair View, Liverpool, to John Webster, Toxteth, agent to the Earl of Sefton, 21 Feb. 1791. (D.D.M. 50/29).

119 Morris MSS (University College Library, Swansea).

October 1764 (25 tons of loose copper ore and 18 casks of packed ore). After 1769–70 the shipments of copper ore brought up to Northwich became fewer and fewer, but calamine continued to move upstream, together with considerable amounts of block and pig copper, indicating that the works in the Macclesfield area were specialising in brass making and the later stages of copper manufacture. By 1775 the shipment of copper ore upstream on behalf of Roe and Co. had ceased. In 1769–70 the flow of manufactured copper and brass articles downstream from Northwich to the Mersey estuary was in full swing, but after 8 October 1776, when a cargo of 11 tons 14 cwt. of copper in blocks and pigs belonging to William Roe paid toll at North-wich on its way to Macclesfield, this section of the traffic ceased entirely, and the tonnage book for 1777–8 contains no evidence that the Macclesfield Company was using the River Weaver at all. This was almost certainly due to the gradual opening of the Grand Trunk Canal, culminating in its com-plete opening throughout in the late 1770s and the transference of the traffic to the new waterway.[120]

William Roe (1746–1827), Charles Roe's eldest son, who had been associated with the business from at least 1770, was the managing partner of this section of the enterprise and carried it on 'with vigour'.[121] In May 1778 he entered into a separate partnership with John Champion, jun., for the use of the latter's sulphur recovery process on Parys Mountain and at the Liverpool smelter. Roe and Champion paid £50 a year to the Macclesfield Company for the privilege of roasting its ores, which were much improved thereby.[122] On 27 March 1779 William Roe was granted letters patent (no. 1216) for a new process for calcining or extracting the sulphur from poor

[120] Weaver Shipments: Navigation Day Books, vols. 6–9, 1757–69, passim; Northwich Ton-nage of Up-Goods, vols. 30–35, 1769–78, passim (County Record Office, Chester).

[121] Holt and Gregson Papers, loc. cit. In 1772 he was described in Gore's *Liverpool Directory* as merchant, Cable Street. Roe Street in Liverpool is said to have been named after William Roe, who in 1779 was living in Duke Street. In later life he resided at 9, Queen Square. (J. A. Picton: *Memorials of Liverpool*, II, 174; *Gore's Liverpool Advertiser*, 21 May 1779). When Dr. William Enfield published *An essay towards the history of Liverpool* in 1773, William Roe subscribed to the work, while his father bought a copy of the plan which accompanied it. William Roe also subscribed to John Corry's *History of Macclesfield* (1817). He was a member of the Common Council of Liverpool, Bailiff of Liverpool in 1786 and Commissioner of Customs. In 1788 he was appointed one of the three Commis-sioners to examine and report to Parliament statements of losses sustained by merchants under the Act of 1788 regulating the slave trade between Africa and the West Indies (*Gore's Liverpool Advertiser*, 2 Dec. 1790; D. Macpherson, *Annals of Commerce* (1805), IV, 174; *Cheshire Sheaf*, 1935, 99).

[122] Mona Mine MSS 3028–32; *Gore's Liverpool Advertiser*, 19 May 1780.

quality copper and lead ores.[123] By 1792 the Liverpool works contained 35 furnaces, employed about 80 people, consumed between 10,000 and 12,000 tons of coal annually and were equipped with 'cranes, sheds, yards, pier, dock and other conveniences'.[124] In addition to the smelter Roe and Co. maintained a copper, brass and lead warehouse in Manesty's Lane, Cornhill, Liverpool, under the supervision of John Johnson, where ingot brass, copper sheathing and copper bolts, nails and battery wares for the West African slave trade could be obtained.[125]

During the War of American Independence, the Macclesfield Company secured an important contract for naval copper to be delivered at Plymouth, but the minutes of the Navy Board show that among other things, the war-time shipping difficulties of 1780 led to a serious delay in its fulfilment.[126] In the financial crisis of 1793 Roe and Co. joined with other Liverpool firms in a public declaration of willingness to support the short-term bills of certain Liverpool banks.[127]

The Liverpool smelter's appetite for coal would seem to be one of the reasons why Charles Roe, in partnership with James Venables (d.1786), mined coal at Brynmally in Broughton, near Wrexham, Denbighshire, from about 1770 onwards. The coal was wound out of the mine by whimseys or whim-gins, 'worked by horses in pairs galloping round,' which were released every two hours. Evidence that the coal was used in industry rather than for domestic purposes is suggested by the statement that, owing to the bad state of the local roads, 'large quantities of coal were stacked in the adjacent fields [in winter] and carted away in the summer' which was the reverse of the usual commercial practice, the demand for coal, and consequently its price, being lowest in the summer.[128]

A few years after Charles Roe's death in 1781 a great change came over

123 *Abridgements of the specifications relating to metals and alloys (excepting iron and steel)* 1861, 22, and *Repertory of Arts*, VI, 386.

124 Holt and Gregson Papers, loc. cit.; *Gore's Liverpool Advertiser*, 3 July 1794.

125 *Gore's Liverpool Advertiser*, 19 May 1780, 5 Feb. 1784, 3 July 1794.

126 Navy Board Minutes (Public Record Office), Admiralty 106, nos. 2603, 2604, 2 and 5 May, 8 June, 7 and 9 Aug., 23 Oct., 9 and 28 Nov. 1780.

127 *Gore's Liverpool Advertiser*, 20 March 1793.

128 G. G. Lerry, *The Collieries of Denbighshire* (1946) 11, 12, 114–5. The Brynmally pit was already open in 1753 (*Chester Courant*, 13–20 March, 1753). It is interesting to note that this colliery was afterwards worked by Richard Kirk or Kyrke (1749–1839) of Martinside, Chapel-en-le-Frith, Derbyshire, and later of Gwersyllt Hill, Wrexham, whose son, George Kyrke of Brynmally (d. 1859) married Harriet Roe, daughter of William Roe of Liverpool, in 1813. (*Cheshire Sheaf*, 1935, 99. See also A. H. Dodd, op. cit., 102–3, 184, 190.

the fortunes of the Macclesfield Copper Company. In 1785 its lease of the eastern portion of Parys Mountain expired, and the Earl of Uxbridge, who had succeeded to Sir Nicholas Bayly's estates, did not renew it, but himself formed a partnership with the Anglesey 'copper king', Thomas Williams of Llanidan (1737–1802), later M.P. for Great Marlow, Bucks, to work the mine. When the Macclesfield Company surrendered the site the mine was in an unworkable condition.[129]

By this time the moving spirit in the Macclesfield Copper Company was Edward Hawkins, merchant, of Congleton, who, in partnership with Abraham Mills of Macclesfield, set up the first bank in Macclesfield in 1787.[130] Hawkins was by no means ignorant of the practical side of the copper and brass trade, for on 30 March 1778 he had taken out patent no. 1189 for the 'art or method of making shaven or bright latten', by rolling, battering, hammering and shaving sheet brass.[131] On 20 April 1785 Roe and Co. wrote to Boulton and Watt enquiring their 'terms for engines of several degrees of power with calculations of the daily expenditure of coals' with particular reference to returning 'all the water now running, with moderate velocity, waste through a space containing 9 square feet'.[132] When James Watt visited Hawkins a few months afterwards he was impressed by the spirit of activity

129 'We yesterday took possession of the [Cerrig-y-bleiddiau] Mine, being first agreed with Roe's Co. for all their engines, stock of tool utensils, implements and iron at the sum of £2013 6s. 0d. which I paid them and they are gone . . . But with respect to the non-performance of covenants nothing is or will be settled but by a suit and a Jury.' (Thomas Harrison, chief agent, Amlwch, to Earl of Uxbridge, 11 Oct. 1785 – Mona Mine Letters, II, 2485, U.C.N.W. Bangor). Details of the litigation between the Earl of Uxbridge and Roe and Co. after 1785 may be found in Mona Mine Letters, II, 3032 to 3034, 3936. For other details of the Parys Mine under Roe and Co.'s management (at one time the Company had 14,000 tons of ore on bank), see B.M. Add. MSS. 38375 (Liverpool Papers) 11 May 1783; A. G. L. Lentin, *Briefe über die Insel Angelsea* (Leipzig), 1800; E. Greenly, *Geology of Anglesey*, II (Memoirs of the Geological Survey) 1919, 824–6; R. Hunt *British mining* (1884), 105 sqq., 445–50, 453.

130 J. Corry, op. cit., 74; P. Barfoot and J. Wilkes, op. cit., III, 895. Hawkins was Mayor of Macclesfield in 1782–3 (Earwaker, op. cit., II, p. 466). In 1787 he purchased Miss Mary Roe's share in the Macclesfield Copper Company from her executor, the Rev. David Simpson, for £1566 (Cheshire Wills, County Record Office, Chester, 1787). There is no evidence that Charles Roe ever became a banker, but he had an account with the London bankers, Sir Charles Asgill and Co. (Mona Mine MSS 3534, 76). Eleven years after Charles Roe's death, John Byng visited 'Mr. R[oe]'s banking house', carried on in close connection with the Macclesfield copper works (*The Torrington Diaries*, abridged ed., 1954, 438). He may have meant the bank run by Mills and Hawkins.

131 *Abridgements of the specifications relating to metals and alloys (excepting iron ore and steel).* 1861, 20.

132 Boulton and Watt Coll. (in-letters). See also Roe and Co.'s letter of 11 May 1785. The project did not materialize.

and solid optimism which he found animating the partners and establishments of the Macclesfield Company, in spite of the loss of the Parys Mountain lease. Watt wrote to his partner Boulton on 16 August, 1785:

> I was at Messrs. Roe and Co.'s Brass works; their consumption of water is amazing. They have 5 wheels; the one belonging to the wire mill requires constant water and may be replaced by a 20 horse rotative engine.[133] Mr. Hawkins (one of the partners) was exceeding kind. After we had seen the mills he took me to dine at Congleton at Mr. Hod[g]son's, his brother-in-law, who is also a partner, and is just returned from Scotland, where the Company have just taken a lease of the lead and copper mines of I[s]lay;[134] he says the latter are very promising and I have heard so formerly. After dinner Mr. Hawkins went to Church and I was left alone with Mr. Hod[g]son. He said that they had 12 years' stocks of ores in hand and besides the fair prospects of the I[s]lay mine, had other resources which were not publicly known,[135] that they would be willing to enter into a treaty of amity with the Cornish Metal Company,[136] and that they would be found always to act honourably. They seem to feel the disgrace of being left out, of which, however, they acquit you, but seem to give [Thomas] W[illia]ms the credit, though they did not say so. For my part I think it would be right to make some bargain with them as to prices, especially as they seem to give up the idea of buying ores . . . and [I] think it would be right to keep on neighbourly terms with those who can subsist without you . . . after sounding your colleagues, if you find anything can be done, I think you should write to them; it is certainly the interest of the Cornish [Metal] Company to avoid competition.[137]

133 Watt had evidently visited the Havannah.

134 For the Kilslevan (Islay) vein of copper ore, discovered in 1770, see G. V. Wilson, *The lead, zinc, copper and nickel ores of Scotland* (Special report on the mineral resources of Great Britain), XVII, Geological Survey, Scotland, (1921), 72–3, 133–4. Robert Jameson noted in 1800 (*Mineralogy of the Scottish Isles*, I, p. 152): '. . . considerable quantities of copper pyrites have been found, but the quantity too small to be of any importance.' See also Gregory Smith, *The Book of Islay* (1895), 464–5.

135 This may refer to the moribund Coniston mine. See *Trans. L. & C. Ant. Soc.*, LXII (1950–51), 141–2.

136 The Cornish ore-selling syndicate, of which Matthew Boulton had been one of the chief promoters in 1785.

137 Boulton and Watt Coll. Some idea of the comparative importance of the Macclesfield Copper Company's brass output may be gauged from the fact that when John Hurd of Birmingham submitted to Matthew Boulton 'a sketch of a plan for the regulation of the brass trade' he allotted the Macclesfield Company a quota of 100 tons out of the total production

NORTH-EAST VIEW OF CHRIST CHURCH, MACCLESFIELD.

The importance which James Watt attached to the Macclesfield Company can be seen from a letter written by him to Matthew Boulton two years later, when the Cornish Metal Company was in danger of falling (as it eventually did) under the sole direction of Thomas Williams:

> . . . if something is not done immediately the whole trade will be in Williams's hands, unless the Duke [of Devonshire] and Macclesfield have a struggle with him first . . . The Duke and Macclesfield can offer about 800 tons [for sale to the East India Company], in Mr. Hurd's opinion.[138]

of 1000 tons by the 10 companies which were to be invited to join the scheme. Only 3 of them were to be offered quotas larger than 100 tons (letter of 22 Oct. 1785, Boulton Coll., Assay Office, Birmingham). Edward Hawkins was in favour of the scheme 'but wishes it not brought forward just at present as he thinks the consumers of brass would be much alarmed.'

138 Boulton and Watt Coll. (Letter Book (Office) 1786–8, 19 June 1787). That the danger of competition from Macclesfield was a reality is shown by Boulton's letter of 21 July 1787 to the Soho firm's Cornish agent, T. Wilson: 'I have just heard that the Macclesfield Co. are selling rolled metal for gilt buttons at 82 [s. per cwt.] but hope it is not true.' It was true – see Watt to Wilson, 26 July 1787 (Royal Cornish Institution, Falmouth).

The 'other resources' which Watt mentioned in 1785 foreshadowed the extension of the Macclesfield Company's interest to Ireland. In 1787 Edward Hawkins, William Roe and partners 'finding it difficult to supply themselves with copper ore for their smelting works, and for the consequent parts of their manufactory', purchased in conjunction with other persons, the copper ore mines of Cronebane in County Wicklow, together with other mines in the same county. This subsidiary concern, the Associated Irish Mine Company, expended more than £40,000 in development of these mines between 1787 and 1799.[139] Abraham Mills was the chairman of the company in 1799.[140] From the evidence given by Mills before the House of Commons Committee on the copper mines and copper trade in 1799 it appears that the Cronebane mine had been yielding about 1000 tons of ore *per annum*, on a three-yearly average. Its quality was similar to that of Cornwall, and the company was making from three to four per cent. profit by importing it from Ireland into Great Britain.[141] From other evidence it would seem that production from all the mines in County Wicklow had been seriously hampered by the Rebellion of 1798.[142]

The shipping supplement to the *Manchester Mercury* for 15 February 1791, recorded the arrival of the Company's brig *The Irish Miner* at Liverpool from Wicklow with 8 hogsheads, 1 barrel and 56 bags of packed, and 83½ tons of loose, copper ore for W. Roe and Co. The supplement for 1 March 1791, chronicled the arrival at the same port of the *Mary Ann*, from Wicklow with 33½ tons of copper ore for the same firm. These shipments are interesting in view of the complaint made in the Company's petition to the House of Commons in 1799, in which the partners alleged that the Cronebane ore was 'charged . . . on importation into Great Britain with a very heavy duty, whereby they are precluded from importing ores of low quality, the duty on such ores operating as a total prohibition'. If the duty were to be removed, a considerable amount of copper would be derived from imports of low-grade Irish ore into great Britain, with favourable

139 *Journals of the House of Commons*, LIV, 22 April 1799, 470. For some interesting details concerning the Cronebane mine, see R. Fraser, *General View of . . . Wicklow*, 1801, 15–17 and J. Williams, *Natural History of the Mineral Kingdom*, 1810, 368.

140 *Report from the Committee appointed to enquire into the state of the copper mines and copper trade of this Kingdom (Great Britain), 1799* (Reports from Committees of the House of Commons, X, 1803), 678.

141 Ibid., 656.

142 Ibid., 678. (Evidence of Turner Camac, chairman of the Hibernian Mine Company, which worked copper mines near Arklow, co. Wicklow). This Company had been founded in 1790 and incorporated by an Act of the Irish Parliament in 1792.

effects on the labour market in County Wicklow and on the supply of copper for British metal manufacturers.[143]

The late 1780s and early 1790s were marked by a large issue of token halfpence by Roe and Company, both in England and Ireland. Between 1789 and 1792 over 11 tons of Macclesfield halfpence, most of them bearing a portrait of the founder of the firm, taken from his monument in Christ Church, were struck in Birmingham (not at Macclesfield, as is often stated) from dies sunk by J. G. Hancock, sen. The edges bore the legend *Payable at Macclesfield, Liverpool or Congleton*, and in a few cases *Payable at Cronebane or in Dublin*. The Associated Irish Mine Company issued a considerable number of halfpence in 1789, payable at Cronebane Lodge or in Dublin. Both issues were extensively counterfeited.[144]

Four years after Roe's death the Company branched out in another direction and joined the band of copper firms which established themselves in the Greenfield district on the Flintshire coast. On 22 September 1785 Thomas Pennant of Downing (1726–98), the celebrated topographer and naturalist, leased land to the Company on the banks of the Nant-hil brook, which formed part of the boundary between Holywell and Whelstone in Flintshire. On this land Roe and Hawkins built the River Bank works,[145] which were in Pennant's words, 'employed for the double purpose of calcining calamine for the brass-works at Cheadle and Macclesfield, and for the smelting lead ore'.[146]

143 *J.H.C.*, loc. cit. This petition was referred to the Committee on the copper mines and copper trade, but no specific consideration was given to the matter. Turner Camac, however, gave evidence as follows: 'Prior to the rebellion, and labouring under the operation of the import duty into England the Wicklow mines employed nearly one thousand people, and if the duty was remitted would give useful employment to many more.' He also stated that 'the Crone Bane ores being richer [than those of Arklow] have always been sent to England.' (*Report* . . ., 678).

144 R. Dalton and S. H. Hamer, *The provincial token coinage of the eighteenth century*, I (1910) 8–23, vol. III, (1917), 524–36, 548; C. Pye, *Provincial coins and tokens issued from the year 1787 to the year 1801* (1801), 15. Unauthorised Macclesfield pennies and farthings were struck in considerable numbers by J. Westwood of Birmingham (1742–92) for sale to collectors. Near Buxton in 1790, John Byng, then on a tour of the Midlands, 'was surprised to receive in change the Anglesea and Macclesfield half-pence; a better coinage, and of more beauty than that of the mint, and not so likely to be counterfeited'. A few days later at Macclesfield, he sent for six pennyworth of these tokens from the copper-works (*The Torrington Diaries*, abridged ed., 1954, 241, 243).

145 There is an excellent engraving showing these works between pages 172 and 185 (*sic*) of T. Pennant's *History of the parishes of Whiteford and Holywell* (1796).

146 Op. cit., pp. 273–4. Power was provided by two 24 ft. diam. water-wheels, one of which operated the refining bellows and the other the bellows for the slag hearth. Hawkins and Roe had also installed 'a curious contrivance for saving the calx of the lead-ore' (ibid.). Pennant

Another source of the Macclesfield Copper Company's ore was the mining site near the village of Llanberis, on the western side of Llyn Peris, where seven levels had been driven into Snowdon. Messrs. Roe, Hodgson, Smith and Mills had leased the derelict workings from Thomas Assheton Smith of Faenol[147] some years before 1798. In that year 80 miners were engaged in blasting the pyrites, which were said to be rich, while women and children hammered the large pieces of ore, and then sorted the fragments according to their quality. The pieces were then washed and taken to a water-driven stamping mill. When pounded sufficiently small, the ore was carried into a reservoir by a stream of water and 'again purified by decantation':

> It is then removed in boats down the lakes, whence it is conveyed by carts to Caernarvon Quay, and shipped to the Company's smelting works near Swansea.[148]

The period 1792–1801 witnessed a shift in the fortunes of the Company. In the first place the Liverpool smelter was dismantled[149] and new smelting works built at Neath Abbey near Swansea in Glamorgan. A note in the Holt and Gregson papers dating from 1792–3 states that William Roe and Co. were then contemplating the removal of their works 'on the account of the scarcity and dearness' of coal at Liverpool.[150] The Company continued [to]

---

gives an engraving of the River Bank works. In 1798 John Wilkinson, the famous ironmaster, offered to buy the Cheadle Company's share in these River Bank works for £350. The Company resolved 'that the same be first offered to Messrs. Roe and Co., and in case they do not wish to purchase ... then the same to be sold and made over to Mr. Wilkinson as soon as convenient' (Cheadle Brasswire Co., Minute Book, 1788–1831, 19 July 1798).

147 Near Bangor, Caerns.

148 Rev. John Evans, *A tour through part of North Wales in 1798 and at other times* (3rd ed., 1804), 184–7; see also Rev. R. Warner, *A Walk through Wales in 1797* (1798), 131.

149 See *Gore's Liverpool Advertiser*, 3 July 1794, where the works were offered for sale or on lease as being suitable, among other things, for 'any business ... that might in a large town, be deemed a niusance. Roe and Co. have removed most of the furnaces to their new works at Neath.'

150 Loc. cit. It is significant that between 2 June and 22 September 1791 Roe and Co. advertised weekly (with one omission in July) in *Gore's Liverpool Advertiser* inviting tenders for contracts for the supply of their Liverpool smelter with coal for 'one or more years from the 1st May, 1792.' H. P. Wyndham (*A gentleman's tour through ... Wales in the months of June and July 1774* (1775), 43–4) noted of the Swansea area: 'The plenty of coals in this neighbourhood, and the convenience of exportation, have induced the copper companies to prefer this spot to all others.' Nevertheless one of the Macclesfield partners, a Mr. Weaver, was complaining as early as 1797 of the unsatisfactory quality and deficient measure of the South Wales coal (G. G. Francis, *The Smelting of Copper in the Swansea district of South Wales*, 2nd ed., (1881), 78. By 1803 Roe and Company had bought a share in a local colliery

VIEW OF MACCLESFIELD SHOWING ROE AND CO.'S WINDMILL.
From an early nineteenth-century tinted engraving dedicated to the Mayor and magistrates of
Macclesfield by John Verga – engraved by D. Havell, London, and painted by J. Parry.

at least 1808.[151]

The move to Neath appears to have been completed by January 1794, for
on 15 February of that year Roe and Company wrote a letter from Macclesfield to the Board of Customs in London pointing out that the firm had been
permitted by the indulgence of the Commissioners to unload copper ore
from Ireland directly on to the quays attached to their Liverpool works 'and
the [customs] officers attended the weighing there', as a duty of 9d. per cwt.
was levied on Irish copper ore imported into Great Britain.[152] In January

concern to ensure a fuel supply for the Neath smelter. (Cheadle Brasswire Co., Minute
Book, 1788–1831, 19 Aug. 1803.)

151 *Gore's Liverpool Directory* (1808).

152 Roe and Co. were 'almost the only importers of Irish copper ore' and consequently almost
the only firm paying the duty. They pointed out to the Board, 'as we hear a commercial
arrangement is in agitation between the two Kingdoms,' the desirability of repealing the
duty, which injured both Great Britain and Ireland, 'for great quantities of ores of a low
quality remain unwrought at the mines in Ireland, because they cannot under the duty be
imported into this Kingdom but at certain loss, whereas, was the duty removed, great

1794 the Company's brig *The Irish Miner* discharged the first cargo of ore from Wicklow on the Company's 'unlawful' private wharf' at 'the Abbey', a mile from the town of Neath (which was a creek of the port of Swansea for customs purposes)[153] and eight miles from the private residences of the Swansea customs officers. These officials had therefore incurred considerable travelling expenses (six guineas) by attending at Neath Abbey to weigh the ore for the payment of duty, expenses which had to be paid by Roe and Co. In addition the master of *The Irish Miner* had to travel to Swansea to make entry of his brig in the Custom House there. Roe and Co. therefore asked the Board of Customs that they should be allowed to make entry of future shipments at Neath and that customs officers, whose fees were to be permanently fixed, should be appointed 'to attend the delivery of the cargoes' at Neath.[154] From the material examined it seems unlikely that the Company's requests were granted immediately.

The Company gave high labour costs as its second reason for leaving Liverpool, and the wages which it paid evidently compared favourably with those ruling in Glamorgan, for on 11 January 1798 the men at the Mines Royal Company's works at Neath struck work, complaining that 'they do now work for less money than Roe and Co.'s men'.[155]

As noted above, the Company was still seeking concessions on the question of the import duty on Irish ores in 1799, in which year the output of the smelter at Neath was 120 tons of copper per year.[156] Roe and Company continued smelting at Neath Abbey until 1811 when it is almost certain that

numbers of his Majesty's subjects might be there employed in procuring the ore, numbers in the transport of it and a supply would be introduced in aid of the expenditure of copper in sheathing and bolting his Majesty's navy, and also for the consumption and consequent exportation of the manufactures of Sheffield and Birmingham.'

153 '. . . the trade of Neath is so trifling as to render the establishing the officers there wholly unnecessary' (Collector and Comptroller of Customs at Swansea to Board of Customs, Feb. 1794, Letter Book, 126).

154 Swansea Custom House: letter book, Collector to Board, 1793–5, 30 Jan. 1794, 15 Feb. 1794 (Roe & Co.'s letter, 124). See also ibid., 125–6 (Library, H.M. Customs and Excise, London) – also quoted in D. R. Phillips, *History of the Vale of Neath* (1925), 281 and A. H. John, *The Industrial Development of South Wales, 1750–1850*, 28. The author is indebted to Mr. C. D. J. Trott of Neath and Mr. R. C. Jarvis of the Library, H.M. Customs and Excise, for help in tracing and elucidating these records.

155 G. G. Francis, op. cit., 78.

156 *Report on . . . the copper trade* (1799), 656. The Rev. R. Warner (*A second walk through Wales . . . in August and September 1798*, 1799, 97) noted 'two considerable copperworks, the one belonging to Messrs. Roe and Co. of Macclesfield, the other to the Mines-Royal Company' at Neath.

the Cheadle Company purchased the works, although members of the former Macclesfield Company retained some interest in the site.[157]

The second change in the Company's operations brings the story to a close. in 1801 the remaining partners in the Macclesfield Company decided to shut down and sell the establishments in the Macclesfield area. A few months before this they had very wisely secured a new title of occupation for the land they were using on the Common from the Corporation of Macclesfield, to which a part of it had been allotted under the awards arising out of the Macclesfield Common Enclosure Act of 1796. It will be remembered that the original lease of common land from the corporation in 1758 concerned 1600 square yards only or about a third of an acre. On September 27, 1800, however, the corporation confirmed the following:

> A lease of two parcels of land on Macclesfield Common (allotted to the said Mayor, Alderman and Burgesses) containing 12 acres, 3 roods, 33 perches of Statute measure to Messrs. Abraham Mills and Brian Hodgson the younger, for the term of thirty-one years, commencing on the twenty-fifth day of March last and under the clear yearly rent of thirty-five pounds.[158]

About a year later in October 1801, the works on Macclesfield Common and at the Havannah and Bosley were advertised for sale both by handbill and by advertisement in the newspapers.[159] The windmill had already been 'fitted up for grinding corn' and only five copper smelting and refining furnaces were standing, 'others having been taken down'. The same properties were offered for sale by auction in April 1806. By that date one of the buildings at Bosley had been converted into a cotton spinning mill, and the windmill at Hunt Hill in Macclesfield was 'in full work' grinding corn.[160]

---

157 G. G. Francis, op. cit., 78: 'Mr. Keates remarks: Roe and Co. had nothing to do with the Cheadle Works. Roe and Co. were Brass manufacturers at Macclesfield . . .' (See also ibid., 124, 131–2, and D. R. Phillips, op. cit., 281); Cheadle Brasswire Co. Minute Book, 1788–1831, 19 Aug. 1803, 11 Dec. 1810).

158 Macclesfield Corporation Minutes, vol. II. According to Mrs. C. S. Davies (Agricultural Change in East Cheshire, 1780–1830, 64, M.A. thesis, 1949, Manchester University Library) the old 'encroachment' of 1758 was allowed under the Enclosure Award of 1804, but Roe and Co. were required by clause 173 to pay £120 10s. for a later encroachment of three acres.

159 Manchester Mercury, 20 Oct. 1801, 3, col. 1. There is a copy of the handbill in the Boulton MSS, Assay Office, Birmingham.

160 Manchester Mercury, 1 April 1806, 1 col. 6.

The Macclesfield copper and brass industry was obviously on the point of becoming a mere memory.

THE ROE FAMILY'S RELIGIOUS DIFFICULTIES

In 1756 Charles Roe's brother, the Rev. James Roe of Disley, who had been admitted a burgess of the town on 30 September 1748,[161] was appointed prime (i.e. senior) curate of Macclesfield Church by John Downes, Mayor of Macclesfield. James Roe had a daughter, Hester Ann Roe (1756–94), who married in 1784 James Rogers of Macclesfield, a noted Wesleyan preacher. She left, besides a mass of letters, a diary kept from the time of her conversion to Methodism in 1773–4 up to a few days before her death. It ran to about 3000 quarto pages and contained a number of references to her uncle Charles Roe and the religious difficulties which divided his family in the last years of his life.[162] The present whereabouts of these documents is unknown, but edifying extracts from them are to be found in various publications, which were frequently reprinted.[163]

Charles Roe's family cannot have been an easy one to manage, even without the disrupting influence of Methodism. He married three times, and there were children by each union. His first wife was Elizabeth Langford, whom he married in 1743. By her he had a daughter and three sons. His eldest son William Roe (1746–1827) of Liverpool has already been mentioned. His third son Samuel (1749–80) carried on business, probably as a button merchant, in Macclesfield,[164] but became consumptive:

161 Macclesfield Corporation Minute Book, I (1734–1768).

162 Earwaker, op. cit., II, pp. 506–7; Rev. T. Coke, *The character and death of Mrs. Hester Ann Rogers* (Birmingham, 1815), pp. 22–3, 53.

163 The following editions have been used in compiling this chapter, and are henceforth referred to in the footnotes as *Account, Spiritual Letters, Extracts* and *Character and Death*: (a) *An account of the experience of Mrs. H. A. Rogers, written by herself, with a brief extract from her diary* (London, 1818), 76pp. This was first published in 1793. (b) *Spiritual letters by Mrs. H. A. Rogers; calculated to illustrate and enforce holiness of heart and life* (London, 1815), 105pp. This was first published in 1796. (c) *Extracts from the journal of Mrs. Hester Ann Rogers* (London, 1818), 286pp. This appears to have been first published in 1818. (d) *The character and death of Mrs. Hester Ann Rogers: set forth in a sermon, preached on the occasion, in Spitalfields Chapel, London, on Sunday, Oct. 26, 1794 . . . also, an appendix written by her husband, with various pieces, selected and transcribed by him from her manuscript journals* (London, 1815). This was first published in 1796, and frequently reprinted.

164 See Boulton and Watt Coll. (Birmingham Public Library) Letter Book (Office), 1775–8, which contains a copy of a letter dated 29 June 1775, from Matthew Boulton to Samuel Roe, who had enquired on behalf of a friend about a 'steam wheel for the purpose of turning a silk

His father said to him once (knowing his peculiar attachment, when in health, to balls, assemblies and all public diversions), 'Samuel, they have got Assemblies this winter in Macclesfield.' But he answered, with a solemn countenance, 'Ah, Sir! they will one day prove the vanity and folly of all such things.'[165]

In the course of 1780, Samuel went to the Hotwells, near Bristol, to take the waters, but his condition became rapidly worse and he died on 28 December 1780. Hester Ann Roe entered in her diary for 29 December:

Late this evening my cousin Robert Roe arrived with the corpse of his brother Samuel, who died at Leek on his way home from Bristol. There was great hope in the end of this once gay young man . . . may those who partook of the follies which employed his youthful years, take the awful warning and seek that . . . which he felt so much the need of in his last hours.[166]

Soon after his first wife's death in 1750, Charles Roe married Miss Mary Stockdale of London, 'who was in the Society at London from a child'. But, as John Wesley noted:[167] '. . . after she was married to a rich man, durst not own the poor despised people'. The second Mrs. Roe, however, had a fairly good excuse for her neglect of Methodism in the shape of a heavy burden of domestic duties for between 1753 and 1763 she bore Charles Roe three sons and five daughters, and eventually died on August 5, 1763, a month after her last confinement. On her death-bed she turned again to Methodism, and, as the Rev. Benjamin Smith unctuously re-marked: 'From one of the best-furnished homes in Macclesfield she . . . passed to a mansion in the skies'.[168] Of her children only her three sons need be mentioned here.

The eldest, Robert (1754–82), after receiving his early education at Macclesfield Grammar School and Manchester, was sent to Brasenose Col-

---

mill.' Boulton ended his letter: 'It's probable I may come soon to Macclesfield, as I want a few female button workers.' When letters of administration were granted for his estate at Chester in 1785 he was described as a merchant (*Cheshire Sheaf*, 1935, 89–90).

165 *Extracts*, 105.

166 *Account*, 60. See also *Extracts*, 95, 96, 101, 104. Hester Ann Roe was confident that he died truly penitent: 'He called in a Methodist physician, and would suffer no other to attend him'! (*Extracts*, 105).

167 *The Journal of John Wesley, A.M.*, ed. N. Curnock, V, 1914, 86. Wesley visited Macclesfield many times between 1747 and 1790.

168 *Methodism in Macclesfield*, 1875, 82.

lege, Oxford, in 1774.[169] His father intended that Robert should enter the Church, and possibly the erection of Christ Church in 1775 was originally planned to provide him with an incumbency.[170] Here his cousin Hester Ann Roe comes upon the scene. In the summer of 1773 she was paying her customary annual visit to her godmother, Mrs. Legh of Adlington, 'a lady of considerable rank and fortune',[171]

> ... when I heard various accounts of a clergyman, whom my uncle [Charles] Roe had recommended to be a curate at Macclesfield, and who was said to be a Methodist. This conveyed to my mind as unpleasing an idea of him as if he had been called a Romish Priest; being fully persuaded that to be a Methodist was to be all that is vile, under the mark of piety.

On her return to Macclesfield she found that public opinion in the town was seriously divided for and against this clergyman, the Rev. David Simpson, M.A. (1745–99).[172] Charles Roe and his children seemed much attached to Simpson, 'but all the rest of my relations were exasperated against him'.[173] In the upshot the Rev. David Simpson converted Hester Ann Roe to Methodism in the course of 1774, aided by her cousin Charles Roe, jun. (1756–91), 'then much devoted to God', who put into her hands in November 1774 'a little pamphlet' entitled *The Great Duty of Believing on the Son of God.*[174] Shortly afterwards her cousin Robert Roe, of whom she was particularly fond, also embraced Methodism. As a result, he was eventually expelled from the University.[175] A third son, Joseph (born 1760) also joined the Methodists.

Charles Roe, sen., appears to have taken alarm at the progress that extreme Methodism was making in his family. Although he had encouraged the Rev. David Simpson, and had protected Hester Ann against her mother's disciplinary measures in 1774,[176] he decided to set his face against a

---

169 *Cheshire Sheaf*, 1935, 91–2; *Account*, 32–3.

170 *Account*, 32.

171 *Account*, 14; *Spiritual Letters*, 3.

172 The Rev. David Simpson had been appointed second curate of St. Michael's, Macclesfield, in 1772 (See *infra*, p. 81).

173 *Account*, 15–6. Her first reaction was as follows: 'I asked, "Is it true that he preaches against dancing?" And said, I was resolved to take the first opportunity of conversing with him, being certain I could easily prove such amusements were not sinful.'

174 *Account*, 28.

175 *Account*, 32–3.

176 'But when my mother heard of it [i.e. Hester Ann's decision to turn Methodist], a floodgate

complete break with the practices of the Established Church and against the identification of his family with the extremer and less respectable followers of Wesley. The Rev. James Johnson summed up Roe's position neatly as follows:

> He was a man of imperious temper, and though far from indifferent to evangelical religion, was much more anxious for the temporal interest of his family than he was for their spiritual and eternal welfare.[177]

Accordingly, a few years before his death, he disowned Robert, Charles and Joseph on their refusal to disassociate themselves from the more extreme Macclesfield Methodists, although Charles subsequently complied with his father's wishes, and succeeded him as an alderman of Macclesfield. A few days before his death in 1781 Charles Roe relented and expressed a desire to be reconciled with Robert and Joseph.[178]

On 23 October 1766 Charles Roe married his third wife at Prestbury. Her name was Rachel Harriott, daughter of John Harriott, Esq., of St. Elizabeth's, Jamaica,[179] and she bore him one child, John Harriott Roe (1768–1833), who was Recorder of Macclesfield from 1804 to 1833 and died at Grafton Hall near Bromsgrove in Worcestershire. Roe's third wife was about twenty years younger than he was and survived him by thirty-eight years, dying in May 1819 at the age of eighty-four or eighty-five. Of her history and character we have very few details, but she may have had some influence on her husband's decision in 1770 to set up the first private carriage, a chariot, in Macclesfield.[180]

In 1775, at a time when the first Methodist chapels were being built, Roe re-affirmed his desire to have at least one foot firmly in the Church of England by building Christ Church, Macclesfield at a cost of about £6,000. Work on it began on 22 March, 1775 and, according to one account, it was completed, with the exception of the tower, on 10 October of the same

---

of persecution opened upon me. In this time of need, God raised me up a friend, in my uncle [Charles] Roe, who prevented my mother turning me out of doors.' (*Account*, 25).

177 *Memoir of the Rev. David Simpson, M.A.* (1878), 24.

178 *Account*, p. 62. Joseph Roe arrived in Macclesfield 'a few hours after his father's decease, having rode on horseback two hundred miles in twenty-four hours' (ibid.). He was Mayor of Macclesfield in 1791–2 (Earwaker, op. cit., II, 466).

179 *Cheshire Sheaf*, 1935, 89–90.

180 Corry, op. cit., 75. In her will Frances Roe left 10s. 6d. each to Mrs. R. H. Roe's 'late coachman' and to 'her present coachman' (Cheshire Wills, County Record Office, Chester, 1783).

year.[181] The tower was built in 1776. The Rev. David Simpson held the first public service in the church, preaching a sermon there on Christmas Day 1775, and it was consecrated on the last day of the year. John Wesley preached in the new church for the first time on 9 April 1777.[182] On 16 November 1779 Roe appointed Simpson the first minister of the new church by virtue of a private Act of Parliament (19 Geo.III, cap. vii, 1779) which vested the right of presentation to the perpetual cure and benefice of Christ Church, which was endowed with £100 per annum, in the coppermaster and his successors.[183] Wesley preached in Christ Church on several later occasions.

It has been stated that Charles Roe built the church 'in fulfilment of an early vow that if successful in business, he would in this way testify his gratitude to the Giver of Success',[184] but it is interesting to note that work began on the project shortly after we have an indication that he was recovering from a serious illness, and there were not lacking people who said that the sale of vault-and grave-spaces yielded a handsome profit on the investment, while building plots around the new church rose in value.[185]

Mrs. Rogers left behind an interesting account of her uncle's last days. After a severe illness in 1780 Charles Roe spent the winter of 1780–81 recuperating at Bath, accompanied by his wife, and returned to Macclesfield in the early part of April 1781.[186] On 26 April 1781 Mrs. Rogers's cousin Robert Roe told her that his father was dangerously ill. Two doctors were called in and on 30 April she made the following entry in her diary:

> Cousin Robert came all in tears; and says, his father is altered much for the worse; that he sees his danger, and calls frequently for Mr. Simpson to pray with him. This morning he gave orders concerning

---

181 P. Barfoot and J. Wilkes, op. cit., III, p. 894. There are also descriptions of the church in the *Gentleman's Magazine*, Part I, March 1796, 181–2, and Corry, op. cit., 128–9. According to Corry, the foundation of the new church was laid in May.

182 *The Journal of John Wesley, A.M.*, ed. N. Curnock, V, 1914, 86, footnote.

183 Earwaker, op. cit., 507, 509. Simpson's relations with the prime curate of St. Michael's Church, Macclesfield, and with Dr. Markham, Bishop of Chester, had been growing steadily worse since Simpson's appointment as second curate of St. Michael's on 1 June 1772. Simpson was actually nominated to the prime curacy of St. Michael's by the Mayor of Macclesfield in 1778, but his appointment aroused so much opposition and criticism on account of his Methodist leanings that he refused the nomination.

184 Rev. James Johnson, op. cit., 16–17.

185 Smith, op. cit., p. 143. An engraving of Christ Church was published on 30 April 1784 by W. Pownall (J. Broad *delin.*, Lowell, *sculp.*, Leeds).

186 Smith, op. cit., 145–8, 153–4, 156.

his temporal concerns,[187] and then took leave of my aunt and all his children.[188]

Roe died on Thursday, May 3, at about 10 a.m.[189] and his niece gives a vivid description of his funeral on 8 May which shows that it was in true eighteenth-century style:

> In the dusk of the evening my uncle's remains were carried in great pomp, by his own carriage and horses, to the New Church; and accompanied by coaches, torches, and a vast concourse of people; the horses, unaccustomed to be adorned with such trappings as black cloth, escutcheons etc., would hardly proceed. He was interred by Mr. Simpson, in the vault he had so lately prepared! Yes, this much *feared*, and much *loved* man is now committed to *corruption* and worms![190]

APPENDIX NO. 1

Charles Roe (Born 7 May 1715; died 3 May 1781)
(A) married 26 May 1743 Elizabeth Langford, who was buried at Macclesfield 1 May 1750.
By her he had four children:

   (1) *Catharine*, born 27 Dec. 1744, baptized 18 April 1745 at Macclesfield, married 7 Feb. 1769 the Rev. Ralph Nicholson of Liverpool (d.1792), and later Rector of Didcot, Berks. (Cheshire Wills, County Record Office, Chester – letters of administration of estate of Charles Roe, granted 14 July, 1781).

   (2) *William*, born 10 April, baptized 1 May 1746 at Macclesfield. Admitted a freeman of Macclesfield, 1 and 2 March 1804. Died 27 March 1827, buried 3 April 1827 at Christ Church, Macclesfield (see pp. 82–3 *supra*).

---

187 This statement is interesting in view of the fact that Charles Roe died intestate, letters of administration being granted to William Roe (acting for all the heirs) on 14 July 1781. William Roe and two Liverpool businessmen entered into a bond of £30,000 with the Bishop of Chester as a guarantee of the honest administration of the deceased's estate (Cheshire Wills, County Record Office, Chester). Mary Roe (d. 1787) stated in her will: '. . . my own relations are all possessed of a decent competency' (Christ Church MSS, Macclesfield).

188 *Extracts*, p. 128. See also *Account* (61–2), where she noted on 2 May: '. . . though scarce able, [he] gets upon his knees in bed to pray for himself.'

189 *Account*, 62.

190 *Account*, 62.

(3) *Charles*, born 3 July, baptized 24 July, 1747, buried 2 Feb. 1755 (The sole authority for this information is *The Cheshire Sheaf*, 1935, 90).

(4) *Samuel*, born 11 Nov., baptized 13 Nov., 1749. Admitted a burgess of Macclesfield 7 Oct., 1774; died 28 Dec. 1780 at Leek, buried 31 Dec. 1780 at Christ Church, Macclesfield (see pp. 93–4, *supra*).

(B) Charles Roe married as his second wife Miss Mary Stockdale of London on 23 April 1752; she was buried on 5 Aug. 1763 at Macclesfield.
By her he had eight children:

(1) *Martha*, baptized 4 Feb. 1753 at Macclesfield, died unmarried, date unknown.

(2) *Robert*, baptized 8 March 1754, died unmarried on 14 September 1782 and buried at Christ Church, Macclesfield, on 17 Sept. 1782. (There are frequent references to him in Hester Ann Rogers's works also in *The Arminian Magazine*, 1783, 521–4, 580–2, 638–41, 1784, 19, 76, 132, 186, 244, 303, 358, 417, 469, 523, 582, 635).

(3) *Mary*, baptized 30 Oct. 1755 at Macclesfield, died unmarried, worth over £4000, at Sutton Hall, near Macclesfield on 18 Aug. 1787; buried at Christ Church, Macclesfield, 21 Aug. 1787. By her will she established 'Miss Roe's Charity School' opened at Christ Church on 25 March 1790 (Christ Church MSS, Macclesfield). She and her sister Frances (q.v.) are frequently mentioned in Mrs. Rogers's works; inclined to Methodism and, to judge by the books and musical instruments mentioned in her will, a woman of some culture (Cheshire Wills – County Record Office, Chester, 1787).

(4) *Frances* ('Fanny'), baptized 13 Dec. 1756 at Macclesfield, died unmarried 2 June 1783; buried 5 June at Christ Church, Macclesfield.

(5) *Charles*, born 25 March 1759 at Macclesfield, baptized 2 April, 1759; married 29 May, 1783 Miss Mary Waller (d.1794) of Carisbrooke, Isle of Wight; admitted a freeman of Macclesfield 5 Oct. 1787, and alderman 3, 10 Oct. 1788. No documentary evidence for the statement that he married without his father's consent has been found (see also *supra*, p. 95), or of the allegation that he 'plunged into gaiety and extravagance' after he deserted Methodism;[191] *died 7 March 1791, buried 11 March at Christ Church, Macclesfield. His house in Chestergate, Macclesfield, was offered for sale by auction soon after his death*

191 *E.g. Smith*, op. cit., 144, 159–60.

(Gore's Liverpool Advertiser, 14 April 1791). To judge by the elaborate safeguards surrounding Miss Frances Roe's legacy to him, he must have been regarded a being in some degree unstable or untrustworthy (Cheshire Wills, County Record Office, Chester, 1783).

(6) *Joseph*, baptized at Macclesfield, 11 May 1760 (see p. 95 *supra*). The date of his death is at present unknown, but it took place before 1836. He may have been the Joseph Roe who was partner in a firm of Macclesfield coach proprietors and carriers in 1791 (*Manchester Mercury*, 22 Feb. 1791, 3, col. 3). Admitted freeman of Macclesfield, 24 Oct. 1788, Mayor 7 Oct. 1791, in which year he was living at the Lower Beach, Macclesfield (*Gore's Liverpool Advertiser*, 14 April 1791). Later he lived at Moody Hall, Congleton.

(7) *Margaret*, baptized 12 May 1761, married William Racster of Bristol at Bristol 5 March 1785. Occasionally mentioned in Mrs. Rogers's works.

(8) *Jane*, born 5 July 1763, date and place of baptism unknown; died unmarried 13 May 1800; buried 16 May 1800, Christ Church, Macclesfield.

(C) Roe married as his third wife Miss Rachel Harriott, daughter of John Harriott of St. Elizabeth's Jamaica, at Prestbury on 23 Oct. 1766. She died 7 May 1819 and was buried on 15 May 1819 at Christ Church, Macclesfield, aged 84 or 85. (The Registers and the memorial tablet in Christ Church do not agree on these points).

By her he had one son:

(1) *John Harriott* born 12 July 1768, baptized 11 Aug. 1768; died 19 Oct. 1833, buried 30 Oct. 1833 at Christ Church, Macclesfield (see p. 96, *supra*). Admitted a freeman of Macclesfield 3 Oct. 1794; Recorder of Macclesfield, 1804–33. His age is given incorrectly as 66 on the memorial tablet in Christ Church.

APPENDIX NO. 2

NOTES ON A PAINTING OF AND A MONUMENT TO CHARLES ROE (1715–81)

1. Oil painting by Joseph Wright of Derby (1734–97) in Christ Church, Macclesfield (see frontispiece to Part I). This portrait was probably painted in 1769, as the name 'Mr. Rowe' (a common contemporary

misspelling) appears in a list of Wright's 'sitters at Liverpool' in that year (William Bemrose, *The life and works of Joseph Wright, A.R.A., commonly called Wright of Derby*, privately published, London, 1885, 118). There is a mediocre copy of this painting in Macclesfield Town Hall, with the following inscription in the bottom left-hand corner: 'After Wright of Derby by H. Beresford, Dec. 19, 1850.'

2. Monument to Charles Roe in Christ Church, Macclesfield,, completed in 1784 by John Bacon, R.A. (1740–99). Genius, holding a broken cogwheel, mourns Roe, whose achievements are shown on the three panels of her seat (*l.* to *r.*: silk-mill, Christ Church, copperworks). The bust of Roe on the Macclesfield Copper Company's tokens is taken from the medallion on this monument.

CHAPTER V

SALT IN CHESHIRE, 1600–1870

Salt is absolutely necessary to human existence and to other forms of animal life. People dwelling in inland districts far from the sea and remote from natural brine springs have therefore always been prepared to pay fairly high prices for small quantities of it, and the internal trade in salt is a very ancient one.[1] In the period up to the early nineteenth century salt was relatively more important in British diet than it is today, and the output was used almost entirely in the preparation and preservation of various food-stuffs.[2] The nineteenth century saw a great expansion in the demand for salt for industrial purposes, as the result of the rise of the British heavy chemical industry, in its infancy in 1800, for which salt was one of the basic raw materials. The expansion of output and the consequent lowering of the price of salt benefited the mass of the population – for example, there was no longer the same incentive to economise the use of salt in the preservation of meat and fish by using insufficient quantities or inferior qualities (often with disagreeable or disastrous results) as there had been in previous centuries.[3]

What were the reasons for the importance of salt in the food processing industries? Firstly, the canning of food was not practised extensively until after the decade 1801–10. Secondly, artificial refrigeration was not developed until after the 1870s, and natural refrigeration in subterranean ice-houses or with ice imported from colder countries, e.g. Norway, was expensive – therefore salt was used in large quantities for pickling (or 'powdering') herrings, cod, and other fish and for salting meat, especially pork and beef, for use during the winter or on sea voyages. Salt was also used extensively in the preservation of eggs and the manufacture of cheese, butter and bread.

1   See W. B. Crump, 'Saltways from the Cheshire wiches', *Trans. Lancashire and Cheshire Antiquarian Society*, LIV, 1939, 84–142.
2   On the general subject of salt in human diet see J. C. Drummond and Anne Wilbraham, *The Englishmans's Food* (1939, 2nd rev. edn. 1957) and C. L. Cutting, *Fish Saving* (1955).
3   The practice of salting down meat at home persisted widely, and many middle-class houses built during the nineteenth century contained salting blocks in the cellars.

In the early seventeenth century three main methods of making salt were practised in Britain.

(a) Natural evaporation in the sun (solar salt)

Where the seaboard was comparatively low-lying, sea-water flowed during high tides over a flat area which could often be artificially extended to form shallow lakes. In the course of time the salt held in solution by the sea-water was deposited by evaporation, and all that man had to do was to collect and dry it; the product so obtained was often polluted by sand, mud and marine refuse and had to be refined. This method of extraction could naturally only be practised in Britain at a few places – the Isle of Wight, the Isle of May in the Firth of Forth, and on certain stretches of the Lancashire coast, especially in the Wyre district.[4]

(b) Artificial evaporation from sea water

This method was far more important than method (a) in this country, and might be found wherever cheap supplies of wood, or later coal, were available. By the early seventeenth century the use of wood as a fuel in salt production had declined very considerably, and the chief centres of manufacture by the method of evaporation were to be found at North and South Shields, along the Flintshire and Denbighshire coasts, and along the Firth of Forth, where cheap coal supplies were at hand in abundance.

(c) Artificial evaporation from natural brine springs

Such springs existed chiefly in Cheshire, Staffordshire, Worcestershire, Hampshire and North Cumberland. The usual method of procedure in the first three counties was to erect a boiling house known as a 'wich house' or 'saltern' containing a number of shallow lead pans for the brine and fitted up with furnaces underneath. The size of a Northwich lead pan was 3½ ft. by 2½ ft., the depth being 6 inches. Observers in the seventeenth century divided springs into those which were 'thrifty', i.e. soon pumped dry, and taking a long time to fill up again, and those which were 'fluent', such as the generous spring at Nantwich in Cheshire.

The discovery of rock salt in Cheshire in 1670 initiated other methods of salt production; the rock was used either in solid or crushed form, e.g. for cattle lick, or was dissolved in fresh water and then boiled down into white salt.

---

4   H. Collins, *Salt and Fishery* (1682), 147–8: 'The manner of making Salt of Sea-sand in Lancashire'.

During the period 1550–1700 a considerable expansion of British salt production took place, partly as the result of the increasingly successful exploitation of the coal measures.[5] Nevertheless, from the later Middle Ages onwards a considerable amount of salt was imported into Britain from France ('Bay Salt'), Portugal and Spain; sometimes these imports reached between two thirds and three quarters of total annual consumption. By 1700 Britain still imported salt from S.W. Europe, but British imports of high grade salt were counterbalanced by exports of coarse salt from the east coast of England to the Netherlands and from the West Midlands and Cheshire to Ireland, North America and the West Indies.

In order to understand fully the problems confronting salt-makers it is necessary to know a little of the chemistry of brine.[6] Both sea-water and brine from springs contain not merely common salt but five other salts, namely calcium carbonate, calcium sulphate, magnesium sulphate, potassium-magnesium chloride and magnesium chloride. The salt content of sea-water is 3% only, while the strongest natural brine (fully saturated brine) contains 26% salt, i.e. it is more than eight times as strong as sea-water. Northwich brine contains 25.32% of salt, i.e. it is almost fully saturated. Therefore, provided plentiful supplies of cheap fuel are available, strong natural brine springs have a great advantage over the sea coast as centres of production by artificial evaporation. Brine from natural springs also tends to contain smaller proportions of the five other salts mentioned above, e.g. at Northwich the brine contains only 0.39% of calcium sulphate and mere traces of calcium carbonate, magnesium sulphate, potassium magnesium chloride and magnesium chloride. In sea-water, on the other hand, calcium sulphate and the other four salts are present in significant quantities. Common salt produced from sea-water is therefore rendered bitter to the taste by the calcium and magnesium salts; this is a drawback in its use on the table and in butter and cheese making. Calcium and magnesium salts also cause a slowing down of the rate at which common salt penetrates the flesh to be cured, e.g. fish or bacon, and the unfortunate results of this may become apparent within a week.

Dr. Jackson wrote in 1669: 'I do apprehend this [Cheshire] salt to be rather more searching than French salt, because I have often observed, that meat kept with this salt shall be more fiery salt to the midst of it, than I have

5   J. U. Nef, *The Rise of the British Coal Industry* (1932), I, 174–9, and passim.
6   A most useful summary is given in A. R. Bridbury, *England and the Salt Trade in the Later Middle Ages* (1955).

observed, when I have eaten powdered meat on ship-board, which was probably done with French salt, I then being on the south-side of England and in a Dutch vessel. 'Tis certain, Cheshire sends yearly much bacon to London, which never yet has any mark of infamy set upon it.'[7]

The Cheshire wiches, given a favourable fuel situation, were therefore in a strong position *vis-a-vis* the coastal production centres whether at home or abroad.

Much has been written on the Cheshire salt industry at various times, but some of these printed sources are not easily available, and the standard work on the subject,[8] while not exactly rare, is notable for the awkwardness of its bulk and the chaotic arrangements of its contents. What follows is an attempt to trace the changing fortunes of the Cheshire wiches in the light of recent research.

The three main salt-producing centres in Cheshire at the beginning of the seventeenth century were the baronial borough of Nantwich, the manorial borough of Northwich, and the royal manor of Middlewich (see Plate 5, p. 123). Of these Nantwich was the most important, its only brine pit, according to a letter of 1605, being divided into 216 shares of 'wallings', each walling, i.e. boiling, being equal to the quantity of brine from the pit which could be boiled down in twenty-four hours (plus two additional hours allowed for kindling the fires and scraping the pans) in six lead pans each of the capacity of twenty-four gallons. It is important to remember that whatever may have been the case in earlier time, by the seventeenth century the number of wallings bore no relation to the number of pans in existence or to the number of wich houses. The number of wallings held by an individual merely represented the measure of his or her right to a share in the distribution of the brine when the officials in charge ('the rulers of walling') fixed the periods during which boiling could take place. Middlewich had 107 wallings of 6 lead pans, plus one of 4, and Northwich possessed 113

7 *Philosophical Transactions* IV, no. 53, 15th Nov. 1669, 1067.

8 A. F. Calvert, *Salt in Cheshire*, 1915. Other printed sources include H. J. Hewitt, *Medieval Cheshire*, Chet. Soc., 2nd ser. LXXXVIII, 1929, pp. 108–22; E. Hughes, *Studies in Administration and Finance, 1558–1825, with special reference to the history of salt taxation in England*, 1934, *passim*; J. Hall, *History of the town and parish of Nantwich*, 1883, pp. 252–67 and *passim*; T. S. Willan, *The Navigation of the river Weaver in the Eighteenth Century*, Chet. Soc., 3rd ser. 1951; T. C. Barker, 'Lancashire coal, Cheshire salt and the rise of Liverpool', *Transactions, Historic Society of Lancashire and Cheshire*, CIII, 1951, 83–101; K. L. Wallwork, 'The mid-Cheshire Salt industry', *Geography* XLIV, July 1959, 171–86; W. H. Chaloner, 'William Furnival, H. E. Falk and the Salt Chamber of Commerce, 1815–1889: . . .' <Chapter VI of this book>.

wallings of 4 pans each plus one odd pan, plus 4 pans given to the Earl of Derby by the burgesses.[9]

Of the three centres Nantwich is the one about which most is known, at any rate in the seventeenth century. Its supremacy at the beginning of this century appears to have been the result of abundant wood supplies in the immediate vicinity which were cheaper than those around Middlewich and Northwich. Nantwich, however, was further away from such coal pits in South Lancashire, East Cheshire and North Staffordshire as were open at this time, and the adoption of coal as the fuel under the salt pans led to the rapid decline of Nantwich in the late seventeenth and early eighteenth centuries. In August 1636 Henry, fifth Earl of Huntingdon, visited Nantwich, entering the town along the Newcastle-under-Lyme road. As his description is neither well-known nor readily accessible, it is here given in full:

> Nantwich is a market town bigger than Loughborough and at the coming in thereof fair wooden houses and a broad street, but towards the middle of the town and where the market is kept the streets are but narrow. From the one end of the town to the other beyond the bridge is a long mile. The chief trade is making of salt. There is but one salt pit and spring. The pit is about 4 yards square and 10 yards deep, and when the water comes to such a height it runs out at a waste, which waste water, had they not abundantly enough, would serve to make salt for half of England.
>
> The manner how they make it is this. They set pumps within the pit within a yard of the bottom, which they pump up into a cistern or reserve, from whence it runs through troughs of wood which are both narrow and shallow into 55 houses, where they boil it to salt, taking the water with a bucket out of a little cistern and putting it into great square pans of lead which are not deep and are to be removed up and down, for that after every day's working those leads must be soldered and mended. They use in some of the houses wood, in some coals, and after three hours boiling it comes to be perfect salt. Each house work(s) not above two or three days in a week and some not so many because they cannot have vent for the salt. The expense of fuel in wood and coal amount yearly to about 3000*l*. and the charges of utensils brings it that the best houses gain not (*de claro*) above 100 marks *per annum* and some but 40*l*. or 30*l*.[10]

---

9 Calvert, op. cit., 75–6.
10 H.M.C., *Report on the MSS of the late R. R. Hastings, Esq.*, IV, 1947, ed. F. Bickley, 339.

From this account it will be seen that the transition from the use of wood to the use of coal for boiling down the brine had begun, and that pumps had been installed in the pit to replace the manual labour of the briners, who raised the brine out of the pit in buckets. The Earl of Huntingdon's reference to the use of pumps at Nantwich in 1636 appears to be the earliest known.[11]

By 1669 another innovation, the use of iron pans instead of leaden ones, was noted by the 'learned and observing William Jackson, Doctor of Physick' acting on behalf of the Royal Society:

> ... they have a rich brine in their chief pit at Middle-wich, which yields a full fourth part of salt, like the rich Burgundian Springs ... yet this is so thrifty in its brine that the inhabitants are limited within proportions out of it ... Our pitt at Nantwich yields but a sixth part; but then 'tis so plentiful a spring that whereas they seldom *wall*, that is, make salt in above 6 houses at a time, and there are or should be about 50 wich-houses in the town; this pitt is judged sufficient to supply them all ...
>
> Their manner of working is this: They have formerly boyled their brine in 6 leaden pans with wood-fire; upon which accompt they all claime their interest in the pitt by the name of so many six leads walling; by which they each know their proportion; but in the memory of many alive they changed their 6 leads into 4 iron-pans, something better than a yard square, and about 6 inches deep, still fitting the content of these to that of the leads; and of late many have changed the 4 iron-pans into two greater; and some wall but in one ... They use for their fewell, pitcoals, brought out of Staffordshire.[12]

Iron pans had been used in the salines on the North East coast since at least the late fifteenth century, but the Cheshire wiches appear to have adopted this innovation only in the second quarter of the seventeenth century. The growing use of iron pans and the change from wood to coal were to some extent connected, because the higher temperatures generated by coal damaged the lead pans more severely than those obtained when wood was burned under them. Another reason for the change from lead to iron was that larger pans could be constructed from wrought-iron plates than from the less rigid lead sheeting.

11 During the summer of 1656 'greate works' costing about £300 were carried out at the · Nantwich brine pit under the authority of the Rulers of Walling (Hall, op. cit., 259), but their nature is not stated.

12 *Philosophical Transactions*, IV, no. 53, Nov. 15th, 1669, pp. 1063–4.

According to Dr. John Ray, the famous seventeenth-century naturalist, writing in 1674, the ownership of the Nantwich pit was divided among a considerable number of persons, who could either carry on production themselves or rent their rights to others.[13] Ray stated:

> Saltwater taken out of the brine-pit in two hours and a quarter boiling, will be evaporated and boil'd up into salt. When the liquor is more than lukewarm, they take strong ale, bullocks' blood and whites of egg mixt together with brine in this proportion: of blood one egg-shell full, the white of one egg and a pint of ale, and put it into a pan of twenty four gallons or thereabouts . . . They do not evaporate *ad siccitatem*, but leave about a pottle or gallon of brine in the pan, lest the salt should burn and stick to the sides of the pan.

The wet salt obtained by this scraping was placed in cone-shaped wicker baskets called 'barrows' and allowed to dry in hot-houses between the furnace and the chimney tunnels. Twenty-four gallons of Nantwich brine produced three and a half pecks of salt, i.e. seven gallons, Winchester measure. Alternatively, it was said that 6 lb. weight of Nantwich brine would produce 1 lb. of salt. A 'barrow' held six pecks, which according to Ray, sold for 1s. 4d. on the spot.[14]

At an early stage it had become apparent to the owners of the pits that unrestricted competition would cause low prices and small profits[15]; and so the proprietors of the brine pits at Nantwich and Northwich had established in the course of the centuries elaborate codes of regulations for the restriction of output; no information appears to be available as to what happened at Middlewich. The Nantwich regulations of 1563 have been printed[16] and were conveniently summarised in 1675 by Thomas Brancker, headmaster of Macclesfield Grammar School, as follows:

> All owners of Brine contribute to maintaining the common pit, for cleansing it, and reparing ye walls and timber, &c.
> And because all ye owners had their title from one, they are now a society or coporation; and have lawes to preserve ye community &

---

13 For example, in the seventeenth century Macclesfield Grammar School owned the right to 6 leads' walling (36 days' boiling) and one wich-house, but did not exert the right directly (Hall, op. cit., 260–2).

14 John Ray, *A Collection of English Words not Generally Used*, 1st ed. 1674, 142–7.

15 For suggestions for reconciling discrepancies between the various figures see Hughes, op. cit., 385.

16 Hall, op. cit., 256–8.

each man's proportional propriety.

Hence it follows, that no man must wall beyond his proportion that, within ye same compass, as he that is greatest hath walled his, he also that is meanest may wall his also.

And to this end there be at every Michaelmas Court Leet, 4 Rulers chosen who are sworn to their office for one year. These Rulers are –

1. To estimate the price and vent [sale] of Salt, and
2. To allot the time of every man's walling according to proportion, and to see that none of ye houses be left so unemployed that they decay for want of use.
3. To be present (one or more of them) at ye beginning and end of every fire that is kindled in any wiche house, to see and be able to make oath of it that their kindlings began and ended according to right.
4. To keep an exact account of every day's walling in each house throughout their year, and also to record in what houses and for how many dayes any man borrowed or hired his walling. And to register ye names of ye chiefe workman in each kindling and under whom he wrought
5. To make taxes that concern ye charge of ye wich-houses and brine-pit.

Other officers they have but ye particulars I have not met withall. These Rulers order that account which they call their Making Meet; that is, according to rise or fall of salt, so they may all of them wall sooner or later their whole course. Of this, the Rulers, as was said, are judges; and they order that in such or such a time all the proprietors shall have all their wallings according to kale (or call).

And because in this making meet perhaps the time may be (by reason of ill trade) so long as that those that have but small interest would not have sufficient employment for their houses, therefore the Rulers have power to debar any man from walling all his whole number in his own wiche-house, that soe he may sell it, or set [i.e. let] it to be done in some other house, that all ye houses may be preserved.[17]

Dr. John Ray added:

When there is occasion for salt to be made, the Rulers cause a cryer to make proclamation, that so all parties concerned may put to their fires at the same time; and so when they shall cease at a determinate hour,

17 Ibid., 260–1.

at which they must give over; else they cause their salt to be marred by casting dirt into it or the like.[18]

At Northwich the regulation was carried out by 'lead lookers'. This policy of regulation and control was not one which could deal with competition from outside the boundaries of the three wiches. Salt production in the Northwich area increased during the late seventeenth and early eighteenth centuries because five pits were outside the town and only one was inside it.

The adoption of coal as the fuel for salt boiling and the greater availability of coal led to some very interesting results. On the North East coast it took between six and eight tons of coal to produce one ton of salt from sea-water. In Cheshire in the 1660s it took only twelve cwt. to produce one weigh at Northwich, fifteen cwt. to produce one weigh at Middlewich and one and a half tons to produce one weigh at Nantwich. A weigh, or forty bushels, was equivalent to nearly one and a half tons, so that if we ignore the difference between coal costs in Cheshire and on the North East coast, even the comparatively inefficient brine pit at Nantwich was producing salt between six and eight times more efficiently than the North Eastern works.

The comparative cost of coal cannot, however, be ignored. On the North East coast and along the Firth of Forth coal lay ready on the spot. It was much cheaper than coal in Cheshire. Low-grade waste coal unsuitable for shipping coast-wise or overseas could be used under the North East salt pans. On the other hand none of the three Cheshire producing centres stood less than twelve miles overland from a coal pit and consequently the cost of coal in the Cheshire wiches was much higher than on the North East coast.

Fortunately we have some statistics of salt production in Cheshire for the mid-seventeenth century which give some idea of their comparative importance. They were printed in 1682 by John Collins, 'Registrar and Accomptant of the Royal Society of London' in his book *Salt and Fishery*, an indication of the interest shown by that Society in economic matters at the time.

At Northwich 186 tons of coal were used every week to produce 12,214 bushels of salt; at Middlewich 79 tons of coal were used in a week to produce 4,300 bushels, and at Nantwich 152 tons were used to make 4,200 bushels of salt.[19] Northwich was already the first producing centre. It is also significant that these quantities of coal are given in the original document in

18 Ray, op. cit., 142–7.
19 Collins, *Salt and Fishery* (1682), 3. The figures were 'according to a Calculation thereof made long since by his lordship [William Brereton]', ibid., 2.

loads of which eight went to the ton; the coal was carried by horse-drawn waggons from the North Staffordshire mines and from the North East Cheshire coal pits. The Lancashire and Welsh coals were brought to the Cheshire bank of the River Mersey around Frodsham in vessels called 'flats', but then had to be transported by horse.

The changeover to coal furnaces was almost complete by the 1660s, and prospecting then began with a view to discovering coal in central Cheshire.[20] In the course of one of these borings for coal the rock salt which lies under Cheshire was first discovered about March 1670 by John Jackson of Halton in the lands of William Marbury at Marbury, one and half miles north of Northwich.[21] This discovery did not produce a crisis in the brine trade for about a quarter of a century. The famous woman traveller Celia Fiennes visited Northwich some years (1698) after this event and noted as follows:

I entered Cheshire 3 miles before I came to the town, its not very large, its full of salt works the brine pits being all here and about – so that the town is full of smoak from the salterns on all sides; they have within these few yeares found in their brine pits, a hard rocky salt that looks cleer like suger candy, and its taste shows it to be salt; they call this rock salt.[22]

In 1682 William Marbury, or his son, was granted a patent for draining brine pits. By 1699 the Marbury estates were hopelessly encumbered with debts amounting to about £25,000; they were therefore seized and the creditors leased the salt-works from William Marbury's daughters for £260 per annum. It is interesting to note that Celia Fiennes was later one of a group of mortgagees who advanced money on the security of these estates to Earl Rivers, who himself purchased them from the descendants of Marbury in 1701–2.[23]

Miss Fiennes went on to say:

... this rock salt ... will make very good brine with fresh water to use quickly, this they cary to the water-side into Wales and by those rivers that are flow'd with the tyde [i.e. to be near to the coal] and soe they

20 For the development in the early seventeenth century of techniques for boring for coal with rods see J. U. Nef, *The Rise of the British Coal Industry*, II, 1932, 446–8.
21 See *Philosophical Transactions*, IV, no. 66, Dec. 12, 1670, 2015–7 (extracts from two letters of November 12th and 26th, 1670 by Adam Martindale to the publisher of the Royal Society.)
22 *The Journeys of Celia Fiennes*, ed. C. Morris (1947), 224.
23 Op. cit., XXI.

boile these pieces of rock in some of the salt water when the tyde's in, which produces as strong and good salt as the others.[24]

This is corroborated in the *Autobiography of William Stout*, the Quaker grocer and wholesale ironmonger of Lancaster (1665–1752), whose account under the year 1689 suggests that the war against France, which raged with a short break from 1689 to 1713, gave a stimulus to the British salt industry and particularly to the rock branch, by cutting off the normal French and Spanish imports. Stout wrote:

1689 . . . the war with France, by being prohibited trade with them . . . put us upon the silk, linen, paper, and many other of the manufactures, to the enriching this nation and particularly in the south of this country . . . As to wine and salt, we now had them from Portugal and Spain, who took from us the double value in goods of what we had from them. Also at this time the salt rock was found in Cheshire, from the brine by which they formerly made fine salt, but now they digged out the rock and carried it by sea to all parts of England and Ireland, and melted it with sea water, and boiled it up into a stong salt, as good [as] French [and] Spanish salt.[25]

On the other hand, the export of rock salt from Cheshire to Scotland seems to have been injured.[26] By 1698 the disastrous effects of rock salt mining on the old salt interest, the brine men, had become clear. A pamphlet published in that year stated that the cost of coal for refining dissolved rock salt at Dungeon, on the Mersey estuary, ten miles south east of Liverpool cost only 5s. 6d. per ton because the refinery was near to a coal mine, whereas by the time it had been carried to Northwich coal cost 16s. 8d. per ton.[27] The proprietors of brine pits tried to get a prohibitive rate of tax laid upon rock salt, but were unsuccessful.

The total quantity of coal used every year in the three Cheshire salt towns was at least 20,000 tons, and transport costs proved to be a considerable item in production costs. By the beginning of the eighteenth century there were refineries of rock salt in Essex, Suffolk, Devon, Somerset, Cornwall and North and South Wales, as well as in Ireland, and the land carriage of this

24 Op. cit., 225.

25 Ed. J. Harland, 1851, 24–5.

26 For the importance of the Scottish trade in salt beef and fish, see A. R. B. Haldane, *The Drove Roads of Scotland* (1952), 225–6.

27 For details see Barker, art. cit., 87 and fn 2.

rock to Frodsham Bridge, the point of shipment at the head of the River Weaver, might double the prime cost of the rock itself at the mouth of the mine. It is to the desire for export outlets and to the search for economy in transport costs by the salt interests that we must look for the reasons for the improvement of the shallow River Weaver in the eighteenth century.

The scheme is first heard of in 1663 during the extraordinary burst of activity in river improvement which took place between 1662 and 1665: as a contemporary states:

> ... it [river improvement] easeth the people of the great charge of land carriage, preserves the highways, which are daily worn out with waggons carrying excessive burdens, [and] it breeds up a nursery of watermen, which upon occasion will prove good seamen.

The scheme was revived in 1670 and 1709–11. On this last occasion great resentment was aroused among the Cheshire gentry on the grounds that the bill was introduced into the House of Commons by a Liverpool alderman, Sir Thomas Johnson, M.P. 'who hath not one foot of land either in our County or our city [Chester], and whose design in it (obvious to everybody) was only to promote his trade of exporting rock salt to Ireland and Denmark'. The bill was, therefore, opposed by the Cheshire landowners and their tenants, who made a great deal of money carrying coal ('cricking') and rock salt in their spare time. It was also opposed by the owners of the brine pits on the grounds that it would favour the owners of rock mines.

The project appeared again in 1720, the year of the South Sea Bubble, when the Common Council of Liverpool took the matter up and appointed Alderman Squire and Isaac Green to go to London 'to attend and assist in the solicitation for an Act of Parliament for making the River Weaver navigable in concert with our members of Parliament'. Charles Cholmondeley, one of the chief opponents, wrote to Sir Thomas Aston, M.P., on February 5, 1720, suggesting 'some little subscription among ourselves to carry on the opposition'. But Aston was incapacitated and all the opposition to the scheme proved in vain; it passed into law in March 1721.

The implementation of the River Weaver Act between 1721 and 1733 undoubtedly benefited Northwich and Liverpool most, but by a second act passed in 1721 the River Dane was to be improved from its junction with the Weaver at Northwich to its junction with Wheelock Brook at Wheelock Bridge, as 'the best means to preserve the present equality of [the] trade of salt', and so give to Middlewich the same advantages for river carriage as those enjoyed by Northwich. A third act, designed to extend the navigation of the River Weaver from Winsford Bridge to Nantwich reached the statute

book in 1734.[28] Unfortunately for Middlewich and Nantwich these exten-
sions of the main navigation never materialised and this undoubtedly
contributed to their decline as salt producing centres.

In the Weaver Act of 1721 three Cheshire gentlemen, John Egerton, John
Amson and Richard Vernon of Middlewich ('the undertakers') were
empowered to carry out the work of deepening the river and providing it with
locks. Eighty commissioners – for the most part members of local landowning
families – were also appointed by the act with the duty of arbitrating on all
disputes between the undertakers and the property owners whose rights might
be affected by the carrying out of the works. The undertakers and their friends
eventually spent £20,500 on the project up to 1760 (against the original estimate
of £9,000) and were allowed 6% interest on the capital advanced. They were
empowered to levy tolls on merchandise passing along the river; surplus revenue was to be handed over to Quarter Sessions at Chester to be spent primarily in
improving the county bridges; the work was to be completed by 1731.

The work on the locks was, however, not completed throughout the
whole length until 1735; the first regular entries in the Weaver Toll books of
tolls received date from 1733, although certain sums had been received up to
this date. Eleven wooden locks were constructed at Butty Meadow, New-
bridge, Vale Royal, Hartford, Hunt's Lock, Northwich, Winnington, Salters-
ford, Acton Bridge, Dutton and Pickerings. The total fall from Winsford
Bridge to sea level was fifty feet. Besides coal, cheese and salt the navigation was soon carrying stone, timber, corn, and cotton, together with flint
and clay for the Staffordshire potteries.

On the completion of their main task the undertakers lost practically all
interest in the navigation, but it was not until the late 1750s, when some of
the works were found to be 'greatly damaged' and decayed, that the Liverpool salt shippers made bitter complaints about the way in which the
navigation was conducted and offered to take over the whole business from
the commission and undertakers for £20,500, plus an annual payment to the
county of £800. This stirred the Weaver Commissioners to action and they
secured another Act in 1760, which abolished the commissioners and undertakers and vested their powers in 105 trustees. The Act of 1760 directed that
all the locks upon the navigation should, as soon as possible, be increased in
size to the one at Pickerings (90 feet long and 18 feet wide) and provided
that a minimum depth of 4 ft. 6 ins. should be maintained.

---

28 Later attempts to link Nantwich with Middlewich by canal (1770–2) and with the North
Staffordshire collieries by horse-railway (1806) both came to nothing.

The finances of the Trust were soon in a flourishing condition. By 1776 the old debt of £20,500 had been cleared off and in 1778 the first payment of surplus money was made to the county funds. Between 1747 and 1777 shipments of rock salt down river were almost quadrupled and white salt shipments almost doubled.

	Rock	White
1747	13,310	16,101
1777	54,176	31,000

After this the rock salt shipments remained pretty steady down to 1800 but the quantities of white salt shipped down river every year rose rapidly to 100,000 tons.

In 1792 the Trustees received a petition from Liverpool, Northwich and Winsford salt proprietors, requesting that the Trustees of the Weaver 'would cause a towing path to be made along the said river for the purpose of hauling vessels [upstream] with horses instead of men'. In 1779 the first 'railed road' on the Weaver Navigation was built at Anderton basin, on the model for the iron railways at Coalbrookdale in Shropshire, for facilitating the trans-shipment of rock salt.[29]

Meanwhile what was happening in the wiches? Middlewich and Nantwich declined as salt producing centres in the eighteenth century, the latter more rapidly than the former. In the case of Nantwich the decline was not entirely the result of failure to cheapen transport costs, but can also be in part attributed to the policy of deliberately restricting output. This policy, which discouraged business enterprise, did not break down until 1696–1713. An additional reason was the burden of the salt tax.[30] At Northwich the growth of the industry was stimulated by the sinking of new pits outside the town boundaries in the 1690s and by vigorous intervention, first by London investors and, secondly, by Liverpool merchants.[31] The investment from Liverpool and S.W. Lancashire proved to be of permanent importance. Dr. T. C. Barker, in his article 'Lancashire coal, Cheshire salt and the rise of Liverpool'[32] has already shown in some detail the way in which Lancashire

---

29 The early history of the Weaver Navigation is well covered by T. S. Willan, *The Navigation of the River Weaver in the Eighteenth Century*, Chet. Soc., 3rd series, III, 1951.

30 Hughes, op. cit., 385–90.

31 Ibid., p. 394.

32 *Trans. Hist. Soc. L. & C.*, CIII, 83–101.

mercantile and industrial capital penetrated the Cheshire saltfield. Liverpool merchants were the driving force behind the legislation for the improvement of the Weaver, and Liverpool merchants secured the Sankey Navigation Act of 1755 which made it possible by 1757 to ship St. Helens coal down the Mersey estuary and up the Weaver in sailing flats. The chief proprietors of the Sankey Navigation were John Ashton, owner of Dungeon salt refinery on the Mersey estuary, and John Blackburne, jun., who had inherited the family rock salt refinery at Liverpool. The construction of the Sankey Navigation led to a triangular traffic, for the same flats could take white and rock salt to various points on the Mersey estuary, but principally to Liverpool; having discharged their cargoes of salt they would return to the Sankey navigation for more St. Helens coal which was peculiarly suited for use in salt boiling owing to the great heat it generated. In the 1790s excise surveyors reported eighty-three sailing flats at Liverpool unloading salt simultaneously.[33] As Dr. Barker has so clearly put it:

> By the early 1830s every coal proprietor in and about St. Helens owned saltworks in Cheshire. The process which started during the seventeenth century had reached completion. Liverpool men had brought new life to the Cheshire salt industry by intervening in the rock salt trade. Then they had stimulated production by cutting out the land carriage between the wiches and Frodsham Bridge and, when this was so successful that it caused an acute shortage of coal, they had created a waterway up to the coalfield to connect with the Weaver Navigation. When the salt boilers of Cheshire set limits to their production, they went into the salt industry and when the coal proprietors attempted to do the same thing they became coal proprietors as well. Thus, over a period of a century and a half, relentless pressure from the men of Liverpool had brought the coal and salt trade to a high degree of economic organisation with Liverpool as its focal point. Only by such constant agitation and by such ruthless rationalisation could the production of rock and white salt have risen from a mere 15,000 tons in 1732 to 150,000 tons in 1800, 500,000 tons in 1840 and 1,000,000 tons in 1870.

The second important change in the salt field in the eighteenth century was the discovery and exploitation of the lower or main bed of rock salt from 1779–81 onwards. It will be remembered that the original or upper bed

33 Hughes, op. cit., 401.

of rock salt had been struck in 1670 about 100 feet from the surface. In 1779 a search for brine in the Lawton district of East Cheshire revealed the existence of the normal rock salt deposit at 120 feet, 'and at a farther depth of 30 feet a bed of 12 feet of rock-salt was discovered. This was afterwards bored through and at a farther depth of 45 feet another bed of rock-salt was found'.[34] Up to 1915 this had not been bored through, although the drills had pierced it to a depth of 72 feet. This discovery stimulated the Northwich proprietors to bore deeper. They had been reluctant to do this earlier owing to the danger of flooding, but in 1780 or 1781 the lower bed of rock salt was discovered 30 feet beneath the upper bed by boring through the sole of Marston Old Top mine near Winsford.[35] After this date all fresh mines in the Winsford–Northwich area were sunk to the lower bed.

After so much has been said about Liverpool enterprise in the saltfield it is gratifying to record that the engineer responsible for this boring operation at Marston Old Top mine was John Gilbert (1724–95), agent and confidential adviser to the Duke of Bridgewater at Worsley near Manchester.[36] Gilbert owned a share in the Marston rock pits and installed a Boulton and Watt rotative engine in them about 1788 for winding rock salt out of the pit and for pumping brine out as well. It was capable of raising half a ton of salt 120 yards and this more or less agrees with the depth of the mine as given by Calvert in 1915 – 330 feet.[37]

The third important change was the introduction of the steam pumping engine into the salt field in place of the horse-driven whim gin or whimsey. Here again development began near Lawton, probably stimulated by the opening of the Trent and Mersey or Grand Trunk Canal through the township in 1777–8; this made it easier to bring coal in and to send salt out of the district, although the canal tolls and charges were said to be higher than

---

34 Calvert, op. cit., 776.

35 Calvert, op. cit., 249.

36 For John Gilbert see Hugh Malet, *The Grand Duke* (1961), *passim*; W. H. Chaloner, 'Francis Egerton, third Duke of Bridgewater (1736–1803): a bibliographical note', *Explorations in Entrepreneurial History*, vol. V, no. 3, March 15th, 1953, 181–5.

37 Calvert, op. cit., 245–6. This engine was giving some trouble by 1795, apparently owing to bad servicing. Boulton and Watt's engine erector, James Lawson, wrote to one of his employers, James Watt, jun., on 23rd March 1795: 'I this morning went to Mr. Gilbert's engine which I find in a damnable plight – as there was only the engine man and a clerk, two stupid dogs . . . The noise of the working gear may be heard almost a mile'. Later he reported to young Watt: 'I have a letter from Mr. Gilbert on Monday desiring me to get the engine at Northwich put in order as soon as I conveniently could as they expected large orders for salt when the [war-time] embargo [on shipping] was taken off at Liverpool'. (17 April 1795, Boulton & Watt MSS, Birmingham Public Library.)

those on the River Weaver. Lawton saltworks, described as 'newly-erected' in 1779, and situated at Thurlwood, were owned and operated by Edward Salmon of Hassall Hall near Lawton and a Dr. Penlington. No evidence has been found to connect these two salt proprietors with the borings made in 1779–80. Salmon and Penlington installed a small Boulton and Watt steam engine in 1778 capable of pumping 24,000 gallons of brine in twelve hours out of their pit to a reservoir 300 ft. above the level in the pit.[38] John Gilbert followed, as we have seen with a rotary steam engine about 1788, and Thomas Marshall installed the third Boulton and Watt steam engine in the saltfield on his mine at Dunkirk near Northwich in 1796, 'to draw 1200 lb. 115 yards deep at the utmost'.[39]

Fortunately a fairly detailed description of Marshall's mine, with a tinted engraving of the interior, has survived, and, as it is not well known, a summary and extracts from it follow.[40] The anonymous writer pointed out that public attention had been called to the Cheshire salt mines by George Canning's visit to one near Northwich during he summer of 1813. After giving details of the upper and lower rock salt beds he went on to describe the large pillars of salt supporting the roof, which were between eighteen and twenty feet square. There were at this time eleven or twelve mines in the area 'from which there are raised, on an annual average, fifty or sixty thousand tons of rock salt. The greater part is exported, and the remainder employed in the Cheshire district, in the manufacture of white salt by solution and subsequent evaporation.'[41]

The visitor was especially impressed by the number and tonnage of the flats employed in the Weaver and coal and salt trades – 'nearly seven hundred such vessels, the average cost of which is nearly one thousand pounds)':

From the number of steam-engines pumping up brine, or working up rock from the pits, the air was dark with smoke, and the roads to the works black with the falling soot, among which, particles of salt glistened in the sun-beams. The blackness of the salt-houses and lofts,

---

38 See Chapter III, pp. 38–9.
39 See Chapter III, pp. 45–6.
40 Anon., 'Account of a visit to the Rock-Salt Mines at Northwich, in Cheshire', *Repository of Arts, Literature, Commerce, Manufacturers, Fashions and Politics*, ed. R. Ackermann, XI, no. 66, Jan.–June 1814, 322–7 (with coloured plate showing interior of mine). For an account by an American visitor in the 1790s, see *Trans. Newcomen Society*, XXXIII, 1960–1, 61–2.
41 Ibid., 323.

and their age and condition, give the place a rather dismal and ruinous appearance.

Our visitor caught a glimpse of the upper salt bed as he descended into the pit and found that the roof of the mine in the lower stratum was twenty-two feet from the floor. The rock was mined by drills and gunpowder, about three tons being blasted away at each shot from a slice three feet deep at floor level:

> The workmen usually descend into the pit about half past six in the morning, to begin their labour by seven o'clock; and they continue, with little intermission, till three in the afternoon, and then quit. They work by companies, and are paid rateably by the ton, according to the quantity of rock sent up and of which an account is kept by an excise officer, who always attends whenever salt is drawn from the pit.

The eighteenth century and the first four decades of the nineteenth century witnessed the supremacy of Northwich. During the 1840s, however, the Winsford area eclipsed Northwich as the source of most of the white salt shipped down the Weaver, as the following figures show (although Northwich remained pre-eminent in the rock trade):

WHITE SALT SHIPPED DOWN THE WEAVER[42]

Year ending April	From Northwich	From Winsford
1840	245,075	169,081
1850	283,146	324,250
1860	274,934	420,838
1870	261,003	640,155

The reasons for this were many: the successful efforts, from the 1840s onwards, of H. E. Falk of Winsford, and, later, by the Salt Chamber of Commerce, formed in 1858, to extend overseas markets for Winsford salt, particularly in India, so that by the 1870s over a million tons a year were being exported.[43] They formed, after coal and iron, Britain's most bulky raw material export. In addition the depressing effects of the subsidence problem on production in the Northwich area, which was the first to be affected, undoubtedly told in Winsford's favour.

---

42 Calvert, op. cit., 485–6.
43 For Falk, see Chapter VI, 'William Furnival, H. E. Falk . . .'

There remain certain other problems worthy of further research. What, for example, caused the links between the St. Helen's coalfield and the Cheshire saltfield to be broken one by one after 1850? Drs. Barker and Harris have suggested several possibilities: the closing down of collieries which had been particularly associated with saltworks, e.g. Gerards' Bridge colliery, owned by Speakman, Caldwell and Co., the rise of alternative markets for St. Helens coal (although Cheshire salt and chemical works consumed an increasing tonnage of coal). Certain links remained, however. The *Annual Reports* (1858–89) of the Salt Chamber of Commerce, with its headquarters at Northwich, show that the Ravenhead Colliery Company Ltd., of St. Helens (previously Bromilow, Haddock and Co.), continued in membership of the Chamber until as late as 1876–7, while the colliery firm of the Executors of William Cross of St. Helens was a member as late as 1870–1. It is possible that further research will reveal that steam shipping and the new railways, particularly after the 1860s, had a powerful effect on the pattern of trade in the Mersey-Weaver basin in general and on the development of the salt district in particular, both by bringing in coal from regions other than South Lancashire and by creating alternative markets for South Lancashire coal itself.[44]

44 T. C. Barker and J. R. Harris, *A Merseyside Town in the Industrial Revolution, St. Helens, 1750–1900*, 1954, 181–201, 338–44 and *passim*. The St. Helens colliery company Richard Evans, Ltd. possessed salt interests in Cheshire in the late nineteenth century.

CHAPTER VI

WILLIAM FURNIVAL, H. E. FALK AND THE SALT CHAMBER OF COMMERCE, 1815–89: SOME CHAPTERS IN THE ECONOMIC HISTORY OF CHESHIRE

In the second volume of his *Economic History of Modern Britain* (p.145), Sir John Clapham, writing of the chambers of commerce and trade associations which multiplied rapidly after 1860, suggested that between 1850 and 1875 'there was rather less co-operation among 'capitalist' producers than there had been in the more difficult first and second quarters' of the nineteenth century. He mentioned that in the British salt industry there had been price-fixing associations 'based on a local monopoly' in the early nineteenth century, and added that after 1825 the industry 'witnessed alternations of gentlemen's agreements and "fighting trade" ' until the formation of the Salt Union in 1888. This combine has been called 'the first British trust', but to the salt proprietors of the time it was merely 'a new device, made easier by limited liability, for handling an old problem'.[1] The purpose of this study is to examine in greater detail the business organisation of the natural local monopoly enjoyed by the Cheshire saltmakers in the nineteenth century and to trace the part played by 'The Coalition' and the Salt Chamber of Commerce in fostering price regulation and output restriction between the end of the Napoleonic Wars and 1889.[2]

---

1 Op. cit., pp. 147–8; see also *Accounts and Papers*, 1817, III, 123, p. 22, and E. Hughes, *Studies in Administration and Finance , 1558–1825* (1934), pp. 359–77 passim.

2 The study is based chiefly on William Furnival's *A Statement of Facts . . . submitted to the consideration of His Majesty, His Majesty's Ministers and both Houses of Parliament* (1833), a copy of which may be found in the Manchester Public Reference Library (P2049/5), and on the *Annual Reports of the Salt Chamber of Commerce of Cheshire and Worcestershire*, from 1858 to 1889, preserved in the Library of Manchester University. The first is hereafter referred to as *Statement*, the second as *A.R.*, followed by the period covered

THE FURNIVAL EPISODE (TO 1833)

The Cheshire salt industry of the early nineteenth century was strongly localised in the valley of the River Weaver, mainly in an area twelve miles north to south and two miles east to west which included the townships of Anderton, Winnington, Marbury, Marston, Wincham, Witton, Winsford, Over, Northwich, Leftwich, Moulton, Middlewich, Sandbach, Betchton and Wheelock.[3] Production took two forms, of which one, the older, consisted of boiling down the natural brine with the aid of coal imported by sea, river navigation and canal from Lancashire and North Staffordshire.[4] The second, and younger, branch of the industry entailed the mining of rock salt, which had been first discovered in the township of Marbury (Bucklow Hundred) in 1670, during boring operations undertaken for the purpose of finding coal. Demand was usually brisk during spring and summer with a marked tendency to slacken about September.

The salt was exported from the district mainly down the River Weaver. Since the Act of 1721 the navigation of the Weaver had been controlled and improved from Winsford Bridge to the Mersey estuary at Weston Point, near Frodsham. The ships[5] used in this trade were small sailing flats which plied to Liverpool, Birkenhead and Runcorn.[6] At these ports the salt was loaded into larger vessels for export and the coasting trade. Later, in the 1860s and 1870s, a direct export developed from the new docks at Weston Point. Flats also brought coal supplies into the salt districts. Writing of conditions in the 1820s William Furnival alleged that 'The greater part of the flats . . . were . . . owned by the old salt proprietors, who charged 3s. per ton on the carriage of salt to Liverpool (which was paid by the purchaser on delivery) . . .'[7] Besides the flat-owning proprietors, there were smaller salt manufacturers who sold their product at the works to the Liverpool salt brokers or to the independent watermen. From the 1840s the independent watermen ap-

in the report, e.g. 1875–6.

3   By the 1820s salt production at Church Lawton, Nantwich and Frodsham was unimportant.

4   The Trent and Mersey (Grand Trunk) Canal passed through the salt district and was connected to the Weaver Navigation by a lift at Anderton.

5   The plan and elevation of Furnival's Wharton, i.e. Winsford, salt works in his *Statement* contain representations of these vessels.

6   Runcorn was 'the small draft port . . . chiefly frequented by French craft' (*A.R.*, 1876–7, pp. 9–10).

7   *Statement*, p. 4. Some salt proprietors had important interests in Lancashire collieries and canal companies.

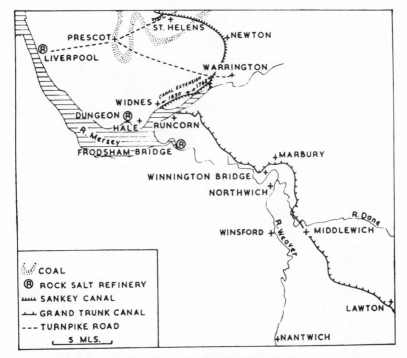

THE MERSEY–WEAVER SALT DISTRICT

pear to have been one source from which new entrepreneurs and fresh capital entered the industry:

> Many watermen commenced by either getting a small flat of their own or joining another person in buying one. In this flat the watermen carried salt for proprietors who had no flats of their own or too few, or they carried for the merchant who purchased salt at the works and paid the Weaver dues. In busy times the watermen bought a cargo on their own account and took it to Liverpool as a speculation . . . When dull times came around the flat owner often found himself with nothing to do . . .[8]

These periods of slack trade provided the incentive to the more enterpris-

8   A. F. Calvert, *Salt in Cheshire* (1915), p. 631.

ing carriers to extend their businesses and thereby enter the ranks of the 'old proprietors':

> As soon as a waterman by carefulness had accumulated a little money, if he was a pushing man, he took a little set of works of two or three pans and made salt enough to keep his flat working steadily. As trade grew he put down more pans and got more flats. Two or three often combined in both works and flats, and the salt brokers of Liverpool sold their salt for them and became practically their bankers, while the more successful among them opened offices of their own.

Until the 1860s the independent watermen 'through a solid combination . . . and most tyrannical rules' successfully maintained 'a very high rate of transport'.[9] Then, in 1863, Hermann Eugen Falk, of Winsford, one of the most important saltmakers and the largest exporter, launched the first iron steam barge, the 'Experiment', on to the River Weaver from his works at Meadow Bank. This was followed in 1864 by a second, the 'Improvement'. Within a few years this revolution in the method of transport broke down the power of the independent watermen and 'brought about also a material alteration in the system of manufacture . . . the small proletariat makers, who were chiefly flatmen, became gradually absorbed into the larger works . . .'[10]

In 1823 the total amount of salt made and raised in Cheshire amounted to less than 300,000 tons, of which 170,400 tons were exported. By 1850 the figure of production had risen to 1,000,000 tons; twenty-six years later exports alone equalled 1,000,000 tons, leaving 750,000 tons for British domestic consumption. The pre-eminence of Cheshire as a producing area even after the discovery of new salt deposits north and south of the Tees between 1859 and 1874 is shown by the output figures for 1887. Out of the total British output of 2,206,951 tons in that year, Cheshire accounted for 1,769,719, Worcestershire for 252,000, Durham and North Yorkshire for 136,267, Ireland for 43,155 and Staffordshire for 5,810.[11]

The export trade in salt had an important bearing on the profitable

---

9   In 1859 one James Southern was instructed, presumably by a committee of watermen, 'to issue out [to the Northwich and Winsford captains of flats] another list of prices' for the carriage of salt and fuel on the Rivers Mersey and Weaver (Falk Papers).

10   *A.R.*, 1887–9, p. 11; see also p. 10 and *A.R.*, 1863–4, p. 12, 1869–70, pp. 29–30; Calvert, op. cit., p. 459.

11   Clapham, op. cit., Vol. II, p. 515; H. W. Macrosty, *The Trust Movement in British Industry* (1907), pp. 182–3; *A.R.*, 1883–4, p. 13.

EAST VIEW OF THE SALT WORKS AT WHARTON IN CHESHIRE
Erected by Furnival, 1828–32.

operation of that portion of the British mercantile marine which frequented the Mersey estuary. Generally speaking the most characteristic sections of the British export trade in the nineteenth century consisted of manufactured goods which took up comparatively little cargo space in comparison with their value, good such as cottons and woollen cloth, pottery, rails and machinery. On the other hand, British imports tended to consist of less valuable but bulkier raw materials such as timber, corn, raw cotton and iron ore. One of the most pressing problems of the men who operated the British mercantile marine was therefore to find bulky outward cargoes from British ports to fill the holds of the ships which had brought in these raw materials. In spite of their efforts many British ships had to sail from British ports in ballast because bulky outward cargoes were lacking.[12]

Liverpool owed its rapid rise partly to the proximity of the Cheshire salt deposits, and by the mid-1870s the salt export trade of between 900,000 and 1,000,000 tons employed one third of the port's loaded export tonnage. In

12 *A.R.*, 1866–7, p. 16: 'The numerous vessels going out to the Southern States to load cotton require to ballast themselves with salt, which they can afford to take at a cheap rate'; and also *A.R.*, 1886–7, p. 32: 'One-fourth of the export is to America, and a large proportion thereof is carried at nominal rates by the mail steamers'.

weight salt ranked third amongst British exports, being surpassed in this respect only by coal and iron.[13] It could be said of Liverpool in 1874 that'... captains of vessels trading to that port will take several shillings per ton less freight, knowing that they can always calculate upon getting a cargo of salt in the absence of dry goods'.[14] The Cheshire salt proprietors were well aware of the importance of their product to the trade of Liverpool and of the part it played in fostering the development of distant markets, as the following extract from the *Annual Report* of the Salt Chamber of Commerce for 1875–6 shows (p. 16):

> The course of trade from all distant countries, since the coal measures of each country become more and more developed, tends to make the exports over-whelmingly to exceed the imports in bulk, and the consequence is, that ships are compelled to take salt out at ballast freights everywhere. Freights to all American ports from Liverpool, which used to rule at an average of 20s. per ton, have during the last twelve months never exceeded 5s. per ton, and in most cases they have carried salt across the Atlantic freight free. We anticipate that the great Indian ports will follow suit at an early date.

The *Annual Report* for 1886–7 (p.31) indicates that in the case of one port at least these anticipations had been fulfilled '. . . the import of salt into Calcutta has provided the tonnage at practicable rates for the great extension of [Indian] exports of jute and wheat'.

The embarrassing bounty of Nature in the Cheshire salt district produced an early development of restrictive practices which had been noted by the famous naturalist, John Ray, F.R.S., when he was studying the method of saltmaking at Nantwich in the 1660s: 'The Lords of the [salt] pit appoint how much shall be boiled as they see occasion, that the trade be not clogged'.[15] The fear of 'clogging' still existed in the years immediately following the Peace of 1815, when price-fixing and output-regulating associations of the Cheshire salt proprietors 'situate at different places' exercised a powerful influence over the trade. On the basis of the evidence given before the Parliamentary Committee on the Use of Rock Salt in the Fisheries in 1817 Sir John Clapham considered that the merchant element

---

13 *A.R.*, 1876–7, p. 6; 1873–4, p. 16. For the period before 1815 see T. C. Barker, 'Lancashire coal, Cheshire salt, and the rise of Liverpool' in *Transactions of the Historical Society of Lancashire and Cheshire*, vol. 103, 1951, pp. 83–101.

14 Morris, *Directory of Cheshire* (1874), p. 500.

15 *A Collection of English Words not generally used*, 1st edn. (1674), p. 142.

rather than the manufacturing element predominated on these committees.[16] Further evidence, however, suggests that the actual producers of salt were the preponderant force in the trade at this period, just as they were the chief beneficiaries from the attempts at monopoly. From about 1815 until January 1825 the prices of common, stoved and certain other varieties of Cheshire salt made from brine were regulated by a group of saltmakers known as 'The Coalition' on lines reminiscent of the Newcastle Limitation of the Vend in the coal trade. William Furnival described them as follows in his *Statement*:

> . . . this society was governed by rules and regulations of their own, exceedingly detrimental to the interests of the public . . .
>
> Each proprietor was bound not to deliver more than a certain quantity of salt, according to the extent of his works, except under a penalty of six shillings per ton, on any excess.
>
> One general agent was appointed by 'The Coalition', to whom was forwarded the quantity to which each respective proprietor was restricted.
>
> The society held their general meetings; appointed committees to fix their own prices; and thus, as they truly boasted, they 'could command their own profits', and make the public pay whatever they demanded.
>
> . . . to the boast already named, they added that of their amazing riches, which enabled them to ruin all, or any who should dare to enter the lists against them.
>
> Besides, this, they imposed the most galling restrictions on the various merchants; insomuch, that premiums were offered by them [i.e. the merchants] at various periods to any who would erect saltworks, to oppose the old proprietors.[17]

It is important to remember that the above account, and indeed most of what we know about restrictive policies in the salt trade at this time, comes from an extremely hostile source. That source is the pamphlet published by William Furnival from his lodging in the debtors' section of Horsemonger Lane Gaol, London, under the date 4 May 1833. In so far

---

16 Op. cit., Vol. I, pp. 200–1 (quoting *Accounts and Papers* 1817, III, 123, p. 22).

17 Op. cit., p. 3. Furnival continued in a sentence which may reveal the source of his financial backing: 'Some of the more independent of them [i.e. the merchants] resolved to break in upon this overbearing monopoly, and offered £10,000 to assist any who would come forward to establish themselves against the coalition'.

as it is possible to check Furnival's story, however, his statements of fact appear to be substantially correct, and interpreted in the light of the evidence given reluctantly before the Parliamentary Committee of 1817, his allegations appear to be well-founded, even if they are somewhat exaggerated.

William Furnival entered the salt trade in 1822 and was one of several men of the time who were interested in the problem of using steam to boil down brine. A. F. Calvert, in his *Salt and the Salt Industry*, published about 1920, considered that Furnival 'anticipated the revolutionary improvements which were achieved some three-quarters of a century later by the Vacuum System and the Hodgkinson Patent Saltmaking Process' (p.76). Furnival himself claimed that in 1823 he and James Smith, engineer, of Port Seaton, had taken out a patent, on the basis of their joint research, for an 'apparatus for the applying steam to the boiling and concentration of solutions in general, [and] chrystalizing the muriat of soda from brines containing that salt'.[18] He took out further patents in his own name in 1824 and 1831, and one in partnership with James Craig, all bearing on the first.[19]

In 1823 he erected salt-works at Droitwich, in Worcestershire, and sold them as a going concern to S. Fowler, Farden and Co., a year later, when he leased brine-bearing lands at Anderton, near Northwich in Cheshire, close to the point at which the River Weaver Navigation was connected by an inclined plane with the Trent and Mersey canal. He sold his interest in these lands to the British Rock and Salt Company in April 1825.[20] In April 1828 he acquired control over salt-bearing lands at Winsford, on which he erected, between that date and 1832, salt-works covering about twelve acres at a cost of over £135,000. In them he installed some three miles of pannage, and the whole property had an estimated output of 130,000 tons per annum. In 1829 he started to build a smaller works covering nearly six acres at Marston. Furnival claimed that these works were 'the only two in the

18 *Abridgments of Specifications of Patents relating to acids, alkalies, oxides and salts, 1622–1866* (1869), p. 91 (19 June 1823, no. 4805). The patent is in Smith's name alone. See also pp. 83, 93–4, 95, 98–9, 100, 103 (other salt inventions).

19 Ibid., pp. 95, 96, 105. Furnival claimed that the adoption of his processes meant a fuel saving of 50%, a saving in speed of production of 50%, and a superior quality of salt, while his mines could 'deliver rock salt at full 25 to 30 per cent less than any other in the country' (*Statement*, p. 68).

20 Between 1825 and 1828 Furnival was busy in the Netherlands, Belgium and France (Isle of Rhé and Dieuze) advising on the erection of salt-works on his principles, but the misfortunes attending him in these Continental speculations contributed to his failure in England (Calvert, *Salt in Cheshire*, pp. 659, 663–5; W. O. Henderson, *Britain and Industrial Europe, 1750–1870*, p. 47, n. 30).

H. E. FALK (1820–98), FOUNDER OF THE SALT UNION.

Kingdom possessing the peculiar advantages of inexhaustible brine fully saturated and dry rock salt on the same premises'.[21] Owing to the variety of

21 *Statement*, p. 68; see also pp. 1–8, 70; the old salt proprietors tried to prevent Furnival from mortgaging his properties by threatening that 'the moment any rock salt came into the market from the Wharton mine, they would lower the price 50 per cent and ruin everyone concerned, whether proprietor, partner or mortgagee'.

circumstances, not the least of which was the combined hostility of the men already in the trade, he was forced to lease both the Winsford and Marston properties to various people in the course of 1830–31. In Furnival's own words:

> The rapid progress of my concerns . . . brought the whole body of salt proprietors on me with a malignity scarcely to be conceived, and as a means of crushing (as they thought) all my undertakings, the prices of salt were at once lowered from 30 to 50 per cent., and on some qualitites even more as will be seen from the Liverpool Price Current of that period . . . The moment they (the Coalition) feared I was making progress, down went the price of salt. When they thought I was crushed by their arbitrary measures . . . they raised the price again, – causing, as it were, my situation to be the regulating index of the price at which the public were to be furnished with this necessary article of life.[22]

He was arrested on 28 August 1832 for an alleged debt of £8. 18s. contracted to a Frenchman in 1826–7, and lodged in the Horsemonger Gaol, London. Little is known of his activities after 1833.[23]

According to Furnival the older salt proprietors 'viewed with a deadly hatred the man who had broken in upon their hitherto undisturbed monopoly',[24] while they rejected the use of his process under licence on equitable terms. His engineer 'was instantly expelled from a farm he held under one of the body', while another declared that 'he would lay by £4,000 a year' to accomplish Furnival's ruin.[25] .

---

22 Ibid., pp. 6, 16–22. The Marston works remained in production until 1847, while the Winsford works were managed by trustees until 1847, when they were taken over by a body of lessees known as the National Patent Salt Company. In 1875 the sole remaining lessee transferred his interest in the property to R. & J. Stubbs, salt proprietors (Calvert, *Salt and the Salt Industry*, pp. 77–9).

23 *Statement*, pp. 12–13, 25. Furnival was still in the Horsemonger Gaol on 13 June 1836 (*The English Reports*, Vol. 132 (Common Pleas, Vol. 10), 1912, pp. 346–7). Since this paper was sent to press a most interesting document has been brought to light by Mr. V. I. Tomlinson of Salford, to whom the author is indebted for the loan of it. It consists of a printed excerpt (with many illustrations) from a larger work (foolscap size), labelled 'Descriptions and Views of the Wharton and Marston Patent Salt Refineries and Rock-Mines'; the label describes the contents as Vol. II, Part XII, and the pagination runs from 247 to 290. This document appears to form part of printed legal proceedings in two volumes concerning a Chancery suit which Furnival was carrying on against the tenants of his works and others. The latest date in the document is 31 March 1836.

24 Ibid., pp. 4–5.

25 Ibid., p. 6.

On Furnival's refusal to join 'The Coalition' that body reduced the price of common salt, which had been 20s. per ton 'for about eight years prior to October 1824', to 14s. 'and (it) continued at that price till January 1825 when the association appears to have been dissolved.' By October 1826 the price had sagged to 9s. per ton under the stress of free competition, and remained at this level until, in January 1827 'an arrangement was made among the proprietors not to sell below 12s.'. By the following October the price was back at 9s. again, but in January 1828 'the price was fixed by agreement at 13s.' After another collapse the prices were again raised by agreement to 12s. in May 1829.[26] In the latter half of the year a meeting of salt proprietors found themselves obliged to pass the following resolution: 'They deeply lamented the low price of salt, but considered . . . it would not be prudent to raise the price until Mr. Furnival was disposed of'.[27] On 17 August 1829 the salt proprietors of Northwich and Winsford issued an appeal to the trade which claimed that 16s. per ton was 'a fair remunerating price to the maker, and one to which no objection is made by the exporter'. Those responsible for the appeal calculated that in the four and a half years which had passed since January 1825 the salt trade ('the only trade . . . which those engaged in have within themselves the power to render with so much certainty a beneficial one') had thrown away 'the enormous sum' of over £280,000 owing to the lack of effective regulation. Saltmakers were said to be disposing of their salt at cost-of-production prices, prices just enabling them 'to make more salt to sell in the same ruinous way'. Only a determination on the part of every maker 'to lay aside all jealousies and . . . to act in the most honourable manner in adhering to every regulation which may be agreed on' could ensure a fair profit.[28]

It is difficult to say whether this appeal had any immediate effect, but on 6 April 1830 a correspondent wrote to Furnival: 'Salt is down to 10s. per ton, and old . . . told me yesterday, that it was done against you. That had you not started again, it would have been at 14s.'[29] Under the date 5 December 1830 we hear of a meeting at which resolutions were passed 'to hold meetings at Northwich, Winsford and Liverpool three days in every month; prices fixed at 12s. common, 15s. butter, 18s. stoved, 25s. British bay, 30s. large'. This association remained in being for almost a year. In August 1831

26 Ibid., pp. 71–2.
27 Ibid., p. 11.
28 Ibid., pp. 74–5.
29 Ibid., p. 77.

a new scheme came into operation. The proprietors entered into a formal agreement and 'appointed one sole agent for the sale of their salt', but unfortunately for them Furnival's Winsford works came into production about this time, whereupon

> ... the price in October (1831) was reduced by general consent to 10s. without any other apparent cause than a general feeling of hostility to those works, and as 10s. offered no grounds for continuing together, and many of the proprietors becoming much dissatisfied, the association broke up, and soon afterwards the price was reduced to 8s., at which rate it has continued till now with little variation.[30]

Furnival's Winsford correspondent had some justification for describing the members of the association as 'the most extraordinary set of devils that ever congregated'.[31]

A similar combination controlled the price and output of rock salt. In 1825–6 the price of the lowest quality rock salt was 12s. per ton, but towards the end of the latter year it fell to 10s. 6d., at which price, '... an association was formed ... and one agent appointed for the sale of all the produce of the pits included in the Association'. The price remained steady at 10s. 6d. until September 1832, although the meeting of October 1831 is said to have raised this figure to 12s. again. However, on 10 September 1832 John Garnett, Furnival's Liverpool agent, informed him 'that a deputation of the Rock Salt proprietors had waited upon him, and told him that unless the proprietors of the Wharton and Winsford Rock Salt mines joined the Association they should lower the price of Rock Salt from 10s. 6d. to 6s. per ton on the 1st of October'. This threat they duly carried into effect, although 'the foreign export houses were ready to purchase at 10s. 6d. as they had been accustomed to do'.[32]

THE FALK ERA, 1842–89

Little evidence has been found of combination in the salt trade from the end of 1832 to 1837 but the material for 1841–50 reveals not only the continuance of price regulation in the white salt trade, but the existence of a fully-fledged scheme for the production and sale of white salt. A general

---

30 Ibid., p. 72. See also pp. 77–8. At the meeting of October 1831 the prices of butter and stoved salt were reduced to 12s. and 16s. respectively.

31 Ibid., p. 78.

32 Ibid., p. 27; see also pp. 35–6, 72–3.

meeting of the 'White Salt Trade' attended by nineteen saltmakers or representatives of salt companies was held at the Angel Inn, Northwich, on 4 March 1841, and began by taking steps to recover £1,206 'due to the late Association' which two individuals named Dean and Tomkinson had decided to detain until they received an indemnity 'against legal proceedings brought against them by Messrs. Worthington, Court and others'. These parties were requested by those present to stay further proceedings and the meeting adjourned for a week. The crisp, business-like air of the document suggests a certain amount of familiarity with such proceedings. The Association was governed by a small committee, and the second document available consists of the minutes of this body, which met at the White Salt Office at Northwich on 21 January 1842. By reading this in conjunction with a printed 'Statement of White Salt delivery, with overs and shorts' for the month of April 1842, and a manuscript agreement of the same year between the participating firms, one can piece together the main features of the quota scheme.[33] Two members of the Committee, Henry Waterton and John Cheshire, had obtained the consent of nearly every proprietor to a plan whereby they were to purchase all the salt manufactured by the trade at certain fixed prices as from 1 February 1842. The salt district was divided into two divisions, Northwich and Winsford, with twenty-seven members each, and to each member was allocated a sales quota for so many tons. Each firm was entitled to a fixed proportion of the yearly total of 645,000 shares. Makers who exceeded their allotted quotas paid a fine of 5s. per ton to the funds of the Association, but in actual practice, arrangements for the transfer of quotas from one firm to another seem to have been in existence, e.g. during April 1842, the firm of Robert Falk, Son and Co., which was entitled to ship only 202 tons, exceeded its quota by 1,569 tons, while seven other firms in the Winsford division alone failed to ship a single ton. The total number of 'over' shipments for April 1842 exactly equalled the 'short' shipments for both divisions. Cheshire and Waterton were empowered to undercut the 'few remaining outstanding firms' who might not consent to join.

It is not known how long this particular arrangement lasted,[34] but a similar document dated July 1850 revealed that a modified version of the

---

33 Falk Papers, Manchester.

34 On 28 March 1845 51 of the salt manufacturers of the United Kingdom met at the Angel Inn, Northwich, and passed unanimously a resolution which contained the following passage: '. . . in the present depressed state of the salt trade and with a great excess of production over demand . . .' (Falk Papers). See also Calvert, *Salt in Cheshire*, pp. 514–5 for the arrangements made in 1846.

scheme was in operation during the years 1848–50. It shows an increased membership (twenty-nine active makers in the Northwich division, thirty-nine in the Winsford division). This scheme was apparently an elastic one, for on 1 October 1849 an arbitrator named Harper had awarded 10,200 extra shares, both of common and stoved production, to several firms 'for new plans', i.e. in order to bring newly-constructed salt-works or additions to existing plants into the scheme. It is, however, by no means clear why 39,600 additional shares had been distributed between seven canal proprietors.[35]

On the subject of price-fixing, the next two available documents are two letters, one from John Cheshire to Christopher Robinson, salt proprietor of Winnington, dated 31 May 1845 and the other a reply to Cheshire from Henry Manisty, of the National Patent Salt Company, dated 3 June. Cheshire wrote that there was no salt proprietor more anxious than he was to improve prices,

> but really after what happened about this time twelve months ago I cannot make up my mind to join in any agreement again, except every firm in the trade is a party to it, and there is some appearance of the contract being more durable than the one entered into on 15th April 1844 . . . It is true 8/– nett was obtained until the following Autumn (which was some benefit to us) notwithstanding the secession of the National Patent Company from the first agreement (on May 27th 1844) and your refusal . . . to sign the second. Demand, however, falling off in September, prices fell as usual, at once showing how valueless all partial arrangements are to sustain them . . .
>
> The present state of the trade is lamentable, but the cure is pretty obvious . . . Let every man limit his powers of production. Unless this is done there can be no profit . . .
>
> I am free to confess that until lately I held the free trade doctrine, that the trade would right itself if left to the natural impulse of demand, but I now feel convinced that this generation will pass away before any increased demand can arise to enable all of us to work at even a small profit.

The gist of Manisty's severely logical reply was as follows:

> It is really idle for the trade to complain of the loss which they are inflicting upon themselves. When every proprietor comes to the

---

35 Calvert, *Salt in Cheshire*, pp. 516–8. The 645,800 shares of 1842 had grown to 761,900 by 30 September 1849.

resolution upon which the directors of the National [Patent Salt Company] are acting, and intend to act, namely, to leave supply and demand to regulate price, and never to sell at a loss, *then*, and not till then, will the trade right itself.[36]

In spite of this Spartan advice, another general meeting of the White Salt Trade attended by twenty-two saltmakers, or representatives of salt companies, was held at the usual place on 21 May 1846. It appointed a Committee'. . . to ascertain the stocks of salt now on hand, and to recommend such a curtailment of make as they may think proper with reference to such stocks and the prospect of demand, and afterwards to carry the same into effect if adopted by a subsequent Meeting'. A second resolution fixed the prices of various kinds of salt

until some plan is arranged by the proposed Committee for curtailing the Make, as under:–

Common	10s. 6d.	
Butter	12s. 6d.	Less 6d. per Ton for
Shute Stoved	15s. 6d.	Cash in 10 days.
Handed Lumps	16s. 6d.	

The salt men then adjourned until 28 May, after passing a third resolution to the effect that members should not enter into fresh contracts until after the further meeting.[37]

Whatever arrangements were entered into do not appear to have had much effect, according to the anonymous appeal to the salt proprietors of Northwich and Winsford issued in December 1846 and attributed by H. J. Falk to Henry Waterton. As the result of a variety of circumstances, including 'the present high rate of coal', salt was said to be selling at an extremely low price, and besides having produced results disappointing to those who had 'embarked their capital in it under the sanguine expectation that they were making a safe and lucrative investment', the trade had become 'a by-word for everything that is fickle and inconsistent'.

For this state of affairs the anonymous author blamed a body of men of whom little had been heard in current salt trade controversies up to this

36 These two letters appear to have been generally circulated to salt proprietors (Falk Papers).
37 Calvert, *History of the Salt Union* (1913), pp. 15–16, and *Salt in Cheshire* (1915), p. 55.

juncture. To right it he propounded a plan which would make the brokers the agents of the salt proprietors:

> . . . premising in the first place that salt – generally speaking – is sold through the medium of brokers at Liverpool; and in the second place, that the brokers are, and have been, an irresponsible body of men to whose irresponsibility may be traced the first cause of the present depression in price:
>
> Let the salt trade abolish the irresponsibility of their brokers, and require them to unite and form a union to be called THE SALT BROKERS' UNION:
>
> Let every member of such union be required to deposit the sum of £500, in some approved banking establishment, as security for his good faith. The depositor to receive the interest on his deposit, but to be debarred from withdrawing the principal, so long as he shall continue a member of the union.
>
> Let the salt trade employ no brokers, but those, who are members of the Salt Brokers' Union.
>
> Let the prices of salt be agreed upon by a committee of the trade at periodical meetings, similar to those held by the ironmasters.
>
> If any member of the Union sell, or offer salt for sale, under the prices agreed upon by the Committee, let his deposit be forfeited and be equally divided among the other brokers. He himself being incapacitated from ever again acting as a salt broker . . . (Falk Papers).

In 1850 there was in existence a committee of syndicate, composed of all the saltmakers of Northwich and Winsford, and statements were regularly issued giving the number of shares held by each proprietor, the number being regulated by the output of salt.

The years from 1850 to 1875 were marked by a considerable, if somewhat uneven, expansion in production, combined with a greater degree of competition than had existed formerly. The period saw a rapid turnover in the personnel at the head of the trade; of the names on the *Saltmakers' List* for 1842 only two, viz., Worthington and Falk, were to be found among the firms which went to form the Salt Union in 1888.[38] Nevertheless, this period, commonly believed to have been the heyday of unfettered trade, both internal and international, was by no means free from the restrictive practices of earlier generations.

---

38 *A.R.*, 1887–9, p. 10.

The next landmark in the history of association in the Cheshire salt trade is the foundation of the Salt Chamber of Commerce of Cheshire and Worcestershire on 30 August 1858, after 'a numerous meeting of Salt Proprietors' had been convened by H. E. Falk, who was at this time the largest exporter.[39] Shortly after its formation the Chamber comprised forty-two out of the fifty or sixty firms in the trade and included several joint stock companies. Brokers who were not themselves salt manufacturers could become members of the Chamber. On the other hand, the watermen salt proprietors could not join the Chamber and the exclusion is all the more interesting because one of the most significant developments in the salt industry during the 1870s and the 1880s was that new men, and especially the watermen, found it increasingly difficult to enter and maintain themselves in the trade. The Salt Chamber of Commerce therefore soon became an organisation of the larger proprietors, and in 1862–3 it turned down a proposition from the watermen salt proprietors 'as to joining the Chamber, provided it would undertake the regulation of prices at Liverpool', on the grounds that it had hitherto been one 'of the fundamental principles of the Chamber not to interfere with, or set itself up as an arbiter of prices'.[40] By 1859 it could be said that 'The only two concerns of any importance who have not joined the Chamber are the British Salt Company and Mr. Joseph Verdin. It is difficult to understand on what grounds they hold aloof, as no trade in the country of any magnitude is without an organisation of some kind to protect its interests . . .'[41] The objects of the Chamber were 'the opening up of new markets, the watching over treaties and tariffs in foreign countries where salt was or might become an article of import, and to impress on the Government and Legislature that in the category of our export trade salt played a very important part'.[42]

---

39 *A.R.*, 1858–9, p. 3, 1887–9, p. 10. The two Verdin firms joined the Chamber in 1865–6. By 1876 the firm of which Robert Verdin (d. 1887) was a partner had an annual make of 250,000 tons. Soon after its creation in 1885 he became the first M.P. for the Northwich Parliamentary Division, which corresponded roughly with the boundaries of the salt district. The Chamber took part in the successful opposition to the original proposals contained in the Redistribution of Seats Bill, and rejoiced that 'the interest is not to be divided, but . . . comprised as one representative body' (*A.R.* 1884–5, p. 25).

40 *A.R.*, 1862–3, p. 3. By 1877 the number of individual salt proprietors had fallen to 40 (*A.R.*, 1876–7, p. 6). There was a feeling among the saltmakers that they had been 'made the sport of jobbers and shippers', who have 'so long exercised an undue influence over the destinies of the Salt trade'. (*A.R.*, 1871–2, p. 6).

41 *A.R.*, 1859, pp. 18–19; see also *A.R.*, 1858–9, pp. 4, 15. Representation of the Worcestershire salt area in the early Chamber was confined to John Corbett, Stoke Works, near Bromsgrove, and William Clay of the Patent Salt Works, Droitwich.

42 *A.R.*, 1865–6, p. 7.

Vigilance was particularly necessary in the case of India and China, where the salt trade formed the subject of various forms of State taxation and monopoly. In 1845–6, after a great struggle, in which H. E. Falk played a prominent part, British exporters had finally been allowed to land cargoes of salt in bonded warehouses at Calcutta without previous payment of duty. It should be remembered that at this time the manufacture of, and the whole-sale trade in, salt were State monopolies in the Bengal Presidency (established by Clive in 1765) and there were heavy duties on imports from overseas. Falk is said to have sent the first cargoes in 1846 and although the export trade in salt to India from Liverpool fluctuated considerably, for the four years ending 1858 the average export was about 78,000 tons per year. Between 1858 and 1863 the Salt Chamber kept up such a pressure on the British Government, largely through the Cheshire M.P.s, that in 1863 the Government of India agreed to abolish the State salt manufacture in the Bengal Presidency and get its revenue from the high customs duties on imported salt.

The Chamber opened offices in Liverpool and Northwich, and by 1868–9 was issuing once a month to its members 'a complete statement of the salt trade of the country' on the basis of daily figures of output and delivery from individual works. This statistical service enabled the salt proprietors, fortified by knowledge of existing stocks, to give more exact instructions to their brokers in Liverpool.[43] During the first few years of its existence those who counted in the Chamber disclaimed any intention of regulating prices and output, but the very existence of the organisation, with its regular monthly meetings, promoted the habit of co-operation between the saltmakers and provided opportunities for the establishment of other bodies which did perform these tasks. The *Annual Report* of 1864–5 (pp. 5–6) put the position quite clearly: '. . . the members of the Chamber, when drawn together for these general objects, have wisely considered that the opportunity might also be availed of to discuss the all-important subject of supply and demand, with a view to exercise its influence in asking for a remunerative scale of prices'.

In May 1862 considerable changes took place in the organisation of the Chamber. H. E. Falk replaced Mr. Darsie, of Darsie and Gibson (Northwich and Liverpool), as the representative of the Salt Chamber on the Liverpool Chamber of Commerce for reasons which are obscure but seem to indicate a disagreement on policy between Darsie and the other members of the association. The Liverpool office was closed down, the whole of the official

43 *A.R., 1868–9, p. 25; 1869–70, p. 30.*

business of the Chamber concentrated at Northwich, and a small executive council set up to carry out day-to-day business.[44] The history of the Chamber from this point becomes increasingly identified with the activities of that enterprising industrialist, H. E. Falk.

H. E. Falk (1820–98) was born at Danzig and came to this country in 1838–9; from 1839 to 1842 he worked for his two elder brothers at Hull, where they were timber merchants trading under the name of Robert Falk, Son & Co. In 1842 Falk moved to Liverpool. Besides owning the Meadow Bank Works and rock salt mines at Winsford, he was also a Liverpool salt broker and the publisher of *Falk's Salt Circular*. He became vice-president of the Salt Chamber of Commerce in 1864, chairman in 1865, and president from 1867 until its demise soon after 1889, with short breaks in 1881–3 and 1884–6. In the winters of 1874–5 and 1879–80 he made business trips to the East in order to explore the possibilities of establishing fresh markets there for English salt. The first took him to India, Indonesia, China, Japan, and California; in the course of the second he made a detailed study of the salt trade in the various provinces of India, Burma, Ceylon, Malaya and the Straits settlements.[45]

Falk was also the prime mover in the foundation of the Salt Trade Committee.[46] The 'trade committee' was first mentioned in 1864 and was later said to have been formed 'in the Chamber.'[47] The duty of this committee 'became to adapt the make to the demand and regulate prices'. It was generally recognised as being an offshoot of the Salt Chamber of Commerce, in spite of the fact that officially the Chamber disclaimed all responsibility for its actions. General references to the Salt Trade Committee's activities in the *Annual Reports* of the Chamber are frequent enough to enable a continuous account of this new association to be pieced together, but exact details of prices and output are scarce. The underlying reason for the formation of this new restrictive committee was the low price of salt

44 *A.R.*, 1861–2, p. 26; 1862–3, p. 14.

45 *A.R.*, 1864–82, passim. John Corbett was president for the year 1881–2, and Robert Verdin for the years 1884–6. (*A.R.*, 1884–6).

46 (*A.R.*, 1887–9, p. 11). On 21 November 1866 Falk was presented with 'a handsome piece of plate' in acknowledgment of his services 'as the originator of the Chamber and Salt Trade Committee' (*A.R.*, 1866–7, p. 34). This Salt Trade Committee should not be confused with the Executive Correspondence Committee or Council formed on 20 May 1862, and consisting of the chairman, vice-chairman and four other members 'to pen and issue Documents and Correspondence of a public nature, on the business of the Chamber, two to' form a quorum'.

47 *A.R.*, 1887–9, p. 11.

consequent upon the outbreak of the Civil War in the U.S.A. The losses in the American export trade more than counterbalanced the advantage gained by opening up the Indian markets: 'The only possible remedy for such a state of things was recognition of the laws of supply and demand, proprietors agreeing to stop their make of salt at the recommendation of a Committee representing the whole body . . .'[48] Another result of the labours of Falk and the Chamber in the years 1865 and 1866 was the formation of the Liverpool Salt Brokers' Association: 'The brokers are a most influential and important body whose interests are closely identified with those of the Salt proprietors but until the formation of the Salt Trade Committee it was difficult to bring about any unity of action amongst the brokers, upon whom depends in a great measure the maintenance of prices fixed by the Salt Trade Committee'.[49]

The period from 1866 to the beginning of 1869 saw steady prices, partly due to a curtailment of the make immediately after the commercial crisis of 1866, but throughout 1869 there were signs of over-production and 'unremunerative prices' due to new pannage coming into operation, and this in the face of an 'immense demand' for salt, both at home and abroad. By the middle of 1870 the Salt Trade Committee of 1864 was defunct, in spite of numerous attempts to 'revive and resuscitate old arrangements'.[50] Prices fell to such a low level in the course of 1870 that in September 'a Trade Committee was again called into action and maintained prices' at a steady paying figure throughout 1871. The new scheme depended on close co-operation between merchants and producers: 'The meetings of the brokers in Liverpool are presided over by Mr. Marwood, the paid chairman, and the meetings at Northwich, which regulate the working pannage and fix prices are presided over promiscuously by one of the proprietors at each meeting.'[51] In the *Annual Report* for 1872–3 the council sounded a note of warning. The boom of the prosperous early 1870s was about to reach its peak. Already the coal shortage had led to a suspension of production at

48 *A.R.*, 1865–6, p. 5. The *Report* continued: 'In some respects the stoppage of our exports to the United States may have been fortunate in showing the urgent necessity for the adoption of the principle now laid down by the trade' (p. 6).

49 *A.R.*, 1865–6, p. 6.

50 *A.R.*, 1866–7, p. 5; 1868–9, p. 5; 1869–70, p. 5.

51 *A.R.*, 1874–5, p. 10; see also *A.R.*, 1870–1, p. 5. Later Falk noted of this period: '. . . the Salt Trade Committee had the extreme satisfaction of guiding the prices of Salt up to figures not known by this generation. From 8s. to 10s. and 12s. to 15s., the prices of common salt were officially raised to 20s. per ton at the works, and 27s. 6d. per ton for Calcutta salt, f.o.b. Liverpool' (*A.R.*, 1887–9, p. 11).

some works, and what was more disturbing: 'there can be no doubt that under ordinary circumstances there is an excess of pannage in existence of 20 to 25 per cent'.[52]

In spite of these gloomy prognostications prices remained steady until 1875–6 when a disastrous fall occurred, owing not to any substantial cessation of demand 'but to a departure from those salutary restrictions which had previously been so beneficial'.[53] The salt trade had at last entered its 'Great Depression'. Falk attributed this departure to what he called 'the proletariat element', i.e. the self-made 'watermen' types among the producers, who could not withstand the temptation to take advantage of the sellers' market in salt which had existed since 1866–7. These men, according to Falk, increased 'quite beyond the necessities of the demand, their capacity of production and although the old steady traders were not carried away by the spirit of extension, over-production again led the way to very disastrous results'.[54]

Fresh arrangements entered into in 1877 worked well and prices were on the whole 'fairly supported' for two or three years. In September 1880 we catch a glimpse of a salt meeting which had 'put sixpence on the price of salt'.[55] Nevertheless by March 1881 the formation of a new association had become necessary. This body had to contend with a diminution in the demand for salt, which meant that artificially high prices could not be maintained. The natural consequences of this state of affairs was a 'break up of the arrangement by which prices had been upheld, up to the 1st April [1883]'. Prices immediately fell from 7s. per ton to 4s. per ton for common salt and from 13s. to 8s. per ton for Calcutta shipments, the lowest figures on record.[56]

---

52 A.R., 1872–3, p. 5. That the figure of 20–25% for surplus capacity was substantially correct may be seen from Falk's statement during an interview with Sclater Booth, President of the Local Government Board, in 1879: 'We are not employing by 20 to 30 per cent the number of men we could do if the trade were better' (A.R., 1877–9, p. 22).

53 A.R., 1875–6, p. 5.

54 A.R., 1887–9, p. 11.

55 The information came out accidentally during the agitation for subsidence compensation of 1880–1 in the salt district. The proprietors (who for three-quarters of a century had pinned their faith to price regulation and the inelasticity of demand for salt) claimed that the proposed levy of a mere 3d. per ton on all salt in brine raised to the surface would interfere seriously with their profits. On the other hand Thomas Ward, himself a saltmaker and supporter of the Cheshire Salt Districts Compensation Bill, came to the conclusion 'that the price of salt was independent of the demand, and that foreign competition was so slight that all [sic? any] advance in the price of several shillings per ton, maintained for many months, did not detrimentally affect the trade'. (Calvert, Salt in Cheshire, pp. 388–91, 397–8. See also A.R., 1877–9, p. 5).

56 A.R., 1881–2, p. 5; 1882–3, pp. 32–3; 1883–4, p. 5. One cause of the falling off in the

In June 1884, when an otherwise unrecorded pool scheme terminated after a short existence, Falk circulated to the trade his first scheme for the formation of a Salt Union, but 'although approved of by the large members, it could not be carried, and as a substitute a syndicate of the makers of Calcutta salt was devised upon a legal basis, which enable them to carry on for a couple of years their business without utter ruin'.[57] The success of this scheme, which lasted until 1886, naturally aroused the jealousy of the makers who catered for the other markets and received lower prices. Just before its breakdown, Falk, still pursuing the idea of a complete union of interests, wrote:

... every mind in the Chamber is now addressing itself earnestly to a remedy of that extraordinary anomaly which allows a price of 9s. f.o.b. for common salt to co-exist with 13s. f.o.b. for Calcutta salt. It may be urged in partial explanation that we have a monopoly in Calcutta more exclusive than in any other part of the world ... The moral to be drawn is that makers of common should combine with the same firmness and ready self-sacrifice as their more judicious friends![58]

With the collapse of the Calcutta syndicate in July 1886, 'a war of annihilation' broke out, extending to 'all and every description of salt manufacturer', and complete chaos ruled in the trade. Prices touched new low levels and manufacture was said to be carried on at a very serious loss. Falk continued to stress 'the enormous advantages of a complete consolidation' of all salt proprietors 'in one well-designed corporation'. He realised from bitter experience that 'no scheme which does not absolutely control the make as well as the market' could be practicable – 'Deposits of large sums and guarantee funds we know are illusions'. In addition to this, Falk went on: 'the tendency of the age is for an amalgamation and co-operation of all manufacturers, in order to lay the giant bully competition'.[59] And so, at one of the customary meetings of the trade in December 1887, he made his historic second and stronger plea for the formation of a Salt Union. His scheme attracted attention in the London press and, what was more to the

demand for salt was the widespread adoption of the new Solvay process for the manufacture of chemicals.

57 *A.R.*, 1887–9, p. 12; 1884–5, p. 18; 1885–6, p. 5. Falk's project of 1884 was not the first of its kind. In 1871–2 some leading Manchester capitalists had 'invited the Salt Trade to a conference, having for its object the absorption of the Salt Trade into a limited company'. In spite of the great interest aroused by this scheme and a well attended meeting of salt proprietors at Northwich, no tangible result followed (*A.R.*, 1871–2, p. 6).

58 *A.R.*, 1885–6, pp. 5–6.

59 *A.R.*, 1885–6, p. 26; see also p. 7.

point in London financial circles, so that after prolonged negotiations Falk's Salt Union, Ltd., was registered as a company with a capital of £3 millions on 6 October 1888. It comprised not only the works, but all the really proved brine lands of Cheshire and Worcestershire, as well as the Irish salt-lands, mines and works, together with the most important works at Middlesbrough.[60]

The history of the Cheshire salt trade in the period under review seriously modifies the generally-accepted idea of the mid-nineteenth century as an era of unregulated competition, although the various restriction schemes did in fact tend to break down after a few months' existence. These early attempts at the regulation of salt prices and salt production met with only partial success because of the ease with which new competitors could enter an expanding trade. In the more difficult business conditions of the late 1870s and the 1880s, therefore, the drive towards regulation began to include efforts to discourage the small producers, efforts which seemed to have succeeded by 1888.

FALK AND HIS WORKERS, 1868–88

Falk appears to have had very mixed ideas about labour management. He built cottages for his workers and founded the Meadow Bank Friendly Society in 1860 for their benefit, but labour troubles in the later 1860s show him in a different light.

In 1868 a great strike for higher wages took place among the workers in the salt district and lasted for two and half months. It involved about 7,000 men. There were three classes of labour in the salt boiling works: (a) skilled tradesmen, such as carpenters and blacksmiths; (b) the 'wallers', who drew the crystallised salt to the sides of the evaporating pan with a large rake and then lifted it out with a spade;[61] (c) labourers employed 'at common work, shifting coal and cinders'.[62] The wallers had a strong trade union, the Winsford Salt Makers' Association, dating back to at least 1849, which forbade overtime, and, at the time of the 1868 strike, demanded a rise of 3s. from 24s. to 27s. a week. It is not clear whether the labourers, who got 16s. a week, were concerned in this strike. The 35 employers, and particularly the small men among them, 'being largely men who had risen from the ranks themselves and being in great sympathy with the labouring population,

60 A.R., 1887–9, pp. 5–6.

61 A.R., Evidence before Select Committee of the House of Commons on Emigration and Immigration (Foreigners), 13 July 1888, Qus. 3237, 3240.

62 Ibid., Qu. 3273.

gradually gave way', according to H. J. Falk.[63] Falk junior made the point that a number of the salt-works proprietors employed relatives as wallers and labourers – in one works, apparently, as many as 43 relatives of the chief proprietor,[64] besides his 7 brothers, were employed. As Falk junior remarked 'The [salt] trade of Cheshire is of a most peculiar kind'.[65]

Falk senior refused to give in, and during the course of the conflict he had a series of conversations with his great friend the pastor of the German church in Liverpool. He also got in touch with the 'German' (presumably Prussian) consul at Liverpool. These two gentlemen helped Falk to recruit about 80 workers from the floating German population of Liverpool and with them he filled the vacant places of the strikers at Meadow Bank works and mine. The Germans accepted 20s. per week as wallers (reduced later in 1868 to 18s.), and as labourers asked for only 12s.

At this time heavy emigration was in progress from Germany *via* Britain to the United States and Canada. The emigrants generally left the Continent from Bremen or Hamburg, crossed to Hull and took the train from Hull, arriving in Manchester over the lines of the Manchester, Sheffield, and Lincolnshire Railway; Falk's son said he had seen a large number of them at Central Station, Manchester, en route for Liverpool. When they arrived in Liverpool a number of them found casual work; others drifted to the Liverpool workhouse, and a number were employed in the chemical works at Widnes. Once Falk senior was known to be willing to employ foreigners, the master of the Liverpool workhouse and the Liverpool Society of the Friends of Foreigners in Distress[66] naturally began to send groups of these men on foot into Cheshire, sometimes as many as 30 or 40, or single men sometimes carried a piece of paper on which was written 'Please direct the bearer to Winsford'.

All went well for a time: the Germans, although inclined to be pugnacious, were hard and satisfactory workers, who were prepared to do an extra half hour's labour, i.e., from closing time at 5.30 p.m. until 6.0 p.m., if necessary. Neither did they object to longer periods of overtime. As H. J. Falk explained: 'They are better [than English workers] because they are much more docile, and they will accommodate themselves to our circumstances, for instance, to tidal necessities. We have to load our barges [with salt] at certain periods of the tide, which are just the same as the tides in

63 Ibid., Qu. 3237.
64 Ibid., Qu. 3362.
65 Qu. 3362.
66 Qus. 3428–30. In 1888 the Secretary of this society was 'a former charge clerk' of H. E. Falk's.

Liverpool'.[67] Most of the Germans, however, regarded England merely as a stepping stone to North America. While at Winsford they would learn a little English, and save about £5 or £6, with which they would buy their tickets for the transatlantic trip, or else relatives already in the U.S.A. would send them the tickets. Others drifted away to work in the Liverpool sugar refineries and a few, but only a very few, went to other salt-works.[68] Over a period of twenty years (1868–88) not one foreign worker stayed more than seven and a half years in Falk's employ, but fresh arrivals from Germany via Liverpool were constantly taking the places of those who left.

At first there was great resentment among the English workers and the general population of the Meadow Bank district against the foreigners: '. . . we had a few rather serious fights when the Germans came in 1868. I remember, as a boy, going out myself amongst the cottages and having some rather difficult peace-making to do . . .'[69] Then towards the end of 1876 and the beginning of 1877 a complete change in the character of this influx began: the Germans were rapidly replaced by what were loosely called 'Hungarians' or 'Russian Poles' but in actual fact were for the most part Poles from Austrian Galicia, subjects of the Emperor Francis Joseph. The reasons put forward for this new wave were, first of all, agricultural depression in Galicia, and, secondly, the desire to escape military service which was more rigidly enforced in Austria as a result of the Russo–Turkish War of 1876–8. It was even said that there were a few Bosnians and Herzegovinians among the new arrivals. The Poles were mainly agricultural labourers, although a few of them had worked in the salt mines of Hallein, near Salzburg, and Wieliczka, near Cracow. Curiously enough they were said to be much more docile than the Germans.[70] At times, when they arrived at Meadow Bank in gangs of about thirty to forty, Falk found himself quite unable to employ all applicants.[71]

By 1888 the foreign colony at Meadow Bank numbered eighty-seven men and five women. How were they housed? Falk owned about one hundred cottages at Meadow Bank, and eight of these were allocated to the foreign workers. They were built of clinker or 'basses' as the material was called locally, and do not appear to have been particularly attractive.

67 Qu. 3320.
68 Qu. 3316.
69 Qu. 3303, evidence of H. J. Falk.
70 Qu. 3419.
71 Qu. 3370.

Theoretically only four persons were supplied to inhabit one cottage. Each cottage was in charge of a captain, who paid Falk 4s. a week and collected a shilling each from the other three occupants. Besides these cottages there was a large dwelling house, formerly the residence of Falk himself, containing a billiards-room 50 ft. by 24 ft. and a dining room 40 ft. by 25 ft. Originally Falk had tried to run it as a private lodging house for the foreigners, but this plan had not been successful. So he had partitioned the house into flats, and in 1888 twenty-eight persons (ten less than capacity) were living there, eight of them in either the former billiards-room or the dining-room. There was also a stable cottage attached to this property which housed seven people.[72] Between eight and twelve persons lived in each cottage, some of which had two rooms, some three, some four.[73] The occupants dressed very roughly; in their native country they were said to wear leather suits, but in Cheshire they wore clothes made of sacking, in which they slept. Their beds were described as large trays on which were placed sacks full of straw. Their diet was Spartan, 'cow's lights chopped and boiled with cabbage being regarded as a toothsome, not to say luxurious dish'.[74] The sanitary arrangements were primitive and filth and fleas abounded.

One feature of the foreign community which disturbed public opinion was the disparity between the sexes, as there were very few women. The special commissioner of *The Umpire* asked a local informant a number of questions on this point in 1889, referring to the time when the colony had numbered between 100 and 120 persons:

'Did they marry?'
'Not much'. This was said with a meaning laugh.
'Do you wish me to understand their morals were only indifferent?'
'Indifferent – no. They were bad – very bad . . .'[75]

The first public comment on conditions at Meadow Bank came in 1885, when Dr. John M. Fox, Medical Officer of Health for Cheshire, attended a meeting of the Winsford Local Board to report on the place with the object of awakening 'the community to a sense of serious alarm and indignation'.[76] Little seems to have happened as a result of this action, but in 1886 the foreign

---

72 Qu. 3441–3.
73 Qu. 3444–5.
74 *Sunday Chronicle*, 5 September 1886.
75 *The Umpire*, 10 March 1889.
76 Newspaper cutting, unidentified, dated 4 July 1885 (Falk Papers).

colony at Meadow Bank attracted the attention of the *Sunday Chronicle,* which printed a long report on 5 September, from its 'special commissioner', the general tone of which can be gauged from the headline: 'A Cheshire Salt Hell'. The newspaper followed this up on 12 September, with an editorial condemning the employment of cheap foreign labour in degrading conditions when English workmen were 'idle or half-employed'. A full-scale public investigation did not take place until 13 July 1888 when Herman John Falk, one of H. E. Falk's sons, gave evidence before the Select Committee of the House of Commons, which was looking into the whole subject of the immigration of foreigners into, and their emigration from, this country.[77]

In the previous May the surveyor to the Winsford Local Board had reported on the overcrowding and insanitary conditions in the hostels inhabited by Falk's foreign workers; legally these hostels were 'houses let in lodgings' and the Local Board's bye-laws relating to such dwelling had been both ignored and contravened.[78] H. J. Falk promised to put the irregularities straight, and during the ensuing months the number of the foreigners seems to have been reduced. Rather late in the day another Sunday newspaper, *The Umpire,* took up the matter and published a long and highly-coloured article on the subject on 3 March 1889 in which the special commissioner promised another instalment[79] of revelations in the next issue 'which will convince my readers, I fancy, that it is quite time England was for the English alone, instead of being the dumping ground for unsuitable, half-starved, servile foreigners, who rob the British workingman of work and his children of bread.'

In the course of time the colony withered away, as its members departed in ones and twos for the New World. The clinker cottages were demolished in the mid-1940s and today the only memorial in Cheshire to these unhappy victims of political and economic change in Central Europe is contained in the parish registers of Whitegate, which record the burials of those who found a resting place from their wanderings in the soil of the salt district.[80]

---

77 Among those who questioned Falk was W. R. Cremer trade unionist M.P. and one of the founders of the First International in 1864.

78 *Chester Chronicle, 9 June 1888; see also Warrington Guardian,* 9 June 1888.

79 This duly appeared in *The Umpire,* 10 March 1889.

80 Among the names are: Louisa Koenig (11 August 1868), Emil Agatzou (7 May 1873), Hermann Dittberner (15 November 1874), John Andrew Poislow (14 November 1878), Maria Magdelena Bederski (3 September 1881) and Lugviet Majura (6 August 1886).

CHAPTER VII

THE MOVEMENT FOR THE EXTENSION OF OWENS COLLEGE, MANCHESTER, 1863–73

In the evening [of 7 October 1873] a conversazione was given at the college, the whole building being thrown open and brilliantly lighted. All the rooms and corridors were crowded to excess with ladies and gentlemen who desired to take part in the opening of the extended college, or who wished to see the 'lions', and to enjoy themselves.

Joseph Thompson, *The Owens College* (1886)

By the mid-1860s Owens College, founded in 1851, had survived those teething troubles which had earlier caused the *Manchester Guardian* of 9 July 1858 to pronounce it 'a mortifying failure', although the numbers both of its staff and of its students were still minute by modern standards. In his autobiography (*The Life and Experiences of Sir Henry Enfield Roscoe*, 1906) Roscoe later reminisced about these days:

The institution was at that time nearly in a state of collapse, and this fact had impressed itself even on the professors. I was standing one evening, preparing myself for my lecture by smoking a cigar at the back gate of the building, when a tramp accosted me and asked me if this was the Manchester Night Asylum. I replied that it was not, but that if he would call again in six months he might find lodgings there! That this opinion as to the future of the college was also generally prevalent is shown by the fact that the tenancy of a house in Dover Street was actually refused to me when the landlord learnt that I was a professor in that institution.

During the period from 1859–60 to 1864–65 the number of day students on the books at Richard Cobden's former house in Quay Street, off Deansgate, had risen from 57 to 127, while the number of evening students increased from 77 to 312. By the time the College moved to its new premises in 1873

OWENS COLLEGE, QUAY STREET, MANCHESTER.

the figures had risen to 334 day and 557 evening students. The College prepared students for the examinations of University College, London, and such students could attend either the day or the evening courses. In addition there were certain evening classes for school teachers from Manchester and Salford. The foundation of Manchester Working Man's College in 1858 also led indirectly to the expansion of Owens College. This College, which had been formed in order to provide more advanced courses than those generally available in mechanics' institutes, had originally held its classes on the premises of the Manchester Mechanics' Institution, but in spite of the encouragement provided by the presence of such Christian Socialist celebrities as Thomas Hughes and the Rev. F. D. Maurice at its first annual meeting in January 1859 the numbers of working-class students had fallen off so much that by the autumn of 1861 the classes had been absorbed into Owens College.

The change in the fortunes of Owens College after 1857–58 was to a large extent the result of the drive and good judgment of three men, John G. Greenwood, Principal from 1857 to 1889, who had a passion for productive committee work, Thomas Ashton (1818–98), a public spirited Manchester cotton manufacturer, and Henry Enfield Roscoe (1833–1915), the young

OWENS COLLEGE, OXFORD ROAD.
The new buildings as they appeared *c.* 1876.

Unitarian professor of chemistry appointed by the Trustees in 1857, who as Sir Henry Roscoe was to become a politician of science, <a phenomenon> more common today than in Victorian times. During the writing of his remarkable book *Fifty Years of Work without Wages* (1912) Charles Rowley of Ancoats persuaded Roscoe to give some reminiscences of this period. Roscoe wrote:

> Coming from Heidelberg university, I saw that the only chance of making a successful college in Manchester was to give importance to scientific studies, and in this Greenwood fully agreed. So after a few years of active work in chemistry I induced the trustees to appoint a Professor of Physics – and Clifton came and was a tower of strength. From 1857 onwards things looked up. Our students increased in number, original scientific work began, students were gradually in-oculated with the spirit of research, and the College became known as a place where a manufacturer could send his son to learn something that would prove useful to him. Our men took high honours in chem-istry year after year in the University of London, so that the name of Owens became a household word to people interested in scientific

education throughout the land. There was certainly 'go' and fervour about the dwellers in those old premises in Quay Street. All the 'old men' of the years 1857–67 look back with feelings of fond regard to the shabby rooms, crowded laboratory, and squalid surroundings of those times. And when Clifton and I with dear John Holme Nicholson met the men of those forty years (or so) afterwards at dinner in the 'Randolph' at Oxford, we might all be looking back at days spent in an Oxford College centuries old, instead of in a back slum in smoky Manchester, so bright were the reminiscences recalled and so sincere the gratitude expressed.

Similarly, George Harwood, MP for Bolton and a master cotton spinner, wrote to Rowley:

He [Greenwood] had only been the Principal a few years when I became a student [in 1861–62], but already he had made everything in the College hum.

Overcrowding had become so noticeable in the Quay Street building by 1863–64 that on 25 January 1865 the Trustees of Owens College decided to appoint a small committee to consider the subject of more accommodation, particularly as the Manchester Natural History Society, founded in 1821, and in possession of a large and valuable museum, was in rapid decline, and wished to dispose of its collections. Admissions to its museum had fallen from 18,000 in 1853 to 5,000 in 1863 and subscriptions had decreased alarmingly. The Society would be prepared to hand over its collections and property to Owens College provided they could be adequately housed and serviced, which they could not be in Quay Street. The valuable collections of the Manchester Geological Society, founded in 1838, were also in danger of dispersal if no suitable home could be found for them. In addition the Trustees wished to establish a School of Medicine in collaboration with the Board of Manchester Royal Infirmary and the directors of the Manchester Royal School of Medicine. Clearly there existed plenty of solid ground on which to build an academic empire.

The committee of Trustees asked Principal Greenwood and the professors to submit a report on 'the extent and nature of the accommodation required for the purposes of the College'. This report (February 1865) pointed out that in 1864–65 more students were being taught in the Owens College Quay Street building than were studying in the main departments of University College, London in 1862–63, the last year for which a return existed: 'probably . . . in no institution of the kind in the kingdom are so many persons under instruction in so confined a space'. The forty-eight students of the professor of physics, Clifton, had to squeeze themselves into desks built to seat 37, and Roscoe's chemistry laboratory, equipped for 39 students, had been extended by converting ten of the ordinary working benches into twenty half-benches. It had proved impossible to form the department of civil engineering proposed in 1863 because of the lack of space:

> It is plain that there should be found in the North of England some one central school of Civil Engineering, Surveying, Architecture, and Mining. A school with these aims exists, but is not very successful, in Durham, and attempts have been made to found one in Sheffield and in other towns. We think that Owens College contains the nucleus of a very efficient school of these branches of Art and Science, and that such a school attached to the College would be warmly welcomed, not only by Manchester, but by the many populous and busy manufacturing towns around and would give us a hold on those towns which would react beneficially on the other branches of the College. While we can never hope to rival the ancient Universities in the study of Literature and Mathematics, we see no reason why Owens College should not aspire to be the first school of applied and experimental Science in the country.

The early stages of growth of the examinations industry also gave rise to problems. The Owens College was the only institution in England which held the complete series of degree examinations for the University of London and the lack of a large examination hall had begun to cause considerable difficulty. Clifton and Roscoe also submitted alarming reports showing the growing vitiation of the atmosphere of lecture rooms by carbon dioxide during the progress of lectures, vitiation which arose not only from the presence of students and lecturer, but also from ten gas lighting jets. This portion of the report was not publicized at the time 'lest an alarm should be raised among the students and their parents', and indeed appears to have been unduly alarmist.

The Principal and professors had also carried out some consumer research into the catchment areas from which students came and on the site of any proposed extension. In spite of its proximity to Deansgate, Quay Street was in the mid-1860s not considered to be 'on or near any great leading thoroughfare', and the immediate neighbourhood to the north and east was alleged to be 'of the most disreputable character'. In addition, plans were then afoot to construct a railway (never in fact built) parallel to Deansgate, which would run between that thoroughfare and Quay Street.

The choice therefore lay between a new and more central site, where the cost of sufficient land would be enormous, and a comparatively suburban site, 'within easy distance of the centre of the city and the principal railway stations and not unfavourably placed as regards any of the principal suburbs'[1], where land would be cheaper. It should be remembered that the Trustees of Owens College had no power to spend any portion of the original endowment on the purchase of land and the erection of buildings.

An appeal to the public of Manchester and the surrounding towns was to be made for money with which to buy land and erect theron 'commodious and stately buildings', so that Owens College would virtually provide 'the foundations of . . . the University of South Lancashire and of the neighbouring parts of Cheshire and Yorkshire'. The appeal made much of the fact that the example of Glasgow, where an appeal for money for new university buildings had recently been launched, showed that there was no incompatibility between 'the spirit of ancient learning and the spirit of modern enterprise'.

The Overend–Gurney commercial crisis of 1866 led to a postponement of the appeal, but towards the end of the year the second attempt to found a department of civil engineering and mechanical engineering succeeded. On 11 December 1866 the leading master engineers of the Manchester district, including Joseph Whitworth, William Fairbairn, Charles F. Beyer and John Robinson, met 'with a view to raise £10,000' for the establishment of a chair in these two subjects at Owens College, an appeal which brought in over £9,500 during the following year.

Meanwhile Roscoe had become somewhat impatient at the slow progress of the extension scheme and had resolved to bring in powerful outside help. One Sunday afternoon in 1866 he walked out to Ford Bank, the Didsbury villa of Thomas Ashton (1818–98) in order to enlist his powerful support for the plans to extend Owens College. Ashton was a member of the Ashton family of Hyde, cotton spinners, and had received his higher education at Heidelberg, partly because as a Unitarian, he was debarred from attending either Oxford or Cambridge. Although Roscoe's account of this interview with Ashton was written down much later and cannot be accepted without some reservations[2], it appears that the cotton magnate was at first

---

1   'Suburbs' in 1866 meant Cheetham Hill, Broughton, Harpurhey, Smedley Lane, Ardwick, Longsight, Victoria Park, Rusholme, Plymouth Grove, Hulme, Old Trafford, Whalley Range and Greenheys, together with Salford and Pendleton.

2   According to Roscoe (*Life and Experience*), he said to Ashton: ' "You must help us in placing this college of ours on a footing worthy of the city". To this he objected, with the remark that the Governors of the private trust were strong Churchmen and mainly Tories, with whom he had little sympathy. The place, he said, was moribund, and he did not like to

unenthusiastic, but finally agreed to place his energy, enthusiasm and very considerable wealth (he left an estate of well over £500,000 in 1898, in spite of considerable benefactions during his lifetime) behind the movement.

In the winter of 1866–67 the New Buildings Committee of the Trustees issued two further reports suggesting that the time was now ripe for the Trustees to meet privately well-wishers who had already promised to subscribe. This meeting took place on 23 January 1867. It decided to raise a fund of £100,000 or upwards, and the appeal was to be launched at a public meeting in the old Manchester Town Hall. The steering committee consisted of Alderman W. Neild, W. H. Houldsworth, and John Robinson (trustees of Owens College), Principal Greenwood, Professors Christie and Roscoe, and J. L. Kennedy, Thomas Ashton, Richard Johnson and C. F. Beyer, all prominent Manchester industrialists either in cotton or engineering. This public meeting of 1 February 1867 produced a large and influential attendance, and a resolution proposed by the Very Reverend the Dean of Manchester, Dr Cowie, and seconded by Oliver Heywood, the banker, called upon 'the public of the district to unite for the purpose of developing the College on a more comprehensive scale, and in appropriate and convenient buildings'. Another resolution constituted all those present a committee for raising a fund of not less than £100,000, and £150,000 if possible. On the motion of W. R. Callender, sen. (d.1872)[3], one of the leaders of Manchester Liberalism, and John Platt, Liberal MP for Oldham, a strong and representative Extension Executive Committee was set up. It met for the first time on 13 February at the Royal Institution in Mosley Street (now the City Art Gallery) and appointed four sub-committees for canvassing and finance, the selection and purchase of a site, the general planning of the new buildings, and a 'constitution committee' for 'matters connected with the extension and rearrangement of the courses of study, and of amalgamation with an application to other educational institutions'. A general secretary was appointed in the person of John Watts, Ph.D. of Giessen (1818–87), the former follower of Robert Owen, and a prominent local educationalist. Local committees were later set up in Bolton and Oldham. They performed some useful work in fund-raising, but the other towns of the cotton district, with the exception of Stockport, did not exhibit much collective enthusiasm for the cause. By 1869 over £91,000 in all had either been paid or promised.

undertake the task of resuscitation.'

3   Not to be confused with his son W. R. Callender, jun. (d. 1876), who served on the Constitution Committee and was the chief architect of the revival of Manchester Conservatism in the 1860s and 1870s.

The chairman and most influential member of the Site Committee was Murray Gladstone, chairman of the Manchester Royal Exchange 1865–75 (d.1875), cousin of W. E. Gladstone, and a Manchester merchant with Indian connections. A number of sites were considered at or in the vicinity of All Saints, but the Committee found that as soon as its intended purpose in buying any plot of land became known, the asking price increased. Finally, in March 1868 Gladstone purchased secretly a large and cheap site of about 4 acres 'which was being offered for private sale on favourable terms' in his own name and at his own risk. It contained 19,164 square yards, and cost £29,100, forming 'an oblong plot, with a frontage of 127 yards down Burlington Street on the south, and 177 yards down Coupland Street on the north'. Gladstone's bold speculation received the approval of the Executive Committee and the land was later conveyed from Gladstone to Ashton as chairman. In the period of disappointment in 1869 when it became evident that no government assistance would be forthcoming, alternative sites in Ardwick on the Stockport Road, in the Cheetham Hill district and in the Nelson Street area were considered and rejected.

Meanwhile the Building Sub-Committee had obtained plans and details of newly-erected 'academical accommodation' in Glasgow, Oxford, Cambridge, London, Cork, and Belfast. During the summer vacation of 1868 Principal Greenwood and Professor Roscoe made a tour of inspection of the universities and high schools of Bonn, Göttingen, Hanover, Berlin, Leipzig, Freiberg (Saxony), Heidelberg, Karlsruhe, Munich and Zurich and particular reference to those 'of peculiarly scientific note, for the purpose of gathering information as to the practical working of those establishments'. Their report (December 1868) is a valuable document on the state of German scientific and technical education. In May 1868 Roscoe had attended a meeting of the Lancashire Alkali Manufacturers' Association at Liverpool in an attempt to secure the support of the leaders of the local chemical industry and on 18 March 1869 Ashton, Greenwood and Roscoe circularized them again; a sum of between £10,000 to £15,000 would be needed to build and equip a chemical laboratory at Owens for about 100 students and adequate for the needs of the North West:

> A recent inspection of the Chief Chemical Laboratories on the Continent . . . has convinced us that in England we have no Chemical Schools which, as regards buildings and appliances, can be compared with many in Germany.

The cost of the recently erected chemical laboratory at Bonn was £18,000,

of that at Berlin £45,000, at Leipzig £12,000 and at Zurich £20,000. Informed opinion in Britain was at this time becoming uneasily aware of those
deficiencies of British higher education, as compared with Germany,
particularly in science and technology, which the Royal (Devonshire) Commission on Scientific Instruction was to investigate between 1871 and 1875
and it is against this background that Roscoe's activities must be viewed.

By the end of 1868 the Executive Committee had enough subscribed
funds to decide to go ahead with the buildings, and early in 1869 appointed
the great Victorian architect Alfred Waterhouse, RA, to design the new
Owens Extension College. After prolonged debate, centring around C. F.
Beyer's wish to see the proposed buildings fronting on to Oxford Road, the
Executive Committee decided to site them some distance back from but
parallel to the west side of Oxford Street. These final plans were accepted by
the general committee in December 1868, and allowed the later formation
in 1888–98 of the present quadrangle. Although £40,000 had been mentioned earlier as the maximum cost, the final contract awarded to Thomas
Clay and Son was for £54,329. The contractors began to dig the foundations in May 1870.

From the first hopes had been expressed in Manchester that the Government might be persuaded to contribute towards the cost of extending Owens
College, and the Executive Committee made strenuous efforts to persuade
successive administrations that the North West, which at this time provided
about a third of the country's exports, had at least as good a claim on the
public money voted for higher education as Glasgow and the Irish colleges.
As early as 1 May 1867 Roscoe had called the attention of the Executive
Committee to the rather surprising news that the Lords of the Council on
Education and of the Treasury were proposing to reconstruct an institution
known by the depressing name of the Museum of Irish Industry as a new
college of science in Dublin at an annual cost of £7,000 by endowing ten
chairs of mathematics and natural science and founding nine scholarships.
In the financial year 1868–69 the Government grants-in-aid for higher
education and learning in the whole of the United Kingdom amounted to
£57,405 for buildings (Aberdeen, London, Glasgow and Queen's University, Ireland) and £69,733 for other purposes to institutions ranging from
learned societies, the Belfast theological professors, the School of Mines in
London (which was a long way from the nearest mine of any sort) and the
Scots universities and colleges. Of the total of £127,138 Scotland managed
to secure no less than £39,384 and Ireland £25,000, leaving England and
Wales proportionately extremely under-endowed.

On 13 January 1868 the future Sir Bernhard Samuelson, bt. (d. 1905), MP for Banbury, who had managed a Manchester engineering firm from 1842 to 1846 before embarking upon a highly successful and adventurous career as an ironmaster and agricultural implement maker elsewhere, waited upon the Executive Committee to give them the benefit of his investigations into technical education abroad. He also mentioned some recommendations which he had made about the work of the Owens College Extension Committee to the Vice President of the Committee of Council on Education (the remote ancestor of the Department of Education and Science). Samuelson had chaired a Select Committee of the House of Commons on Scientific Instruction in 1868 and the evidence of many competent witnesses before this Committee had established that Owens College was 'one of the very few colleges in England which could be developed into a Science School of the first order'. Samuelson clearly could not know what the Government intended to do but made various suggestions as to the tactics the Executive Committee might adopt in applying for State aid. Acting on this advice the Committee circularized MPs and others favourable to the movement.

Ashton, Houldsworth and Greenwood were appointed a committee to arrange interviews with members of Lord Derby's Government, and circulars were sent to the mayors of all the municipalities in Lancashire, Cheshire and the West Riding requesting them to accompany the deputation. The first interview with the Duke of Marlborough, Lord President of the Council, and Lord Robert Montague, MP, Vice President, took place on 5 March 1868, by which time Disraeli had succeeded Derby as Premier (27 February). Ashton explained that £150,000 'would be barely sufficient for present development' of Owens College. The Duke of Marlborough, in reply, stated that 'the time had come when the whole question of such colleges and the education provided in them would have to be taken into consideration by Parliament. He personally was in favour of making grants to such institutions as Owens College, and could scarcely see why it should be less favourably treated than Glasgow, although that was a university. Hitherto grants had been made principally to the metropolitan colleges of the three kingdoms, and it might be inconvenient to depart from that limit.' The committee arranged for a second interview, on 24 March, this time with the new Prime Minister (who had been Chancellor of the Exchequer in the former administration) at No. 10 Downing Street. The reception of the delegation by Disraeli and his Chancellor of the Exchequer, Ward Hunt, has been amusingly described by Joseph Thompson:

> It was an interesting scene and characteristic of the chief actor. The room was well filled and many had to stand. The Premier slipped in

noiselessly and sat with his back to the window. He kept his eyes down when the gentlemen spoke and the addresses were delivered, but he was not insensible to what was going on . . . In his reply he assured the deputation of the great importance he attached to the subject . . . laid before him. The college had evidently done good work and was destined to make its influence felt. It had his fullest sympathy, and would command the greatest consideration from his colleagues when he brought its claims before them. 'But', said he, 'if Her Majesty's government, in the exigencies of the state, should be unable to comply with your request, I am quite certain that the public spirit and the generosity of Lancashire will not allow the interest of the college to suffer.' This was done in his grandest manner. He had a slight cold, and held in his hand a large cambric handkerchief edged with black, which he freely used as a lady would use her fan, as a valuable aid to effect. The impression left on the minds of the hearers varied with their idiosyncrasies; some were hopeful, others feared the politeness was a cover for refusal. Nothing came of the application.

Later, in the House of Commons, Jacob Bright, MP for Manchester 1867–74, and brother of John Bright, pointed out that Glasgow University had recently received from the public funds £120,000 spread over a period of years, and pleaded for a similar grant to Owens College of £100,000, to be paid in five yearly instalments. This plea was followed up in June 1868 by a personal interview with Disraeli by Sir Thomas Bazley, MP for Manchester 1858–80, and the Hon. Algernon F. Egerton, one of the Lancashire MPs.

Disraeli 'freely admitted his approval of the proposal which had been made, but stated that nothing could be done or finally considered before the commencement of the next financial year,' partly because the defence expenditure had amounted to £2m more than the estimates. Later evidence suggests that a Treasury minute in favour of a grant to Owens College was indeed drafted, but Disraeli's Conservative Government fell as a result of the Liberal victory in the General Election of November 1868, and the process of lobbying had to begin all over again. W. E. Gladstone, a firm believer in strict economy, cheap government and leaving money to fructify in the pocket of the taxpayer, was now Prime Minister and his Chancellor of the Exchequer, Robert Lowe, held much the same opinions as his chief.

Between November 1868 and early February 1869 the Executive Committee drew up a memorial to the Lords of the Treasury, which made a reasoned plea for a grant to the Owens College, particularly with a view to developing it as School of Science:

A conviction is now widely spread that there should be in England, as in France and Germany, Colleges giving instruction at once complete and thorough, in all the leading branches of Applied and Experimental Science.

This conviction is justified by the evidence taken in 1868, before a Committee of the House of Commons, on Scientific Instruction. It is felt that what is wanted is the foundation, not of workshops for teaching manufacturing processes, but of Schools of Science.

(1) In which those who are to direct the industry of the country may receive thorough training in Mathematics, and the principles of Physical Science.

(2) In which those artisans who have proved themselves to be possessed of superior parts may, by acquiring a knowledge of Science, fit themselves to fill more important positions, and

(3) In which competent teachers may be trained, both for the higher posts, and for teaching soundly the rudiments of Science in primary and secondary schools.

Such schools, to be of real efficiency and the greatest usefulness, must necessarily be maintained within the immediate neighbourhood of the manufacturing populations and establishments they are mainly intended to serve. It is evident that no place is more fitting than Manchester to be the seat of such a School of Science. The effort now being made to enlarge and refound Owens College, which is already doing a considerable amount of satisfactory work in this very direction, affords an opportunity of *at once*, and with exceptional ease, supplying the need in the place where it is felt the most.

On 18 February 1869 an influential deputation, organized by the Extension Committee, waited upon the new Prime Minister 'with high expectations', but received little comfort.

Mr. Gladstone explained that Mr. Lowe had to find the money. There were great difficulties in the way of meeting such an application, but he would take the views of his colleagues upon it. Mr. Ashton pointed out that Manchester was the capital of Lancashire and district, with a population equal to Scotland; that government had shown a disposition to help capitals with science schools, and Owens College would

soon be a college of science for the whole of England. He referred to
the case of Glasgow, and said that if the grant there had been to a
university Manchester must be made one. Mr. Gladstone thought that
enlarged the question, and made it one to be considered with others.

A further attempt, later in the year, by Jacob Bright, MP, to challenge the
estimates in the debate in the House of Commons on the vote for salaries and
expenses of the Science and Arts Department met with no success, and it
became clear that the money for the extension to Owens would have to be
raised entirely by the freewill offerings of the people of the North West,
'without', as Joseph Thompson put it, 'submitting the college to the interference or subjecting it to the bondage of permanent officials in London'. One
member of the Committee, Thomas Wrigley, stated that he was glad the
Government had refused them a grant: 'There was plenty of money to be had
in Manchester, let them look for that and be independent of government help
and interference'.

The constitutional problem now became paramount. In 1868 the Executive Committee had asked Professor James Bryce, Regius Professor of Civil
Law at Oxford, to advise on the constitution of the extended college and on
14 July the Constitution Sub-Committee recommended the introduction of a
bill into Parliament in the session of 1869–70 for the purpose of incorporat-
ing the Owens Extension College and enabling it to absorb the Owens
College. The draft bill received the approval of the Extension Committee on
3 November 1869 and of the trustees of Owens College on 17 February
1870. Out of the twenty-one Governors of the proposed new Extension
College, ten were to be trustees of Owens College. The bill involved some
modification to the wishes of the founder as expressed in his will of 1845,
for example, it was proposed eventually to admit young persons of *both*
sexes. Although Owens had authorized the trustees of his will to apply for a
charter of incorporation, this had never been done, and the will remained the
basic constitutional document of Owens College. Before being introduced
the Owens Extension College Bill had to pass the Standing Orders Committee and here the Chairman, Lord Redesdale, made some stern observations:

> This is a bill for incorporating a non-existent charity, and enabling it
> to annex the property of another charity, setting aside to a great extent
> the expressed intention of the founders. I don't think anything of the
> kind has ever been done, and it would be a very bad precedent.

The Earl of Derby introduced it into the House of Lords, and on the
motion of Lord Redesdale it was referred to the Attorney-General, Sir

Robert P. Collier, who in general concurred with the observations of Lord Redesdale and remarked that in law any move towards the enlargement of an existing charitable foundation usually proceeded from within the foundation, rather than from outside bodies. The Attorney-General went on:

> Your lordships will observe that, in the proposed institution which is to absorb Owens College, there is no provision resembling one of the two fundamental conditions of the Owens trust, viz.: the preference first in favour of Manchester, and then of South Lancashire; that there is no account given of the collateral foundations which are by section twenty-five transferred absolutely in favour of the proposed institution; that dispositions of property by the proposed body are not made subject to the sanction of the Charity Commissioners; and that it does not appear why the contracts of the proposed corporation should not be regulated by the general law.

It soon became clear, however, that the Attorney-General had not read the bill very carefully and the promoters were advised, first of all to obtain the official consent of the Owens College Trustees to the scheme and then to secure the approval of the Charity Commissioners to the proposed enlargements and modifications to the testamentary wishes of the founder. After consultations with Sir Thomas Bazley, MP, a deputation consisting of Thomas Ashton, R. D. Darbishire and Professor R. C. Christie waited on the Attorney-General and discussed his objections point by point. The Attorney-General agreed to send a second message to the House of Lords in the light of this further information. Unfortunately early in March 1870 a Manchester solicitor, Stephen Heelis, one of George Faulkner's executors, and therefore one of John Owens's personal representatives, objected to a number of features in the bill, mainly the power to extend the benefits of the charity to women, and the possibility that the proposed new 'Owens College, Manchester' might admit students under fourteen years of age and teach them school subjects rather than have older students studying subjects at university level. The Extension Committee was forced to compromise with Heelis, in view of the critical position of the bill, and to excise the clause relating to the possibility of admitting women to the proposed new college. Lord Redesdale still objected strongly to the bill, in spite of another deputation to him (7 March) and in self-defence the Extension Committee drew up two memoranda explaining their point of view for circulation in Parliament. Fortunately the Government, after considering the matter, announced through Earl de Grey (later the Marquess of Ripon) that Redesdale's objections should not be allowed to impede the progress of the bill and it passed its second reading in the Lords by 33–6. Unfortunately neither Redesdale nor Heelis was satisfied and complicated negotiations were necessary before the bill went to the Commons (April–May 1870) where Jacob Bright, MP, exercised his independent judgment as an MP to restore the clause making possible the enrolment of women in the College. After further negotiations Bright agreed, on the third reading, to the substitution of the neutral phrase' such young persons as the proper authorities of the college may from time to time direct' for his original direct mention of 'persons of the female sex'. The bill passed its third reading in the Commons easily and received the royal assent on 4 July 1870. The Owens Extension College was now in being as a body corporate.

By the end of the summer of 1870 things were shaping so well for the Extension Committee that a grand stone-laying ceremony could be organized for the autumn. The seventh Duke of Devonshire consented to accept the position of President of the College and a number of life governors had been appointed – the Lord President of the Council, for example, nominated Sir Thomas Bazley, MP, Thomas H. Huxley, FRS, and Matthew Arnold, DCL. The Duke laid the first stone on Friday, 23 September 1870 in the presence of a large and distinguished company. Thomas Ashton stated that the new buildings would accommodate about 600 day students and a much larger number of evening students. The buildings, the fittings and the site would cost about £90,000, and £30,000 more was needed. When Ashton had concluded, the architect Alfred Waterhouse presented the Duke with an engraved trowel, while Thomas Clay, the contractor, then deposited in a cavity below the foundation stone a glass bottle containing current coins, copies of the three Manchester daily newspapers, the London *Times* and printed documents issued by the Extension Committee. The cavity was covered with a lead plate, bearing on the lower side an inscription: 'The first stone of this building erected for the Owens College, Manchester, was laid by His Grace the Duke of Devonshire, KG, FRS, etc., the first president, September 23rd, 1870. Architect: Alfred Waterhouse, Esq.' Unfortunately the exact whereabouts of this stone is now unknown.

On the same day, after a sumptuous lunch in the old Town Hall, the first meeting of the Court of Governors took place, at which the Registrar of Owens College was appointed Registrar of the Owens Extension College; Alfred Nield was appointed Treasurer; and the Principal and the ten other Professors of Owens College were appointed to equivalent chairs in the new institution. At the same time the Court appointed a new Extension Committee headed by Ashton to raise further funds and 'to conduct the treaty with the trustees of Mr Owens's foundation, and of the trusts attached to his

institution, for the amalgamation thereof with the college . . . and to prosecute the application to the Charity Commissioners of England and Wales for
their approval thereof.'

By November 1870 a draft agreement with the Trustees of Owens College had been prepared and was approved by the Charity Commissioners in
1871 after a long correspondence with their Secretary, Henry M. Vane,
chiefly because of the implied opening of the proposed amalgamated Owens
College, Manchester, to 'young persons of either sex'. The Commissioners
considered that under the terms of Owens's will the education of males
should be considered the primary object of the institution. The Commissioners wished to make two conditions: that the Owens Extension Committee
should be in possession of sufficient funds to open the proposed amalgamated college to women without prejudicing adequate provision for *all* male
students seeking admission and that due arrangements should be made 'for
securing *at all times* the effectual separation of the students of the different
sexes when attending for the purpose of instruction'. After further negotiation the words *all* in the first condition and *at all times* were dropped. The
preference given by the terms of Owens's will to children of parents resident
in Manchester or South Lancashire also gave rise to some difficulty, which
was resolved by the Commissioners' insistence that it should be retained and
applied to the new funds raised since 1867, although such restrictive prefer-
ences had come to be looked upon with disfavour since 1845. The Extension
Committee duly approved the amalgamation scheme in May 1871. Ashton
and his Extension Committee thereupon promoted a second bill in Parliament to ratify the amalgamation of the Owens Extension College and Owens
College, under the title of 'The Owens College, Manchester', as from 1
September 1871. It passed rapidly through all stages in Parliament and
received the royal assent on 24 July 1871.

Once amalgamation was within sight Principal Greenwood took up again
the subject of absorbing the Royal Manchester School of Medicine and
Surgery, a project which had remained dormant for nearly four years. This
School, situated in Pine Street, off York Street, had been established in 1825
by Thomas Turner, surgeon, as a preparatory school of medicine and surgery. It had been the first such school established in the provinces and in
1836 received permission to use the prefix 'Royal'. In 1858 it absorbed a
small medical school operating in Chatham Street, Piccadilly. The School
was a private one, being the property of its founder Thomas Turner and
George Southam, another Manchester medical man.

On 30 November 1870 Ashton, Nield, Roscoe, Greenwood and Johnson
presented a report to the Extension Committee containing proposals for

implementing the scheme, the success of which depended very much on the attitude of the Board of the Manchester Royal Infirmary. The Infirmary, it was stated, possessed advantages as a teaching hospital 'in some respects superior to the London hospitals in the opportunities they furnished to the students of seeing varied practice.' Fortunately the Board of the Infirmary, headed by its chairman Hugh Birley, MP, agreed to give a sealed undertaking to carry out any approved arrangements. The Council of Owens College on its part, agreed to take over the Manchester Royal School of Medicine and Surgery in the Pine Street buildings pending the erection of a new school on the model of the best of the London medical schools. A timely donation of £10,000 by Miss Brackenbury of Brighton, the daughter of a Manchester solicitor, half of which was to go towards a building fund for a new medical school and half towards the endowment of a medical chair, went far towards making this possible. During the period 1871–74 the final arrangements for the taking over of the Manchester Natural History and the Manchester Geological Societies were also completed.

As the work on the new College progressed, the Quay Street buildings became even more congested than they had been in the early 1860s. In the last Quay Street session (1872–73) the day classes contained 334 students in arts, science and law and 557 evening students, besides the 112 students in Pine Street. For the first time Owens College had over 1,000 students in attendance. Naturally the inauguration of the Oxford Road buildings on 7 October 1873 became the occasion of an impressive ceremony in the mid-Victorian style. As president of the College, the Duke of Devonshire was supported by an array of Northern and London notabilities. Thomas Ashton formally handed over the building on behalf of the Extension Committee, praised the architect, and looked ahead by announcing that the building was only a part of the grand scheme. The Extension Committee was £20,000 in debt, but he looked forward to a second appeal for £150,000: 'He had the greatest confidence that before thirty years had elapsed they would see within the walls of Owens College from 1,500 to 2,000 students', a prophecy which was only slightly too optimistic; the figure of 1,500 students was first reached in the session 1908–9. The 'monotony of excellence' of the numerous speeches, which lasted for over three hours, was 'varied by the humour of the students, the 'medicals' being particularly conspicuous . . . Refreshments were served during the evening, but the great crowd made it somewhat difficult to obtain what was longed for.'

On the occasion of the opening lectures were delivered in various rooms in the College by the Principal, the twelve professors and one lecturer. Later these were collected and published in book form. Some of those who participated – Osborne Reynolds, Sir Adolphus W. Ward, W. S. Jevons and James Bryce – later achieved more than national reputations. But the title of Roscoe's contribution, in view of his efforts during the previous decade, was perhaps the most significant: 'Original research as a means of education', with its firm insistence on original research as the essential basis of any institution of University status. The book was noted in the *Revue Scientifique* of 27 March 1875 in the following terms:

> La ville de Manchester possède une institution de haute enseignement de création récente mais devenue vite célèbre en Angleterre et grâce au mérite exceptionnel de ses Professeurs et au caractère special de son enseignement qui l'appelle à rendre bein plus de services aux générations laborieuses de nos jours que les vieilles Universités littéraires et théologiques – c'est le Collège Owens.

The attainment of university status was clearly the next step to be taken.

FURTHER READING

Joseph Thompson, *The Owens College: its Foundation and Growth: and its connections with the Victoria University, Manchester*, Manchester, 1886.

B. Stewart and Sir A. W. Ward (eds), *Essays and Addresses by Professors and Lecturers of the Owens College, Manchester*, London, 1874 (published to commemorate the opening of the new buildings on Oct 7th, 1873.)

P. J. Hartog (ed), *The Owens College, Manchester: (founded 1851): a brief history of the College and description of its various Departments*, Manchester, 1900.

Sir H. E. Roscoe, *The Life and Experiences of Sir Henry Enfield Roscoe . . . written by himself*, London, 1906.

E. Fiddes, *Chapters in the History of Owens College and of Manchester University*, Manchester, 1937.

H. B. Charlton, *Portrait of a University, 1851–1951, to commemorate the Centenary of Manchester University*, Manchester, 1951.

F. I. Jenkins, 'Alfred Waterhouse and the Old Quad', *Staff Comment*, Manchester, Nov 1971, pp. 3–5.

All quotations in the text are from Joseph Thompson (*see* item above), unless otherwise indicated.

CHAPTER VIII

SAMUEL BAMFORD, 1788–1872:
AN INTRODUCTION [1]

The number of British working-class autobiographies dating from the late
eighteenth and early nineteenth centuries is few indeed, and Samuel Bamford may be ranked with Thomas Cooper, Thomas Dunning, Alexander
Somerville, William Lovett and a few others as the chroniclers of a way of
life – that of the artisan-craftsman – characteristic of the pre-factory era. Yet
in spite of Bamford's fame in the annals of the English working class there
has been little systematic and critical study of his career and achievements.
This is partly the result of the very readability and quotability of his *Passages in the Life of a Radical* (1839–41), and, to a lesser extent, of his *Early
Days* (1848–9). Isaac D'Israeli considered him to be 'The raciest writer of
Saxon English since Cobbett',[2] and more recently E. P. Thompson has
roundly declared that *Passages in the Life of a Radical* is 'essential reading
for any Englishman'.[3] The perfunctory entry in the *Dictionary of National
Biography*, with its sadly incomplete list of his works, leaves much unsaid.
The late Humphry House at one time contemplated a re-issue of Bamford's
Passages with a critical introduction, but the Second World War frustrated
these plans, so that his two short pieces on Peterloo are all that remain to us.[4]

Bamford's finest years were spent between 1816 and 1821, and the
remainder of his long life, with its anti-Chartist attitudes and boundless
egotism, proved to be something of an anti-climax. It is easy, however, to

1 From *The Autobiography of Samuel Bamford*, published in two volumes by Frank Cass &
  Co., Ltd., in 1967. Volume I contains *Early Days* and *An Account of the Arrest, etc.*, and
  Volume II, *Passages in the Life of a Radical*. References to these titles within this chapter
  are to this edition.
2 Quoted in *Manchester Guardian*, July 18th, 1861.
3 *The Making of the English Working Class*, 1963, p. 836.
4 'Peterloo I' and 'Peterloo II' in *All in Due Time: the collected essays and broadcast talks of
  Humphry House*, ed. R. Hart-Davis, 1955, pp. 46–57.

SAMUEL BAMFORD
Detail from water colour of Samuel Bamford (1788–1872) about the age of thirty
(reproduced by courtesy of Mr W. J. Smith).

exaggerate the extent to which he moved to the Right during his later career. At least he never became a Tory, and remained to the end, as he liked to call himself, an independent-minded 'Lancashire peasant', a member of Burke's 'swinish multitude'. He was no man's hireling, in spite of a chronic tendency to lapse into poverty and an equally chronic tendency to touch friends, acquaintances and sympathisers for small loans. His unpublished diary covering the years from 1858 to 1861 reveals him as a difficult, crotchety, jealous and cantankerous old man, always ready to bite the hand which had fed him, and on occasion biting before he was fed.[5] At this period of his life he was constantly brooding over imagined slights to his prestige as the 'oldest living reformer' and the 'oldest Radical poet'. He suspected that even his friends and acquaintances had sinister designs to diminish his standing and reputation with the public by devious and highly improbable manoeuvres. As late as 1861 he still believed that Government spies were keeping him under surveillance, and his jealousy bordered on the pathetic. Long after he had become one of the prize platform bores of Lancashire political life, he noted bitterly in his diary that someone else had been invited to give a lecture on parliamentary reform in Oldham Town Hall:

> I was certainly much hurt to see that a young man, a young Parliamentary reformer, should be preferred to give a lecture on that subject whilst an old veteran like myself, who must have large knowledge of the subject from experience, and was on the verge of distress from want of due encouragement in the way of lecturing, should be passed by (May 13th, 1861).

The following pages will, it is hoped, provide a preliminary guide to Bamfordiana and act to some extent as a check on his occasionally vague chronology. The first thirty-three years of his life are well if not fully covered in *Early Days* and *Passages*, although there is a lacuna from 1813 to 1816, and for this period it only remains to try to fill in certain gaps and elucidate chronological vagueness. For the years after 1821 a connected narrative of his life has been attempted.[6] This is not meant to be a definitive account and merely tries to clear the path for future research.

As Bamford omitted to give anything but the most rudimentary genealogical information about his family in *Early Days* an attempt has been

---

5   MS. in 4 vols., Manchester Public Reference Library.
6   In 1852 Bamford himself was writing 'some memoranda' of his life after 1821 (letter to John Harland, March 31, 1852, in Manchester Public Reference Library).

made to be more precise. His father, Daniel Bamford of Middleton, described as a schoolmaster, married Hannah Battersbee of Middleton on October 29th, 1780. Daniel was still described as 'schoolmaster' on July 23rd, 1782, when their first child Mary was christened at Middleton, but by the time their second child, Samuel (I) was christened on February 9th, 1785, Daniel had changed his occupation to that of cotton spinner. This Samuel (I) died in infancy and was buried on January 14th, 1788; our Samuel (II) was christened on April 11th, 1788, having been born on February 28th, 1788. Another son, William had been christened on March 31st, 1786.[7] Daniel Bamford may have changed his occupation from that of cotton spinner to cotton weaver about 1789.

The details given by Bamford of the family fortunes from the 1780s to the Peace of 1815 confirm the impression that the Bamfords belonged to the reasonably well-educated skilled artisan class of the late eighteenth century. They were well able to take advantage of the opportunities which presented themselves of rising in the social scale, but were dogged by misfortunes arising from the unhealthy living conditions characteristic of the period. Bamford's account can here be supplemented by evidence from the *Manchester Mercury* newspaper and the local directories. About 1793 Daniel Bamford agreed to take over the management of a 'manufactory of cotton goods' at the new workhouse for the township of Manchester at Strangeways, of which he shortly afterwards became the Governor. Samuel's uncle Thomas Bamford succeeded his brother Daniel as superintendent of the handloom weavers employed in the workhouse making cotton goods. During a smallpox epidemic in the winter of 1795 Samuel's mother Hannah Bamford died of this disease at the age of forty on December 26th, 1795.[8] His uncle Thomas, his sister Hannah, aged three, and his infant brother James, aged one, had died shortly before from the same cause.[9] Sir Francis Morton Eden visited the Manchester Workhouse at the time of this epidemic of 'malignant fever' and found it 'unsafe to enter'.[10]

Soon afterwards Daniel Bamford remarried. His second wife, Jane, had four children surviving from her previous marriage. They apparently

7   I am greatly indebted to Mr. W. John Smith for extracting this information from the parish register of St. Leonard's, Middleton.

8   R. W. Procter, *Memorials of Manchester Streets* (1874), pp. 63–4

9   See *Early Days*, p. 59; and *Manchester Mercury*, February 16th, 1796, p. 3, col. 5 (advertisement for new male superintendent of cotton weavers employed in Manchester poorhouse).

10   *State of the Poor*, Vol. II, 1797, p. 343.

continued as Governor and Governess of the Manchester Workhouse until the middle of 1799, when they were discharged as recounted by Samuel.[11] Although Samuel suggests, rather than states explicitly, that his father became Governor of Salford Workhouse about 1800, there is in fact a gap in our documentary knowledge of Daniel Bamford's career until 1807 when he appears for the first time in the *Manchester and Salford Directory for 1808 and 1809* as Governor of the Salford Workhouse at Greengate, with his wife Jane as Governess.[12] In the *Manchester Mercury* of September 22nd, 1807 the Overseers of the Poor for Salford announced that Daniel Bamford, Governor of their workhouse, would be glad to receive enquiries from prospective employers of common labourers, jobmen, washerwomen and charwomen, as persons following these occupations were applying for poor relief.[13] The 1813 *Directory* is the last in which he appears holding this post;[14] as in the 1817 *Directory* Mrs. Jane Bamford is described as 'widow'.[15] Samuel nowhere mentions the death of his father.

Bamford's period as a seaman aboard the brig *Aeneas*, which was engaged in the coal trade between South Shields and London, can be approximately dated from his confused recollections (*Early Days*, pp. 244–5) of twice passing close to the expedition lying in Yarmouth Roads 'which under the command of Admiral Duckworth and Sir John Moore, went to the assistance of the King of Denmark against the French'. This apparently refers to the expedition of July – September 1807 which, under the command of Admiral Gambier, bombarded Copenhagen and seized the Danish fleet.[16]

While employed as a warehouseman in Manchester and shortly before marrying his Mima in June 1810 Bamford had fallen into loose, drinking company, and had an affair with a Yorkshire lass as thoughtless as he was. It was not long before he 'became amenable to the parish authorities for

---

11 *Manchester Mercury*, June 25th, July 9th, 1799 (advertisement for new Governor and Governess).

12 Op. cit., p. 9, The 'advertisement' to this directory is dated December 1st, 1807. Compare *Early Days*, pp. 108–11, 174–5, 185.

13 p. 4, col. 3.

14 *Pigot's Manchester and Salford Directory for 1813*, p. 12.

15 *Pigot and Dean's Manchester and Salford Directory for 1817*, p. 13.

16 *Manchester Mercury*, July 28th, 1807, p. 4, col. 3 (cf. *Manchester Mercury*, July 21st, 1807, (p. 4, col. 3): 'Some persons have represented that this fleet is to be sent into the Baltic to act against Denmark. It is sent more with a view of supporting than opposing her, of allowing her to preserve her neutrality'. Sir John Moore had nothing to do with the Copenhagen affair but did undertake a mission to the King of Sweden in 1808.)

certain expences which were about to be incurred'.[17] Bamford could not bear the thought of marriage to the girl, particularly when he found that 'she took the affair less to heart than many would have done, and that the obtainment of a handsome weekly allowance was with her as much a subject of consideration as any other'.[18]

The parish authorities accordingly served him with an affiliation order in 1809.[19] Payments under this order were in arrears a few years later, for he tells us that 'on the 25th of October 1816, the Overseer agreed with my wife to receive the money which I at that time owed, by instalments, at the rate of five shillings per week . . .'[20] Nothing is known of the fate of Bamford's child by this Yorkshire connection.

The circumstances of his marriage in 1810 were peculiar, if not unusual. Bamford married his 'Mima' or 'J. S.' (Jemima Shepherd) in the Collegiate Church of Manchester (now the Cathedral), on June 24th, 1810, the ceremony being performed by the celebrated divine, the Rev. Joshua Brooks.[21] Although Bamford gives a long and amusing account of the ceremony, he nowhere gives the date.[22] But the Bamford tombstone in St. Leonard's churchyard, Middleton, states that his daughter Ann Bamford died on October 15th, 1834, in the twenty-fifth year of her age, indicating that she was born somewhere between October 16th, 1809 and October 14th, 1810. A reference to Ann as his 'love child'[23] and the curious account in *Early Days*[24] of how the infant Ann was placed in his arms on the day after his wedding, i.e. on June 25th, 1810, show that she too was born out of wedlock. A search of the Middleton parish registers revealed the christening of Ann, daughter of Jemima Shepherd, single woman, of Middleton on January 9th, 1810.[25]

The general background of Bamford's adventures between 1816 and 1821 has been well covered in the following sources:

(a) J. L. and B. Hammond, *The Skilled Labourer, 1760–1832* (1919)

---

17 *Early Days*, p. 229.

18 Ibid., p. 230.

19 *An account of the Arrest and Imprisonment of Samuel Bamford . . .* 1817, p. 4.

20 Ibid., p. 8

21 Registers of Manchester Cathedral. I am indebted for this reference to Mr. Roger C. Richardson. 'Mima' signed her own name in the Register in a fashionable hand.

22 *Early Days*, pp. 292–5. Bamford nowhere mentions the maiden name of his wife.

23 *Passages*, Vol.I, p. 75.

24 p. 294

25 I am indebted to Mr. W. John Smith for searching the parish registers for this entry.

where the doings of 'Oliver the Spy' were first seriously investigated (pp. 341–78).

(b) F. O. Darvall, *Popular Disturbances and Public Order in Regency England* (1934).

(c) H. W. C. Davis, 'Lancashire Reformers, 1816–17' (*Bulletin of the John Rylands Library*, Vol. X, no. 1, Jan. 1926, pp. 3–35).

(d) Donald Read, *Peterloo: the Massacre and its Background* (1958), which contains an excellent bibliography, pp. 224–30.

(e) F. A. Bruton, *Three Accounts of Peterloo by Eye-witnesses* (1921).

(f) A. Aspinall, *The Early English Trade Unions: documents from the Home Office Papers in the Public Record Office* (1949), which covers the period 1791–1825.

(g) R. J. White, *Waterloo to Peterloo* (1957).

(h) E. P. Thompson, *The Making of the English Working Class* (1963).

(i) M. W. Flinn, 'The poor Employment Act of 1817', *Economic History Review* (2nd ser., Vol. XIV, no. 1, August 1961) is a useful corrective to the generally-received opinions about Lord Liverpool's Government.

Bamford's pamphlet of 1817, *An Account of the Arrest and Imprisonment of Samuel Bamford, Middleton, on suspicion of High Treason*, adds so much to the somewhat tailored account of this episode given in *Passages* that it has been reprinted in an appendix to *The Autobiography*, vol. I, for purposes of amplification and comparison. Towards the end of his period of bail after his Peterloo arrest the *Manchester Mercury* published the following amusing paragraph, obviously referring to Bamford. It is unfortunately impossible to vouch for its complete accuracy, but it certainly conveys the flavour of Lancashire artisan radicalism at this time, and Bamford's fondness for alcoholic liquor is fully supported by a study of his diary for 1858–61:

A well known Radical Leader, famous for poetry and politics, whose humble muse does sometimes deign to visit him in his 'rocking chair and quiet nook', and who has long had a subsistence without the aid of his loom, lately went to the different sections, to ascertain the cause of the failure in the Radical Funds. On finding some in arrears, and others entirely given over paying, he very feelingly and forcibly told them, if they did not pay up, 'Reform would be lost, as it was only by this means and a disuse of all exciseable articles, that their object could be brought about.' On his return home, forgetting the lesson he had been inculcating, this doughty champion for abstemiousness went to a neighbouring public house and got drunk; not having money to pay his shot, the landlord took the Radical list for security, which proved to be the best pledge, it being released the next morning for fear of a disclosure. Not satisfied with his over-night's cup, and feeling himself a little below par, he went to another public-house, where, after drinking two pints of ale, a person in the room said to him, 'Sam, aw think thow'rt turn'd'. 'Turn'd, whot dost meon?' 'Why, aw thought yo Radicals had nare drunken owt, ot paid th'excise.' 'Yay, for medicine.' 'Medicine, mon, aw'd nare drink cow'd ale for medicine, get a pint o wot ale un rum.' 'Egod, aw think awl tae thy advice, here, lanlort, bring me a pint o wot ale an rum, made good'.[26]

Like many other Radical politicians of the early nineteenth century, Bamford frequently criticised the character and conduct of his fellow-Radicals with a bitterness which ought to have been reserved for their common opponents. The increasingly unfavourable opinion which he had of Henry Hunt from 1819–20 onwards was probably entirely justified, but Bamford seems to have been hyper-suspicious of the motives of his friends, allies and patrons. Few escaped denigration, at the least.

One example may serve to guard us against a complete acceptance of his denunciations. In volume II of *Passages*[27] he fiercely attacked the Unitarian minister at Lincoln, the Rev. James Hawkes, who visited two of his fellow-prisoners, an act which presumably required some moral courage. It is difficult, without having anything of Hawkes's side of the matter, to decide whether Bamford had the right on his or not. Yet it is known that Hawkes, when Unitarian minister at Nantwich in Cheshire, during the early 1830s, strongly supported the trade unionist shoemakers of the town and was described as 'the brave advocate of reforms in Church and State as well as local.'[28]

The period of Bamford's life between his release from Lincoln Castle gaol and 1851 – a period of thirty years – is not well documented. On his release he returned to his silk weaver's loom and removed to Stake Hill near

26 *Manchester Mercury*, February 22nd, 1820, p. 4, col. 5. The punctuation of the dialect dialogue has been corrected. I am indebted to Mr. G. B. Hindle for this and other references.
27 pp. 189, 206–8.
28 'The Reminiscences of Thomas Dunning . . . and the Nantwich shoe-makers' case of 1834', *Trans. Lancs. & Ches. Antiquarian Society, Vol. LIX for 1947* (1948), pp. 97–8. Hawkes (1771–1846) was successively Unitarian minister at Congleton, 1797–1800, Dukinfield, 1800–13, Lincoln, 1813–22 and Nantwich, 1822–45 (A. Gordon, *Historical Account of Dukinfield Chapel and its School* (1896), pp. 64–8.

Middleton.[29] In 1825 he was one of the founders of the Middleton Mechanics Institution, when the founder-members were helped by two London members of the Society for the Diffusion of Useful Knowledge. Bamford, with a characteristic lack of modesty, stated that he was 'the originator' of the Institution, which later, he alleged, withered away under the blighting patronage of Lord Suffield and the disruptive activities of the Chartists.[30]

In 1826 began the process of his separation from the extremist wing of the working-class movement. He became the correspondent of the London daily newspaper, the *Morning Herald*, and, possibly somewhat later, Middleton district correspondent of the *Manchester Guardian*. As Bamford, writing in the third person, stated in the 1860s:

> He had now ceased to be a weaver, and many of the weavers, some of them his old acquaintances, looked upon him as an alien to their class and their interests.[31]

In 1826, too, he dissuaded breakers of power-looms from East Lancashire from descending on Heywood, Rochdale and Middleton. According to Bamford, one Friday evening in the summer of 1826, when mobs of starving hand-loom weavers were breaking machinery in the neighbourhoods of Blackburn, Burnley, Haslingden and Bury 'a young fellow . . . came to my house at Middleton . . . and expressed concern at a plot which he said was being carried on in our vicinity . . . he said that certain persons residing in the neighbourhood, had been in the habit of holding secret meetings, and had once or twice sent delegates to the disturbed districts in the moors, inviting the loom-breakers to come down into our part of the country, where they would be joined by the working population, and might make a clear sweep of the obnoxious machinery, all around by Heywood, Middleton and Oldham . . .'[32]

Bamford therefore walked over to Haslingden, after ascertaining that the Middleton plotters were 'from a dozen to a score of persons of the worst character,' who had hatched the plot to give themselves an opportunity for looting provision shops and public houses. At Haslingden Bamford got an introduction to the local delegates and persuaded them to have nothing to do with the schemes of the Middleton men. As a result of this no mobs of

29 *Homely Rhymes*, p. 9

30 See *Middleton Albion*, 26th November, 1859 (letter of November 23rd from Bamford); see also diary for October 2nd, 1858 and newspaper cuttings annexed.

31 *Homely Rhymes*, p. 9.

32 S. Bamford, *Walks in South Lancashire* (1844), pp. 216–17.

weavers came down from the moors into Middleton as expected and the plot miscarried. A second attempt to start a similar riot, this time by 'about a hundred and fifty, or two hundred strange men, from towards Manchester,' also failed.[33] The disappointed Middleton plotters were naturally furious with Bamford:

> Several hole and corner meetings were held, at which I was denounced as a spy and a traitor; at one of such gatherings held in a chamber at Bury, I was noted to be a fit subject for assassination . . . To my family these things were annoying, but I treated them with contempt.[34]

In 1832 Bamford, according to his own story, 'was compelled to undertake the office of Constable. He evaded the oath until threatened with a prosecution, and he was then sworn at the New Bailey – in that court where he had so frequently appeared under charges of treason and misdemeanor. He felt his position to be a singular one, and having taken the oath, he determined faithfully to carry it into effect . . . A faction was at that time appearing in Middleton which afterwards became the Chartist party, and when, at the expiration of his year of office, he submitted his accounts, amounting to a matter of fifteen shillings, they were, with the exception of one or two small items, disallowed; and ever afterwards the Chartists of Middleton omitted but few opportunities of acting towards him as if he had been their enemy.'[35]

Later he referred in the diary to the exhausting travels of his days as a journalist in the 1820s and 1830s, which were followed by long evenings at home writing up accounts of meetings for the press. As an ardent political reformer he reported the local agitation of 1830–2 for the Great Reform Bill with relish, but stated that 1833 was 'the last year in which I corresponded with the *Guardian* as one of its established reporters'.[36] After that date he sent in only occasional reports. It has not been possible to discover how long his employment with the *Morning Herald* lasted.

In his *Homely Rhymes*, Bamford gave the following amusing and characteristic account of a brush he had with Oastler in the 1830s:

> Richard Oastler, calling himself 'king of the factory children',

33 Op. cit., pp. 226–7.
34 Op. cit., p. 226.
35 *Homely Rhymes*, pp. 10–11.
36 *Diary*, September 15th, 1859.

appeared on the stage, and delivered in various parts of the country numerous orations in favour of a Factory Act, and against the New Poor Law. In one of his perambulations he visited Middleton, and addressed a numerous assemblage of his friend O'Connor's followers, Chartists, in a dissenters' chapel. The Author attended to furnish a report for one of the Manchester newspapers. Oastler, Hart, the Minister of the Chapel, and a Chartist leader from Scotland occupied the pulpit. The reporter stood on the top of the pulpit stairs outside. The place was densely crowded, and Oastler was in the full enjoyment of an abusive speech against the public press, its supporters and contributors. The reporter, in order to catch the light for the taking of his notes, stood with his back to the orator when the words 'Scoundrels of the press!' struck his ear; and turning suddenly he found Oastler looking at him. 'Are those words addressed to me?' he demanded. 'They are,' were [sic] Oastler's reply. 'Then I have to say that you are stating a falsehood,' was the instant rejoinder. This was a choker to the orator, and he made a full stop, during which there was a dead silence. 'Then,' he said, breaking the pause, 'I will not speak another word until that person,' pointing to the reporter, 'is turned out.' The latter, amid indescribable confusion and cries of 'pull him down!' 'turn him out!' and other menacing vociferations, eyed Oastler sternly, and then putting his note-book in his pocket, he buttoned up his coat, and speaking loudly above the uproar, he said – 'Who is to begin, then?' The noise subsided, and he repeated the question, 'Who is to begin, then?' 'Who starts it?' Not a hand was raised; not a foot stepped forth. The reporter stood there with an air of determined self-defence. Oastler looked silly and embarrassed; and his friends in the pulpit, feeling, no doubt, pained at the position in which he had placed himself, pulled him by the button and whispered in his ear, and after a few coughs and a-hems, the orator made a finish of his address.[37]

Bamford's connection with the press as a regular reporter ceased altogether in 1830,[38] although he remained almost to the end of his life a writer of special newspaper articles and a prolific source of 'Letters to the Editor', often under one of his many pseudonyms. He was particularly critical of what he imagined to be inadequate, malicious or inaccurate

37 *Homely Rhymes*, pp. 9–10.
38 *Middleton Albion*, July 16th, 1859.

reporting of his literary readings and his speeches at political or social functions.

While employed the by *Manchester Guardian* he became friendly with John Harland (1806–68), pioneer of the verbatim newspaper reporting of political speeches,[39] and chief reporter of the *Guardian* from 1830 to 1860. Harland, like many of Bamford's acquaintances, did not escape his censure later on, and the diary of 1858–61 contains a number of disparaging remarks to the general effect that Harland had either forgotten his old friend or was deliberately contriving to hide his activities from public notice.

During the Chartist troubles of 1839 he (again according to his own account) became a leader of special constables and 'took means for rendering the party which he directed as efficient as possible. This again was a cause of enmity on the part of the Chartists.'[40] His dislike of Chartism was based on his general philosophy of 'gradualism', as opposed to the all-or-nothing policy enshrined in the six points of the Charter and on a cordial dislike of Feargus O'Connor as a man and a leader. His later writings have a general anti-Irish tone.

A glimpse of the veteran reformer, presumably dating from about 1840, is given by Samuel Chadwick, nephew of the John Heywood who printed a number of Bamford's works. Chadwick stated '. . . it often fell to my lot to visit Bamford's house [at Middleton] with 'proofs' and to bring copy . . . He was sometimes very odd and queer and very hot tempered, more especially so when the proofs were what printers call 'dirty'. I ought to state that his calligraphy was very difficult to decipher and I heard many an oath as a consequence . . . Sam was very fond of dogs and always had two or three.' Chadwick states that at the time Bamford was a silk weaver.[41]

About 1840 he left Middleton, this time for good, and settled for a few years in a cottage near Charlestown in the township of Blackley (or Blakeley as it was then spelt and is still pronounced), near Manchester. One of the few scraps of evidence we have about him during this period is contained in a letter he wrote to John Harland at the *Manchester Guardian* office, dated November 4th, 1840:

At present I am finishing the last number of Passages of my life [*sic*];

39 For Harland see *Dictionary of National Biography; Manchester Guardian*, 4th September, 1957 (article by Donald Read on 'A Pioneer of Precise Reporting') and D. Read, 'John Harland', *Manchester Review*, Autumn 1958, pp. 205–12.

40 *Homely Rhymes*, p. 11.

41 *Heywood Notes and Queries*, ed. J. A. Green, Vol. 2, 1906, Manchester, pp. 86–7. I am indebted to Mr. W. John Smith for this reference.

I hope this week to have finished it and then I shall try something in the dialect.[42]

James Dronsfield of Hollinwood, near Oldham, described his first encounter with Bamford as follows:

It was about the year 1843 or '44 that I first became acquainted with Mr. Bamford, who was then residing in a cottage in the small hamlet of Charlestown, in the township of Blackley . . . I shall never forget the old Poet and Reformer as he appeared as I first fell in conversation with him . . . he a man of about 56 years of age, and I a youth about 18. Mr. Bamford was then a tall, well built man, about 5 ft. 11 in., . . . strong limbed, broad shouldered, walking very erect, with a bold, firm majestic step, and altogether a man of very commanding appearance. He was dressed in thick corduroy knee-breeches and gaiters, and strong nailed shoes. His coat was blue, and somewhat broader in the lap than the 'swallow tail', with steel buttons. He wore a flat-crowned fur cap, with square neb notched out at the corners, a neat neckerchief, and shirt as white as snow, and a plaid woollen rug thrown loosely over his shoulders. In one hand he carried a portmanteau, and in the other a stout oaken walking stick . . . His appearance reminded me of a Scotch drover . . .[43]

His acquaintance with the Carlyles, about which little has hitherto been known, started in the 1840s. Bamford had begun to write and publish his *Passages in the Life of a Radical* in 1839, the year in which Carlyle brought out his *Chartism*. The Carlyles may have got to know about Bamford's book from the reviews which appeared in such periodicals as the *Athenaeum*, and on March 12th, 1843, Mrs. Carlyle wrote to her cousin Jeannie Welsh:

Have you ever tried for Bamford's book?[44]

She described Bamford and the *Passages* enthusiastically to Helen Welsh and recommended it for Mr. Welsh's reading list, although it bore 'a rather questionable name as a book for my uncle'. She continued:

He was one of those who got into trouble during the Peterloo time; and the details of what he then saw and suffered are given with a

---

42 Quoted in *A Lancashire Garland of Dialect Prose and Verse*, ed. G. Halstead Whittaker, 1936, p. xxvii.

43 J. Dronsfield, *Incidents and Anecdotes of the late Samuel Bamford* (1872), p. 5.

44 *Jane Welsh Carlyle: Letters to her Family, 1839–1863*, ed. L. Huxley, 1924, p. 98.

simplicity, an intelligence, and absence of everything like party vio-
lence, which it does one good to fall in with, especially in these
inflated times.[45]

Thomas Carlyle also began to recommend it to his friends and patrons,
and a month later he wrote to Bamford:

5, Cheyne Row, Chelsea, London, 13 April, 1843.
Dear Sir, – Will you be so good as send by the earliest convenience
you have two copies of your book, 'Bamford's Life of a Radical,'
addressed to 'The Hon. W. B. Baring, 12, Great Stanhope-street,
London.' Two copies have been wanted there for some time. Probably
you have some appointed conveyance by which your books arrive
here without additional cost; if so, pray use the earliest of these. Nay,
perhaps your books are themselves procurable somewhere in London?
That would be the shortest way of all. At any rate the coach or railway
remains, and will be of no enormous amount. Be so good as apprise
me by post what way you have adopted, and on what day the books
may be looked for in Stanhope-street, not forgetting to enclose an
account withal. I read your book with much interest, with a true desire
to hear more and more of the authentic news of Middleton and of the
honest toiling men there. Many persons have a similar desire. I would
recommend you to try whether there is not yet more to be said,
perhaps, on some side of that subject, for it belongs to an important
class in these days. A man is at all times entitled, or even called upon
by occasion, to speak, and write, and in all fit ways *utter* what he has
himself gone thro', and *known*, and got the mastery of; and, in truth, at
bottom there is nothing else that any man has a right to write of. For
the rest, one principle, I think, in whatever farther you write, may be
enough to guide you; that of standing rigorously by the fact, however,
naked it look. Fact is eternal; all fiction is very transitory in comparison. All men are interested in any man if he will speak the facts of his
life for them; *his* authentic experience, which corresponds, as face
with face, to that of all other sons of Adam.

Another humbler thing I will suggest – that it seems to me a pity you
had not your book in the hands of some bookseller; such a one could
sell it for you much faster than you yourself will. A friend of mine, for
example, could not find your book in Liverpool at all; and, unless he

45 *Letters and Memorials of Jane Welsh Carlyle*, ed. J. A. Froude, Vol. I, 1883, p. 187.

have written to Middleton, as I suggested, may still be in fruitless search of it. The commission charges of booksellers are in truth entirely exorbitant, unexampled among any other class of *sellers* or salesmen in the world; but, as I said once, 'If you have a wagon to drive to York, you had better pay the tolls, however unconscionable, than try to steeple-hunt it thither!' This, too, is not to be neglected, tho' a very secondary side of the business. Wishing you a right good speed in all manful industry with hand or with head or with heart, I remain, yours very truly,

T. Carlyle.

P.S. What is curious enough: this note was just folded, but not yet sealed, when your letter was handed in to me! Many thanks for your gift. Your remarks on *Chartism* are also very welcome to me. I have now only to add that you had better send Mr. Baring's two copies to Mr. Ballantyne along with the other, and request him to forward them all to me without delay. Do not forget to enclose your account, which will be paid thro' the post-office.

T.C.

Three years later Mrs. Carlyle paid a visit to her friend Geraldine Jewsbury of 30 Carlton Terrace, Greenheys, Manchester. She had intended to stay for only two days, but the novelty of Manchester and the devoted attentions of Miss Jewsbury persuaded her to prolong her visit to a fortnight. On August 16th, 1846, she wrote from Manchester to Helen Welsh:

I 'find myself in a new position', not knowing my own mind! – so much so has Manchester fascinated me! I am not going tomorrow either – Geraldine arranged a pleasure excursion for me tomorrow to the house of Bamford '*The Radical*' and my love of punctuality was not equal to putting a veto on it . . .[46]

She described Bamford as 'a fine sturdy old fellow'.[47] The visit appears to have been an enjoyable and memorable one, for in 1848 Carlyle wrote to Bamford on receipt of the first two parts of *Early Days*, as follows:

46 *Jane Welsh Carlyle: Letters to her Family, 1839–1863*; ed. L. Huxley (1924), p. 280.
47 *New Letters and Memorials of Jane Welsh Carlyle*, ed. A. Carlyle, 1903, Vol. I, p. 206. See also p. 209.

The Grange, Hampshire, 4 September, 1848.

My dear sir, – Both the numbers of your new work, which you were so kind as send me, came safely to hand – the last only a few days before our leaving Chelsea for this place, whither we have come to see some friends, and have a little fresh air while the summer still lasts. I have read the two pieces with great pleasure, in which Mrs. C. your old acquaintance also shares. We find the Narrative full of rough veracity, clear, wholesome description of what you meant it to describe, namely – of an authentic phasis of human life – in which accordingly all human creatures may take a real interest. Withal there is a certain breezy freshness in the delineation, as indeed in former delineations by the same hand – a rustic honesty, a healthy manful turn of mind is nowhere wanting, and that is a pleasant neighbour everywhere, and to all readers and all men. On the whole, if you continue this work in the way you have begun, I think there is every reason to expect a lasting favour for it and all manner of good fruit that you and your friends could have anticipated. There are only two precepts I will bid you once more always keep in mind – the first is to be brief, not to dwell on an object one instant after you have made it clear to the reader, and on the whole to be select in your objects taken for description, dwelling on each in proportion to its likelihood to interest, omitting many in which such likelihood is doubtful, and only bringing out the more important into prominence and detail. The second, which indeed is still more essential, but which I need not insist upon since I see you scrupulously observe it, is to be exact to the truth in all points; never to hope to mend a fact by polishing any corner of it off into fiction, or adding any ornament which it had not, but to give it us always as God gave it – that, I suppose, will turn out to the best state it could be in! These two principles, I think, are the whole law of the matter; and in fact they are the epitome of what a sound, strong and healthy mind will, by nature, be led to achieve in such an enterprise; wherefore perhaps my best 'precept' of all were to recommend Samuel Bamford to his own good genius (to his own honest good sense and healthy instincts) and bid him write or omit without misgivings whenever that had clearly spoken! And on the whole, perservere and prosper: that is the wish we form for you. We are here among high people, to whom the 'Passages' and other writings of yours are known: last night I was commissioned by Lord Lansdowne to ask you to send him a copy of this new work, – or to bid Simpkin and Marshall send it, if that can be done; but in any way to be sure that he gets it soon. I think perhaps you had better send it direct yourself; if the two Nos. are stitched together they will go thro' the post-office for sixpence (six stamps stuck on them); the address is, The Lord Marquis of Lansdowne, Lansdowne House, London; – and you have only to write a little note (a separate post-office note) saying, with your address given, that the book is sent by my order, that you yourself both write and sell it, and that the price is so and so. Pray do not neglect this, however, but set about doing it straightaway. If you write at any time to Chelsea, the letter finds me after one day's delay.

My wife bids me remember her to you and Mrs. Bamford, whom she hopes to see again by and by; Blakely appears to be a place very bright in her recollections.

With many good wishes, I remain, sincerely yours,

T. Carlyle.

Two other letters from Carlyle to Bamford have survived and are self-explanatory:

Chelsea, 9 January 1849.

My dear sir, – Yesternight I read the preface and the last portion of your autobiography. I have followed the work throughout, as the successive instalments of it reached me by your kindness (for which I am much obliged): and now it is ended, handsomely, yet sooner than I quite expected. It seems to me you have managed the affair very well indeed; a manful rustic frankness runs thro' it; a wholesome freshness, energy, sincerity: it is very clear everywhere, very credible; and, to sum up many merits in one, it is singularly memorable, and stands out in distinct visibility and continuity in one's mind after reading it. You will give an innocent and profitable pleasure, I hope, to very many persons by what you have written; and made known, with advantage to all parties, important forms of human life, in quarters where they have not been known hitherto, and much required to be known.

On the whole, however, we must not yet let you off, or allow you to persuade yourself that you have done with us. A vast deal more of knowledge about Lancashire operatives, and their ways of living and thinking, their miseries and advantages, their virtues and sins, still lies in your experience; and you must endeavour, by all good methods, to get it winnowed, the chaff of it well separated from the wheat, and to let us have the latter, as your convenience will serve. To workers themselves you might have much to say, in the way of admonition, encouragement, instruction, reproof; and the captains of workers, the rich people, are very willing also to listen to you, and certain of them will believe heartily whatever true things you tell them; this is a combination of auditors which nobody but yourself has such hold of at present; and you must encourage yourself to do with all fidelity whatever you can in that peculiar and by no means unimportant position you occupy. 'Brevity, sincerity,' – and in fact, all sorts of manful virtue, – will have once more, as they everywhere in this world do, avail[ed] you.

Since I wrote last, I have never seen Lord Lansdowne; know not what he did with those Nos. of your book, or, indeed, whether he has ever yet fairly got hold of them, for his life all this while has been in the country, I suppose, amid a crowd of guests, and with little leisure for considerate reading. Pray tell me how the matter is when you next write. I wish you farther to address a copy of your book so soon as you have got it bound to Lord Ashburton, whose address I enclose; if the book is under half a pound weight it will go by post if you stick sixpence worth of stamps upon it; above a pound and under two it goes for a shilling's worth. And the note you write must bear a cover quite apart. With many good wishes, yours,

T. Carlyle.

Chelsea, 21 April 1849.

My dear sir, – It will not, I fear, be of much use to try a bookseller with the poems. Poetry of all kinds is a bugbear to the booksellers at present, for there is no kind of poetry that they find the public will buy. For my own part, too, I own I had much rather see a sensible man, like you, put down your real thoughts and convictions in prose, than occupy yourself with fancies and imaginations such as are usually dealt with in verse. The time is in deadly earnest; our life itself, in all times, is a most earnest practical matter, and only incidentally a sportful or singing or rhyming one: – Let S. Bamford continue to tell us in fresh truthful prose the things he has learned about Lancashire and the world; that, I must say, would be my verdict too!

Lord Lansdowne has hardly come across me again at all – I think only once – since he commissioned me to bid you send your book. In the huge whirlpool of things great and small, which the like of him lives in, he has doubtless let the transaction go out of his head; and had not you, according to my bargain with you, recalled the memory of it, all had remained forgotten. I have now communicated with his

Lordship, and probably before long you will hear some farther account of it from him or me. Yesterday Lord Ashburton sent me the enclosed draft of £25, which I was in some handsome way to present to you as a proof of his approbation. On being consulted I had said there was a public testimonial set on foot for your behoof some time ago, to which, tho' it was no longer open to the public at large, his Lordship might still fitly contribute whatever acknowledgement of service he thought due to you. This draft is the result, which any Manchester banker who knows you, or knows a responsible man going with you to his bank will at once convert into cash, after which pray be so good as signify that you have received the amount, and that all is safe. –

With many good wishes, yours very sincerely,

Mr. Bamford, Blakeley.

T. Carlyle[48]

According to his later statements Bamford appears to have played an active part in the campaign of 1839–46 for the repeal of the Corn Laws, but precise details are lacking. He was clearly a familiar figure at the League's headquarters in Newall's Buildings, Manchester.

Between 1847 and 1850 the Samuel Bamford Testimonial Committee, with Joseph Brotherton as Chairman, raised about £400 for him, and proposed that the sum should be invested in an annuity on the lives of the reformer and his wife. Bamford would not agree to this, and chose to take the whole sum in cash. An anonymous member of this committee, writing in 1861, stated: 'Of his [Bamford's] conduct towards his committee, and the whole body of the subscribers during the canvass on his behalf, the less said the better.'[49]

In 1851, on the strength of a recommendation from Joseph Brotherton, master cotton-spinner, vegetarian and Radical M.P. for Salford, Bamford secured the nomination to a minor clerical post at Somerset House, London,[50] under the Commissioners of Inland Revenue. The Chairman of the

---

48 These four letters of Carlyle's were printed in the issue of the *Manchester Guardian* for April 16th, 1881, p. 9, col. 4, when they were in the possession of E. W. Binney (press cutting, Chetham's Library, Manchester).

49 *Manchester Examiner and Times*, April 30th, 1861. See also Bamford's not very convincing reply in ibid., May 4th, 1861. According to J. Dronsfield, *Incidents and Anecdotes of the late Samuel Bamford*, 1872, p. 29, the sum handed to Bamford in 1850 was £280.

50 There seems to be no evidence for H. Dunckley's suggestion (intro., Vol. I, p. 22, to 1893 edn. of *Passages*) that the appointment was merely that of a 'doorkeeper or messenger'.

Board of Inland Revenue at this time was John Wood (1790–1856), the son of a Liverpool merchant, and like Bamford and Brotherton, a Radical.[51] Bamford later referred to Wood as 'my honoured friend.'[52] and stated in 1859 that 'an epistolary acquaintance' had sprung up between himself and Wood shortly after the publication of *Passages* in 1839–42.[53]

The London correspondent of the *Manchester Guardian* met Bamford in Fleet Street in the summer of 1851 and mistakenly concluded that he had come up to see the Great Exhibition, 'but it turns out that he has come to settle in the 'Fog-Babylon' . . . I am heartily glad to hear of this fortunate passage in the life of so worthy a radical. In looking after him as he shouldered his way through Temple Bar, in a very characteristic style, I could not help thinking on the marvellous change which has taken place since his first appearance in London thirty-four years ago.'[54]

From London he continued to contribute letters to the Lancashire press, and in 1853, under the pseudonym of 'Stedfast', advocated the adoption of the Public Health Act of 1848 by Middleton township in a letter to Thomas Mills, editor of the *Middleton Albion*.[55]

Although his official duties were not onerous and the hours of attendance reasonable enough, Bamford and 'Mima' do not seem to have been particularly happy in London, although they eventually lived in a comfortable house in St. John's Wood. Bamford had optimistically and over-ambitiously hoped, when he first came to the capital, that '. . . a probation of some years would have ended in an arrangement of some kind, whereby I might be enabled to devote the remainder of my days to the collection and arranging of the materials for Lancashire history which were at the British Museum, materials which I alone could properly select and arrange, inasmuch as they embrace incidents and transactions of many of which I was personally cognizant.'[56]

Instead, towards the end of his seventh year in London he found the work getting more tiring and more uncongenial. He later stated publicly: 'I

51 Wood began as a barrister and was M.P. for Preston, 1826–32; chairman of the Board of Stamps and Taxes, 1833–8; chairman of the Revenue Boards, 1838–49; chairman of the Board of Inland Revenue, 1849–56. (F. Boase, *Modern English Biography*, Vol. III, 1901, col. 1468.)
52 Letter to L. S. Lyne, 24th April, 1858 in MS. Diary.
53 *Middleton Albion*, July 16th, 1859.
54 Quoted in R. W. Procter, *Literary Reminiscences and Gleanings* (1860), pp. 132–4.
55 MS. letter of April 18th, 1853, in Middleton Public Library.
56 MS. Diary, Vol.I, April 24th, 1858. See also his letter from 2, Chapel Place, Portland Town, London, to John Harland, March 31st, 1853.

thought the situation beneath me'.[57] In spite of his wish to undertake historical research he seems to have felt contempt rather than understanding for the
multitudinous and often mouldering documents which he had to sort, catalogue, and arrange on the shelves in the course of his duties as Superintendent of Books and Papers in the Accountant-General's Department in the
Depository, 'the great 'lubber-slum' of England'.[58] After seven years' service Bamford decided to return to Lancashire and gave in his resignation with
effect as from Saturday May 1st, 1858.

He travelled North early on May 10th and narrowly escaped injury in a
railway accident at Nuneaton. He was seated in a second-class carriage, the
third from the engine, but when the second and fourth coaches were completely crushed, Bamford 'threw himself upon the seat of the carriage' and
escaped uninjured.[59]

He and 'Mima' decided to settle in Moston Vale, Harpurhey, which was
reasonably close to Middleton, Oldham, Rochdale and Manchester; travel
between these towns was much easier than before, owing to the construction
of the railway network and the existence of omnibus services. Bamford now
used these frequently but, in addition, although in his early seventies, still
walked for considerable distances. Early in 1859, probably because of
increasing poverty, he and his wife moved a short distance to a 'very good
cottage of four rooms' in Hall Street, Harpurhey, at a rent of 2s. 6d. a week,
with coal at 7d. per cwt. laid down at the door, and other advantages.[60]

In 1859 Bamford, who was by now increasingly poverty-stricken, decided to try to a make living by giving public readings and recitations from
his own works and those of the popular poets of the day. He was jealous of
the ease with which Charles Dickens had earned large sums of money in
Manchester by this means, just as in 1839 he had been spurred on to begin
publishing *Passages in the Life of a Radical* by the vogue for the 'publication of books in weekly parts,' such as *Pickwick, Nicholas Nickleby* and *Jack
Sheppard.*[61]

He accordingly gave readings, or 'literary exercises,' during 1859–61 at
Ashton-under-Lyne, Bury, Chorlton-on-Medlock, Lees, the Manchester
Athenaeum, and the Manchester Mechanics' Institute, Middleton, Oldham

57 MS. Diary, Vol. II, May 19th, 1859.
58 MS. Diary, Vol. I, April 24th, 1858.
59 Undated newspaper cutting in MS. Diary, Vol. I; see also Vol. II, sub May 9–10th, 1859.
60 MS. Diary, Vol. I, February 24th; April 5th, 1859 (letter to Mrs. Shiel).
61 *Passages*, ed. of 1844, Vol. II, p. 245.

and Rochdale. In general these subscription readings were not as successful, either financially or in the matter of attendances, as Bamford had hoped, and he found the selling of tickets for them by means of personal solicitation extremely humiliating. In addition, another and more famous Lancashire fellow-poet notes, among other amusing details about Bamford's readings, that:

His antiquated style of delivery often provoked merriment when it was not intended; and a peculiar stammer which he could not overcome was another source of fun.[62]

At the same time he was pressing his claims to public compensation for his sufferings in 1817–21 by means of printed leaflets and campaigns in the press of South-East Lancashire. Lord Palmerston, the Prime Minister, finally agreed in 1860 to grant him £50 out of the Royal Bounty Fund on the representation of Thomas Bazley, M.P., but this was a single grant only, not an annual pension, and by 1861 he and 'Mima' were again running up debts with tradesmen for daily necessities, borrowing small sums from friends and resorting to 'uncle' (the pawnbroker) as they had been doing two years previously. On June 10th, 1861 he wrote in his diary:

Three years this day since we commenced house-keeping in Moston. How we have been preserved from starvation seems to me a wonder.

At this point, when a second grant from the Royal Bounty Fund was refused, Thomas Bazley, M.P., and Dr. John Watts,[63] the former Owenite Socialist (by 1861 safely ensconced in profitable respectability as Manchester agent for the European Assurance Company) raised a subscription for Bamford with the help of David Chadwick, David Morris and Alexander Ireland, editor of the Radical *Manchester Examiner and Times*. This provided Bamford with about £60 a year for the rest of his life, of which Bazley contributed £12.[64] In addition E. W. Binney, F.R.S. (1812–81), a rich and eccentric Manchester solicitor, who was also a self-taught practical geologist specialising in the proving of coal seams, contributed handsomely to keeping Bamford in his last years.[65] It is characteristic that Bamford should have earlier referred to Binney, who acted as the patron of other working-class *literati*, as follows, after meeting him in Manchester:

---

62 Ben Brierley, *Home Memories, and Recollections of a Life* (1886), pp. 63–4.
63 Dronsfield called Watts Bamford's 'almoner and generous patron' (op. cit., p. 41).
64 Diary, May–June 1861; Dronsfield, op. cit., p. 30.
65 For Binney, see *Dictionary of National Biography* and *Memoirs of the Literary and Philosophical Society of Manchester*, 3rd series, Vol. IX (for 1881), 1883, pp. 447–64.

Mr. Binney got into the omnibus in Market Street . . . he nodded and said, 'How are you?' 'How do you do?' was the reply, and so began and ended our recognition, I never afterwards bestowing a look. This terminates, I suppose my acquaintance with Mr. E. W. Binney, now a F.R.S., and consequently not to be mated with one who has not some sort of ridiculous handle to his name.[66]

In the early 1860s his eyesight began to fail, his deafness became more pronounced, and by 1865 he appears to have been unable to read any longer.[67] His beloved 'Mima' had died in 1861. J. C. Lockhart described him in 1865 as follows:

He has latterly allowed his hair to grow at its pleasure and it now hangs in long silver bars above his shoulders; his beard and moustachios, white as snow, have also attained a great length, covering a goodly part of his ample chest; his straight lower limbs are enclosed in a pair of drab gaiters and on his head, in the house, he constantly wears a peculiar square cloth cap, which, with his long flowing locks and his beard, quite give him the appearance of an old Druid . . .[68]

After Mrs. Bamford's death, Mrs. Hilton, a cousin of Samuel's, kept house for him until his death on April 13th, 1872. His final and protracted illness 'was a gradual wearing out of the system, continually growing weaker and weaker, until, like a clock, whose wheels are worn out with eating Time, the machine ceased working . . .'[69] Bamford's burial in the parish churchyard of St. Leonard's Middleton, became a great political demonstration for the Liberals of Manchester and the surrounding areas, and a number of persons, e.g. Edwin Waugh, attended whose character or conduct or both he had secretly and severely criticised in his diary of 1858–61. The funeral arrangements were in the hands of a committee 'selected from the political and social circles in which the deceased veteran moved'.[70] Among the organisations represented were the Manchester Literary Club, the Manchester Chamber of Commerce, the National Reform Union, the

66 Diary, August 5th, 1858.
67 Wentworth, *History and Annals of Blackley* (Middleton, 1892), p. 190 (from an article by J. C. Lockhart, 'The last days of Samuel Bamford').
68 Philip Wentworth, op. cit., p. 191.
69 Dronsfield, op. cit., p. 39.
70 Op. cit., p. 40.

Reform League, the Salford Liberal Association, the Heywood Reform Club and the Newton Heath Local Board.

Rather inappropriately, having regard to Bamford's early Methodist background and his later anti-clerical attitudes, the Church of England played a large part in the proceedings. The Rector of Middleton, the Rev. Waldegrave Brewster, M.A., conducted the service and delivered 'an address on the character of Samuel Bamford as a politician, poet and husband'.[71] The Bishop of Manchester, James Fraser, wrote on April 18th to John H. Haworth, one of the two joint secretaries of the Funeral Committee, regretting that a previous engagement prevented him from attending the funeral. He continued, in a passage which deserves to be remembered:

> I am afraid, too, that it may wear too much the form of a political demonstration, for me fittingly to have borne a share in it, even if I had been disengaged. Not that I consider 'politics' in the highest sense of the word – an interest to promote what tends to the common weal – to be an interest alien from, or contrary to, the proper functions of a minister of Christ; and I could have cordially united in honouring the man who wrote the *Passages in the Life of a Radical*, and who, in that remarkable book avowed the 'nation to be the only party he would serve' (ii. p. 235); tried to teach the rich and poor, employers and employed, that they had 'been all in error as respects their relative obligations' (i. 281); sought to bring all classes together on the basis of mutual sympathy and co-operation; believed that, 'instead of wishing to create sudden changes, and to overthrow institutions, it were better that ignorance alone were pulled down' (i. 279); and maintained that the self-control and self-amendment of the individual was the only solid 'basis of all public reform.' If I had attended Samuel Bamford's funeral, I should like to have heard the last chapter of the first volume of his memoirs read over his grave. It contains counsels that England seems to me emphatically to need just now.
>
> I remain, Sir, your faithful servant,
> J. Manchester[72]

Mr John H. Haworth

71 Op. cit. p. 43.
72 Op. cit., pp. 46–7

CHRONOLOGICAL LIST OF THE PUBLISHED WORKS OF SAMUEL BAMFORD (1788–1872)

(Excluding handbills, posters, articles and letters in newspapers and periodicals.)

1. *An Account of the Arrest and Imprisonment of Samuel Bamford, Middleton, on suspicion of High Treason. Written by Himself* (Manchester, 1817), pp. 55.
2. *The Weaver Boy: or Miscellaneous Poetry* (Manchester, 1819), pp. 12.
3. *The Queen's Triumph* (London, 1820) – a single sheet, quarto (verses on the acquittal of Queen Caroline).
    This item is only known from the copy in the British Museum; consists of the poem 'The Queen's Triumph' printed in *Homely Rhymes*, 1864, pp. 199–200 (where a footnote states 'This poem was written when the author was a prisoner in Lincoln Castle.')
4. *Miscellaneous Poetry by Samuel Bamford, weaver, of Middleton, Lancashire, lately imprisoned in the Castle of Lincoln* (London, 1821), pp. vi + 102.
5. *Hours in the Bowers. Poems, &c* (Manchester, 1834), pp. 95. (1834 is from the title page; the preface, however, is datelined: Middleton, October 25th, 1835.)
6. A translation into English verse of Charles Béranger's poem *La Lyonnaise* with notes and postscript ('In 1839 . . . I got printed, and circulated by sale, about five hundred copies of my Berenger (*sic*) La Lyonnaise', *Passages* ed. of 1844, p. 244; see also p. 234.
    No copy of this appears to have survived, but it is reprinted in *Homely Rhymes* (1864), pp. 219–27, 242–5.
7. *Passages in the Life of a Radical* (2 vols., Middleton, 1839–1841). This book was published in parts and has a complicated bibliographical history; it was offered for sale in 1843 in 'two neat volumes, post octavo, price eight shillings'. Volume II of the edition of 1844, used for *The Autobiography*, contains five additional chapters. A single volume edition was published in 1857 by Abel Heywood of Manchester, pp. 461, 'revised and corrected by the author'.
8. *Poems* (Manchester, 1843), pp. xi + 159.
9. *Walks in South Lancashire and on it Borders* (Blackley, near Manchester, 1844), pp. 291.

10. *Early Days* (published in parts during 1848–9) (London, 1849), pp. viii + 312. A second edition was published in 1859, 'revised and corrected by the author'.

11. *Dialect of South Lancashire, or Tim Bobbin's Tummus and Meary revised and corrected with his Rhymes, and an enlarged and amended glossary of words and phrases, chiefly used by the rural population of the manufacturing districts of South Lancashire* (Manchester, 1850), pp. xxiv + iii–x + 241. (There is also an alternative title-page in dialect throughout, beginning *Tawk o' Seawth Lankeshur . . .*)

12. *The Lord of the Manor and the Lord of the Mill: or Scenes in Lancashire* (Manchester and Liverpool, 1851). Published in sixpenny parts, of which only Part I, pp. 64, is known to exist (Middleton Public Library). A copy of Part III was publicly exhibited by J. A. Green in 1904 in the 'Old Manchester and Salford' Exhibition of the Lancashire and Cheshire Antiquarian Society (*Illustrated Catalogue . . . City Art Gallery*, Manchester, Spring 1904, p. 51), but its present location is unknown. An earlier version of Part I is printed at the end of *Walks in South Lancashire* (1844). There is some reason to believe that pubication of all the parts of *The Lord of the Manor and the Lord of the Mill* was never completed (see James Dronsfield, *Incidents and Anecdotes of the late Samuel Bamford* (1872), p. 11, where it is stated that Bamford 'intended to have depicted scenes in the plug-drawing days of 1842').

13. *Some Account of the late Amos Ogden, of Middleton* (Middleton, 1853), pp. 15.

14. *Homely Rhymes, Poems and Reminiscences . . .* (Manchester and London, 1864), pp. viii + 248. An expanded reprint of *Poems* (1843), containing about fifty additional pieces.

For earlier work on the bibliography of Samuel Bamford, see J. A. Green, *Bibliography of the Town of Heywood* (Heywood, 1902), pp. 6–9, and the file of correspondence from Humphry House preserved in the Middleton Public Library.

INDEX

Figures in bold type refer to illustrations